MORE BOOKS FI.... ... .

The Swamp: Deceit and Corruption in the CIA
An Elizabeth Petrov Thriller (Book 1)
by Jeff Grant

Chains of Nobility: Brotherhood of the Mamluks (Book 1)
by Brad Graft

Meeting Mozart: A Novel Drawn From the Secret Diaries of Lorenzo Da Ponte
by Howard Jay Smith

Labyrinth of the Wind: A Novel of Love and Nuclear Secrets in Tehran
by Madhav Misra

A Boy and His Dog in Hell: And Other Stories
by Mike Sager

Miss Havilland: A Novel
by Gay Daly

The Orphan's Daughter: A Novel
by Jan Cherubin

Lifeboat No. 8: Surviving the Titanic
by Elizabeth Kaye

Shaman: The Mysterious Life and Impeccable Death of Carlos Castaneda
by Mike Sager

See our entire library at TheSagerGroup.net

SO YOU WANNA BE A TEACHER

by Peter Kravitz

A Memoir

Cover and Interior Designed by Siori Kitajima, PatternBased.com

Cataloging-in-Publication data for this book is available from the Library of Congress
ISBN-13:
eBook: 978-1-950154-68-5
Paperback: 978-1-950154-69-2

Published by The Sager Group LLC
TheSagerGroup.net

SO YOU WANNA BE A TEACHER

A Memoir

32 YEARS OF SWEAT HOGS, TEEN ANGST, HALL FIGHTS AND LIFETIME FRIENDS

by Peter Kravitz

THE SAGER GROUP

Artifex Te Adiuva

To the most-impactful teacher I ever had, my Harriton High School wrestling coach Bill Zimmerman, who inspired me to delete the word can't from my mind.

For Jennifer, my wife

CONTENTS

CHAPTER 1

"I'd rather have a bottle in front of me than a
frontal lobotomy."

—Tom Waits

I t took a beautiful woman and a frontal lobotomy to rescue me
from completing a degree in accounting. My path in life was
altered, for the better.

A manic episode severed my junior year of college, sending
me to the Institute of the Pennsylvania Hospital, a private mental
hospital in West Philadelphia.

I was 20 years old and lost in mania, severely mentally ill. My
psychiatrist fed me a cornucopia of drugs: lithium to stabilize my
mood swings, pills to knock me out at night, more pills to suppress
an erection, pills for anxiety and pills to pretty much turn me into a
compliant zombie.

My shrink wasn't pushing for a lobotomy, which thankfully had
gone out of style, or even electroshock therapy, which was still very
much in vogue. I was so far gone, however, that my doctor's fight to
return me to sanity must have seemed somewhat fruitless.

How did I get there? What the hell happened?

My tumble from the world had begun a month before when
I was infected with a virus, which traveled along the nerves and
attacked my skin, creating large, bubbly blisters.

I had made it halfway through the first semester of my junior
year in November 1980 at the University of Delaware; I was also on
the wrestling team. I had been a happy, healthy, fit student athlete. I
chose Delaware because of one of the team's wrestlers, who gave me
a tour and pointed out that Delaware was nearly 60 percent female.
Unlike my other college tours, which focused on athletic facilities
and academic opportunities, my Delaware campus tour focused on

pretty girls. I was deciding between five colleges and even had a couple of partial scholarship offers for wrestling, but after seeing all of these attractive Delaware coeds I decided that that was the college for me. I hadn't had a girlfriend in high school and hoped that one of these young ladies would become my college sweetheart.

During my first years in Newark, Delaware, I tailgated at football games and spent time in all of the hotspots like the Deer Park Tavern, where the rocker George Thorogood hung out. I was an average student and not doing much in wrestling, but I enjoyed myself. The girls liked me. I had a couple of different girlfriends, who were better looking than any of the girls I had dreamed about in high school.

And then, thanks to the aforementioned virus, I landed on the University of Pennsylvania Hospital infectious disease floor. Nobody visited me without full-protective gear.

Doctors and staff treated me like patient zero in a pandemic—though at that time a pandemic seemed to me an impossibility, due to the advances of modern medicine. I vaguely knew about the "Spanish flu" because family lore said that my great uncle Enoch had died in that outbreak some 60 years before.

Despite my awareness of that horrific pandemic, if someone had told me an estimated 20-50 million people had died worldwide, I wouldn't have believed it.

Several doctors examined me but none could diagnose my illness. My good friend Milton Frank, of Philly's famous Franks soda family (*Is it Franks? Thanks.*) visited me. He wore a gown and a face shield. We laughed. We were 20 years old. Yeah, I was a little freaked out that some mystery virus had pillaged my skin. It's just that Milton looked so goofy in his plastic gown with his big ears sticking out of the face shield.

At that age I thought nothing could take me down, even an affliction that sent scores of open, itchy sores roiling down my arms, my torso, my neck, face and head. Not a single lesion was below my waist.

The Penn doctors in different specialties remained baffled. Several dermatologists examined me. Nothing. My parents were distraught and overwhelmed with worry. The doctors photographed my red, inflamed lesions. Pictures of them are probably in ancient medical texts. Then a dermatologist from the Midwest, just another in the parade of doctors, took one look at me and said, "That's herpes simplex type 1."

A University of Delaware wrestling teammate had herpes on his face but kept wrestling with it and the virus got into a cut on my hand. That 158-pound workout partner shouldn't have wrestled with herpes. He knew he had it. He knew what it was. I had no idea. I thought his sores were acne. While I had wrestled in high school and was beginning my third year of college wrestling, I was incredibly ignorant about skin diseases. I had never encountered one from wrestling.

We felt safer from diseases back then, in part because humanity had cured so many of them. Twenty-five years before, Jonas Salk's vaccine had protected us from the polio virus that killed and maimed so many, including one of our greatest presidents—Franklin D. Roosevelt. Smallpox had claimed its final victim, Janet Parker, an English medical photographer, two years before. That apparent freedom from contagion nearly ended, however, as the first U.S. case of HIV/AIDS would be reported a few months later.

In time, I would come to understand all the types of infectious skin diseases that wrestlers are susceptible to, such as impetigo and ringworm. And today, 40 years later, I now know all about infectious viruses. Who doesn't?

Herpes is a Group I virus along with chicken pox. Group IV includes polio, the common cold and the corona viruses—SARS, MERS and COVID-19. Group V is flu, measles, mumps and ebola; and Group VI is HIV, which since 1981 has led to the deaths of 39 million people. It remains the number one cause of death by infection worldwide.

Luckily, herpes simplex type 1 nailed me and not one of those other viruses. Through four decades of battling it, I've never gotten it below my waist, which would be the type 2 version: a venereal disease. Twenty years ago I got stressed and a herpes patch bloomed across my forehead. Then a dermatologist introduced me to the drug Valtrex. The minute I feel a cold sore I pop two grams—two big pills. That drug and the immunity I've built up limit the damage. The virus hides dormant in the nerves at the base of my neck and when I become stressed, ill or my skin is damaged it travels down the nerve endings and attacks my lips. If it hid in the nerves at the base of my spine it would attack my genitals.

That virus pinned me. I withdrew from Delaware that semester. I never saw myself as an accountant anyway, especially after Intermediate Accounting. No doubt accounting had aided that virus's savage attack—due to how much it stressed me out.

The apparent end of my wrestling career also slammed me. And I had done nothing in my first two years as a Division I wrestler going 3-5. I wrestled one match in the fall of my junior year and sucked down to 167, dropping 15 pounds, even though I vowed I would never cut weight in college. I lost badly.

The painful sores took time to heal. The stress mounted. I was home, my future uncertain. I watched my two younger brothers wrestle for Harriton High School, the other public high school in the Lower Merion School District adjacent to Philadelphia. As my health improved, I helped coach my brothers and other wrestlers. Although I was down about my situation, I was able to coach Harriton wrestlers well—the school's legendary coach Bill Zimmerman appreciated my effort.

Instead of tumbling into depression, a sudden shift in my brain chemistry created a euphoria. I could do anything. I felt invincible. I actually believed I could make myself invisible. I wasn't doing drugs but I conjured weird acid-trip thoughts like I was some kind of stable genius, though to others, I showed signs of intense stress, maybe even mental illness. I had no understanding of mental illness. My life had gone well up to that point, and I believed mental illness happened to weak people with problems. I knew about nervous breakdowns but I had little understanding of exactly what they were. My compulsion with girls and sports overwhelmed any attempt to understand mental health. And certainly, mental illness of any kind could never happen to me.

My parents took me to a shrink and I faked it, saying that I was stressed but I was okay now, and all the crazy ideas were, I knew, crazy. But the minute I left the doctor's office my new super-powers returned. While I had conned the doctor, I didn't fake out my parents. They suspected I had slid into insanity. And they were right: I was severely mentally ill.

My parents' next move really pissed me off. Looking back, they saved my life by committing me.

I had no idea I was in a mental hospital. As I looked out the window at the cold, snowy December streets of West Philly, I believed I was in a CIA safe house in Tehran, Iran. That part of West Philly back then, in my delusional mind, was clearly Iran. Though I wondered where the mountains were—I've always been obsessed with geography—I was convinced the CIA had brought me there where my superpowers would get the U.S. hostages out, who had been prisoners in Iran for over a year. All of America obsessively worried about the fate of the hostages.

Of course, I wasn't in Iran. I was in a locked ward of a mental hospital.

I was convinced that my fellow patients were CIA or hostages. My thoughts ping-ponged between the two, depending on how the drugs, meant to save me, reacted with my delusions. I had youth, strength and a great future; now my future was in doubt. To my parents it looked grim.

I struggled for days in this deranged state. Some days I woke up before sunrise fearful that the sun would not come up and the world would end. I'd wait for light, which relieved me that the world would continue. Those apocalyptic visions were terrifying but infrequent; my delusions were mostly euphoric.

Gradually, I more closely observed my fellow patients (though I didn't think of them as patients) and I tried to sort out who they were as individuals. My thoughts were so disjointed I had no idea who these people were sprawled out around this ward, going to meetings, playing board games, watching TV.

One tall, very old guy ambled up to everyone and mooched cigarettes. He signed out at the locked front door, the only door, as Colonel George Hogue, but he never left the ward, as I never left it either. Other patients were permitted to go to a gym or outside and walk the grounds. I decided that he was Colonel George Washington, alive after 180 years, as part of a CIA experiment. I mean, to me, he looked about 250, give or take a few scores of years. He hobbled around the ward, extended a trembling hand and said, "Cigarette. Cigarette."

I liked George, after all he was our first president. I also liked the most attractive woman in the ward. She had dark hair and blue eyes. Once after Colonel George harassed us she said, "Do you know who that is?"

"Sure," I said. "He's another CIA plant."

She smiled. I stared at her and drooled a little from all of the medication. She wiped the drool off my face. She was 10 years older than me.

"That's George Hogue," she said.

"Yeah I know all about him."

"Oh really," she said. "Did you know they brought him in here in the 1930s."

"What?" I said. That didn't fit with my delusions. I tried to get my mind around how to work that new information into my insane thought pattern.

The woman took a drag from her cigarette and blew the smoke over her shoulder, which attracted George. He ambled over, extended his gnarly hand through the charged air and said, "Cigarette? Cigarette?"

"It's my last one, George," she said. He walked away.

She grabbed my chin and moved her face close to mine. She attempted to break through my illness, to crack open the circle of thoughts that spun in my head: the bars on the windows, the Tehran cityscape, the locked doors, the guards, CIA, hostages.

"Peter, do you know why I'm here?" she said.

"Of course I know what you are doing here. You're a hostage. But I'm not."

Conversing with me was difficult but this woman kept trying to connect to sanity, which she believed still existed somewhere in my brain.

"I got divorced," she said. Her beautiful face, inches from my own, compelled me to listen. "I couldn't handle it. I started drinking too much."

"That doesn't make sense," I said. Again, confused, I struggled to process this new information. It didn't fit.

"Then I tried to kill myself," she said.

Why would such a beautiful woman try to commit suicide? No. That couldn't be. Had she really tried to kill herself?

"Look at George," she said. "Look at his forehead. George was brought here because he was violent. They did an operation on him. Do you see the indents on his forehead? They cut out part of his brain." She squeezed my chin with her small hand, turned my face and said, "Peter, look! Do you see?"

I saw the indentations on either side of his forehead. For the first time in several weeks, reality burst through the delusions that had trapped me. I looked into the beautiful, sad eyes of this woman and said, "Wait, he really had a frontal lobotomy?"

"Yes," she said, starting to cry. "Yes! You see? You understand. Finally! Oh my God."

She had tried for days to get a sane response out of me but I was too mired in mania. Finally, like a miracle, I snapped out of my insanity thanks to this woman.

I know that my psychiatrist would say that the nurses made sure I took the medication and that was what slowly pushed me back to reality. But that woman, that sad beautiful woman who had tried hard to break through had saved me when she forced reality into my delusions. George wasn't George Washington. He had had part of his brain cut out in a barbaric operation and had been in that hospital for four decades.

My recovery began. But the road to sanity was long and filled with potholes—even bigger than those on the Schuylkill Expressway. Because, while I now had an understanding, while reality had a little niche in my thoughts, the big insane thoughts could easily overwhelm it. It was a fight. But at least I was aware I was in one. And I was a battler. A tough opponent, I fought hard to win. And I had an objective now, when I could see it through the haze. Still, it took weeks to get out of that hospital.

Despite the great new drugs, a lot of young people didn't get out of the hospital. I was lucky that this sad, beautiful woman had spent days trying to break through my madness.

I watched on TV from the hospital as the hostages were freed from Tehran after 444 days on January 20, 1981—the same day that Reagan was sworn in to his first term as president.

While the world watched and reacted to that incredible drama, five days later I made it home to my younger brothers and my parents in Penn Valley, Pennsylvania. Upon my homecoming our beloved Philadelphia Eagles played in their first Super Bowl. While Super Bowl XV would be a blowout loss to the Oakland Raiders, it was a great day for me. I was out: fighting to maintain my sanity.

I had been an incredibly fit Division I collegiate wrestler when I went in and now 20 pounds of flab made my belly its home. The lithium gave me muscular tremors, making it difficult to work out and lift weights. But through the spring, as an outpatient at the hospital, I ran and worked out and even wrestled with my brothers. I dropped the weight.

Still, crazy thoughts competed with my rational thinking. I couldn't completely shake them. And I couldn't deal with the lithium, so I went against my doctor's orders and stopped taking it. I fought the weird ideas. I ran, lifted weights and wrestled. That wouldn't have worked for everybody.

I even decided to return to the University of Delaware in September, which I knew would be extremely difficult. To face all my friends and teammates, who all knew about my mental hospital stay, terrified me.

As an athlete, I was friendly with several Delaware football players. I had worked out in the weight room with them and we'd gone to the same frat parties. They had a great football program then. When I got sick, my roommate had been a football player. Upon my return that fall I roomed with another football player, Steve Long. One of Delaware's best players was a defensive tackle named Ed Braceland, from South Philly. As a sophomore defensive end, he helped lead Delaware to a Division II National title in 1979 and he was team captain in 1981, when I returned to Delaware. My first day back on campus, Braceland was one of the first people I talked to.

He stopped me at the dining hall. Usually I loved talking to people, but now I feared what big Ed would say to me. I didn't want to explain what I'd been through. I didn't want to talk about it.

"You okay?" he said.

"Yeah."

"Good," he said, slapping me on the back. "Glad to have you back."

And that was it. The captain of the football team, one of the most recognized students on campus, and in the state of Delaware, had welcomed me back. He didn't question me. He didn't look at me funny. He didn't want to know or care about the cuckoo's nest I'd been locked up in nine months before. He was just glad I was back. And from there I soared.

I changed my major to business finance, fleeing accounting. Since I had most of the business requirements covered I took several elective classes, including writing and journalism. My courses actually interested me and I wrote for the college newspaper, *The Review*.

And while my parents opposed my wrestling return, I trained with the team. I promised my parents I wouldn't wrestle competitively. I just wanted to work out and stay fit. I was a redshirt junior, though I didn't really think of myself as one. I just enjoyed practicing and being a part of the team again. Then, in that season's first meet against the University of Pennsylvania and Division III Gettysburg College, we had no heavyweight. Well, actually we had an outstanding heavyweight, Paul Ruggiero, who had won the conference the year before and won a match at DI nationals. But he said he wasn't going to wrestle his senior year.

I knew Penn's heavyweight. He was a true freshman from suburban Philly. I was confident I could beat him. Our coach wanted me to wrestle rather than forfeit. To wrestle at heavyweight, which was unlimited then, I needed to weigh around 182 pounds. I actually had to drink water to make the weight. My opponent was about 250 pounds. Despite yielding all that weight I beat him 8-3. Then I pinned Gettysburg's heavyweight. That was it. I was back. And our heavyweight saw how well I did and decided to return for his redshirt senior year. So I wrestled 190 pounds that season.

My dad was not happy about my return to the team. Wrestling had, to him, put me in a mental hospital. He was terrified that it would send me back. Clearly there were several factors that had plunged me into that state. Actually, wrestling now helped wipe out the last vestiges of mental illness. I ended up going 17-5 and placed third in the conference tournament. I could have been Delaware's comeback athlete of the year, going from a mental hospital to undefeated in dual meets and All-Conference in one year, but I didn't want to publicize what had happened to me. It's still something that I never talk about with anyone—many of my good friends have no idea.

And later in that spring I met one of those beautiful Delaware coeds, who would become my wife. Jennifer Green was a freshman, from Long Island, with curly blonde hair and blue eyes. She had a boyfriend back home on Long Island from Wantagh. I stole her heart from him, though it took several months.

My nerve-wracking return to Delaware proved quite fortuitous.

I was also fortunate to have that one last year of eligibility for wrestling. My practice room workout group included my buddy Don Philippi at 177. He was a three-time conference finalist and champ his senior year, who was also Delaware's all-time-winning wrestler—until our other workout partner eventually broke that record. David DeWalt, a true freshman from Pennsylvania, would go on to win three conference titles and become Delaware's only DI All-American his senior year. Delaware's wrestling program survived 50 years, from 1941-1991, when it was dropped. DeWalt went 101-9 and set 12 team records.

David and I were pretty even his freshman year and my redshirt senior year. Of course, the five years I had on him made a huge difference. David would go on to improve every year and become nearly unbeatable. Don could beat both of us. But there were days when I got Don, too. We knew each other very well and had different styles. Don was a mentally tough, physical South Jersey wrestler.

My dad, another tough guy from South Jersey—a World War II Marine—accepted what I had achieved junior year. He would have preferred I didn't wrestle as a redshirt senior. Nonetheless he acquiesced.

Don, David and I all reached the East Coast Conference finals, hosted by Delaware. Only Don won, at 177 pounds, and reached the Division I national tournament in Oklahoma. At 167 pounds David lost to Hofstra's Pete Capone, who would reach the national final his senior year. I lost to a 190-pound Rider College opponent who took fifth in the nationals that year.

Both David and Don went on to very successful careers. Don became a highly decorated New Jersey state trooper and then retired. David became a CEO, renowned for running tech and cybersecurity companies like FireEye, McAfee and Nightdragon Security.

And then there's my career. Here is the path that I took and what led me to it.

CHAPTER 2

Paris—Spring of 1988

My wife Jennifer and I were running out of money. We had been traveling for months, starting in Paris, then south to Portugal, Morocco, back across the Strait of Gibraltar to Spain, over to Italy and now back to Paris. It was time to return to the United States. I had spent much of the 1980s escaping from America, Reagan's America. My friends grew wealthy. I traveled and gained knowledge, experienced culture shock and devoured books. But I didn't accumulate material wealth. Married for a year, travel glued and anchored our relationship.

I was 28 and unsure what to do when we returned. Our plan was to live in New York City, as Jennifer was from the suburbs—Long Island.

"What are you going to do when you get back?" she asked me at delicious, cheap meals in the Left Bank.

"Uh, I don't know. I want to write another manuscript." I had completed a fictional manuscript but it was pretty bad.

"No, you have to get a job. You can't just write. You have to make a living. Don't you understand that?"

"Could you pass the wine?" I said politely. "You know we haven't gone down to the catacombs yet. We should do that tomorrow."

"We have to leave. That's it. Traveling is over. We have to begin our lives. We have to think about jobs."

Jobs? Ugh. Really? I didn't want to think about a job. But she was right. We weren't expats or anything like that. I could keep exploring. She was done. She was ready to nest. Children? Not on my radar but I knew the minute we returned, job or no job, an American life would start. She wasn't thinking kids, but kids would arrive. The United States loomed and I had avoided it for long enough.

I strolled alone, listening to my walkman—a little cassette player with headphones. Perhaps Jennifer shopped. Though she was kinda cheap about buying anything, which was great with me. You couldn't beat a beautiful, fit wife who loved to shop but hated to buy anything outside of a bargain.

I promenaded slowly down Rue St. Denis—the street of prostitutes. I wasn't looking for a prostitute. I listened to music, admired architecture and people, and the variety of women who all looked at me and mouthed French that I couldn't hear due to my music.

The Rue St. Denis prostitutes came in all colors, sizes and ages. They were young and beautiful, middle aged, old and a little worn out. Every variety of women sold herself for a few francs. I never asked how much. Though I liked saying, "Avez-vous un preservative?" But just for fun. Just for the reaction.

I blasted the artist then known as Prince into my headphones. The more I walked the more I thought about my future in the United States, in New York. Motion helped my thought process. This one very dark-skinned woman floated words at me. I kept the headphones in. And then it struck me—an epiphany. I'm not sure exactly why. Perhaps it was Prince's lyrics. Or the way this African French woman looked at me. I would go to the rough neighborhoods of New York City and teach African American children. I could teach them literature, introduce them to African American writers like Alice Walker, Toni Morrison, James Baldwin, Richard Wright, Alex Haley. Were those children reading those writers in New York City public high schools? I would teach high school English. I loved literature and nonfiction. I would teach books to children of the inner city even if I had to buy them myself.

Now, my wife takes credit as the inspiration for my going into teaching. And she probably did mention teaching as an option. But she also mentioned several possible careers, most of which were unappealing.

There was no Teach for America back then—that was born a year later. The idea of going into the inner city and trying to help underprivileged minority children was my idea. Jennifer wouldn't have suggested where I teach. But we were planning to live in New York City.

Who could imagine that a career would be born out of a glimpse of a Parisian hooker, with Prince blasting through my head?

CHAPTER 3

Brooklyn—August 1988

I had picked up a map of New York City High Schools at the Board of Education on Court Street, near our first Carroll Gardens apartment, a third-floor walkup on Second Place.

I planned to pedal my Raleigh three-speed, my childhood bicycle, to various Brooklyn high schools until I found a teaching job. It was sweltering late August and administrators had trickled back to the city schools to figure out staffing needs.

I had never taken an education class and had only taken one English undergraduate class. But I had gotten myself a New York City TPD license and I had been fingerprinted.

I didn't know Brooklyn very well, but my map dictated that my first stop would be Boys and Girls High School. So I pedaled there—it was only about two miles away.

Bedford-Stuyvesant had a reputation as one of the more dangerous neighborhoods in New York City. I was fearless, especially when pedaling my three speed—youth often creates an unrealistic sense of indestructibility.

At one point, in a forest of apartment-building projects, I stopped my bicycle to consult my map when my keys fell out of my short's pocket. I was immediately surrounded by about five or six young teenage boys. Despite the neighborhood's reputation, I wasn't alarmed. We'd only recently returned from our sojourn and had spent time in Morocco, where ghostly figures in hooded djellabas had crowded around Jennifer and me and that was far more disconcerting than this. The boys appeared harmless and I wasn't trying to communicate in my limited French to Arabic or Berber speakers.

"Hey guys, what's up?" I said, smiling at the boys.

One of them bent down and picked up my keys. He handed them to me and said, "Don't be losing your keys in Bed-Stuy."

"Thanks," I said. "Can you guys steer me towards Boys and Girls High School? I know it's around here somewhere."

Not long after that, I was perspiring in the office of Boys and Girls High School Principal Frank Mickens. Despite the air conditioning Mickens sweated even more.

He was a big man in a suit and tie with a booming voice. He didn't really talk, he yelled. He studied my resume on his desk.

"You were a newspaper reporter?" he said.

"Yeah, I worked for a few newspapers in Philly including the *Philadelphia Inquirer*," I said. "But then the Inquirer went on strike-"

"And you coached wrestling at Haverford College?" he said.

"And I worked with admissions to get kids into the school. One of my wrestlers came from Brooklyn. I was the head coach."

"But you never taught before?" said Mickens, who was in his third year battling drug dealing and shootings as the principal of Boys and Girls High.

"Well, coaching is teaching—"

"I repeat, you never taught before?"

"Correct, I never taught."

"Then I'm not hiring you!" he roared, hoarsely.

His secretary pulled me into her office and quietly handed me an application.

"We need you," she said.

And so, I had a full-time teaching job, after my bicycle ride to my first high school, after being told that I didn't have the job. Welcome to New York City's world of education.

I commuted to the school via the F-train subway to Borough Hall. Then I walked to the A-train platform. There were hundreds of commuters, packed into the platform, headed into Manhattan on my first day of orientation. My side of the tracks had a sign saying, "To Bedford Stuyvesant." On my side of the tracks was me—not another soul rode the subway into Bed-Stuy at that early morning hour to go to work.

In a crowded auditorium, Mickens addressed his staff at my first-ever teachers' meeting.

"Nineteen years of incompetence!" said Mickens. "Twenty-seven years of genocide to our children!"

He described his enemy, teachers who stopped caring. He's gonna get them, he said. He'll transfer them out of his school.

"I know that some of you have a tendency to be attracted to the children." I looked around. Everybody was looking at the ground. Everybody was nervous. This wasn't deadwood he was talking about. Who knew what was coming next? Would he single out a teacher? He sounded like a preacher. The power of his words rang out like a Martin Luther King speech. "Rid yourself of those tendencies now!"

And then he said something that would become the greatest advice on teaching I have ever heard, words that I carry with me and repeat every day. He lowered his booming voice, and in a softer voice he rarely used he said, "Treat the children as if they were your own."

You could take every education course, every motivational film about teaching, and just throw them into the sewer and begin with: "Treat the children as if they were your own."

A teacher need only be armed with that simple advice. Nothing more. If you like kids, and you are out to help them, and do for them what you would do for your own children, in time you can become a good teacher. Now, I didn't have any children at that time, but I recognized that I had just received the First Commandment of teaching.

Mickens grew up in Bedford-Stuyvesant. He'd taught at Boys and Girls. Before he returned as principal the school had become the most dangerous in New York City. Students attacked teachers, fired guns at each other during basketball games. Teachers appointed by the NYC Board of Ed to Boys and Girls would look for another profession.

Mickens worked 18 hours a day, seven days a week to change the school. If the Board of Ed sent a student with a criminal record there, Mickens focused on that student to the point that the student either turned his or her life around or left the school—though probably more the latter. Bureaucrats ranted: "He's dumping students on other schools."

Mickens responded to the bureaucrats at 65 Court Street with: "These troubled students you are dumping on my school require constant attention. They have attacked teachers and deans. Take them in your office and try to educate them. You don't do anything all day anyway."

Mickens' passion, his concern for his neighborhood and his school, led the city's new chancellor, Dr. Richard Green, to tell him in their first meeting: "So you're the principal they want me to fire."

Mickens was everywhere. If there was a fight, he was the first on the scene to break it up. He knew hundreds of his students' names. He walked in on classes. Older teachers didn't like his omniscient presence, especially Danny Rubin. Rubin had taught at Boys and Girls for 20 years. He and Mickens had taught there together.

While Mickens's only indulgence appeared to be his trademark cigar, Rubin had done his fair share of mind-altering drugs. Though he claimed he'd quit smoking dope six years before and was sober now. When I first saw him, I wasn't sure exactly what he was. His head was a mountain of silver dreadlocks. A huge gray beard and glasses hid the rest of his face. His skin was dark. I assumed he was Jamaican.

The first time I met him I shook his hand and introduced myself.

"Yeah. Alright. Cool. Yeah. Okay," he said before finally introducing himself.

"Man, this year is gonna be so difficult," he said. "I'm 50. There are days I get the idea of just walking out of here. And I can't shake it."

"Well, maybe you should retire," I said.

"I can't man. Besides, Mickens will get rid of me anyway."

"Really," I said. "He seems like a great leader."

"Yeah, he's doing a good job. But he hates me."

"Why?"

"It's my hair. He wants me to cut my hair. I can't. I mean, cut my hair?" His voice reeked of despair. "How can he demand I cut my hair?"

"He tells you to cut it?"

"Nah man. Of course not. But I see it in his eyes every time he looks at me. Now, don't get me wrong, before Mickens took over this place was dangerous. Even I had to be careful and the kids liked me. Mickens has cleaned it up. He's into cleaning, man. He sees my hair as the last bit of filth in the school. He'd probably chop it off and sweep it away himself. The man just doesn't like my hair."

"He doesn't like your teaching style either," said a small man with dreadlocks. He appeared to be African-American but as I had yet to determine what ethnicity and race Rubin was. I wasn't too sure.

"Nah, man, it's not the teaching," Rubin said. "I'm telling ya, he won't let up until I cut the hair. But I'll quit before I cut it. But I can't quit."

The smaller Rasta said, "Yeah, you've got problems. At least you are White."

So, Rubin was White. Hmm.

Teaching English to ninth graders exhausted me. At night I took English classes at Brooklyn College so I could eventually get a permanent New York State Teaching license. I also needed Education classes. And we got a dog. I'd return home from my subway commute dreaming of a big flop on the couch and a nap but first I had to walk the dog. My wife had begun to nest. Unlike traveling around Europe and North Africa, teaching exhausted me. I had little time to write. If I began to read, I fell asleep.

But I liked the kids. Despite the many challenges, right away I knew that this teaching thing could work out because I enjoyed attempting to open the children's minds, especially through fiction and nonfiction. I followed the literature curriculum, but on Fridays I used music, as no doubt countless teachers have. For homework the students brought in lyrics to a song and a cassette tape with that song on it. I'd type up the lyrics and in class we'd read the words and listen to Public Enemy, Big Daddy Kane, Boogie Down Productions. My ninth graders knew the lyrics to every song but they didn't know the meaning of 70 percent of the words. Public Enemy sang: "Revolution a solution. For all our children."

"What is a revolution?" I asked the students.

After about two minutes of quiet, an eternity of solitude with 25 ninth graders, one said, "Ain't that a war?"

"Yes, nice job," I said and thought to myself that I had to do a lot of vocabulary with these kids.

Going off the grid with music seemed like a great idea but it quickly landed me in the assistant principal's office. She was from Guyana. Rubin warned me, "She hates to see you do well with the kids."

She told me not to do any more Friday rap songs.

"These children need the basics," she said. "They need grammar. They can hardly read. All they do is listen to music. Teach them English."

I was relieved. I thought maybe she was going to say I was fomenting revolution. I went with the dusty, ancient anthologies and their less-than-thrilling stories by Guy de Maupassant and O. Henry. Then I got tired of that and went with some Paul Bowles.

Bowles's short masterpiece "A Distant Episode" was way too difficult for the kids. But I read it to them, and explained it, and even tossed in my own tales from my recent journey to Morocco. The kids loved it.

Reading Bowles with the kids sent me back to the Guyanese woman's office. She angrily waved one of my copies of "A Distant Episode" and said, "Has this story been approved by the state?"

"Ah, I don't know," I said.

"How can you let the children read this? A man has his tongue cut out and is turned into a clown? Do you think that is appropriate?"

"It's actually kinda upbeat for a Bowles story," I said.

"The children should not read it."

I wanted to tell her how much the kids enjoyed it. They actually wanted to read more Bowles. When do you get kids to say they want to read more? I felt like I was on to something if I could create the desire to read in children. All of the literature she directed me towards turned them off. Plus, Bowles was the 20th century's Poe. And all of the Poe stories of murder, torture and being buried alive were state-approved. I mean, this was New York not Alabama. In addition, these kids had experienced real violence on the streets. I had had six students lose friends or family to violence in my first month. But I didn't say any of that. I figured that this administrator didn't want to debate with me. I had to do what she said.

"No more of these stories," she said. "You only teach what the state permits. We could lose our funding if the auditors see this."

My most incensed student was my most difficult one: James Britton, a skinny boy, brilliant, with a rubbery face, an Eddie Murphy sense of humor, a disdain for verbs, a voice cracking with puberty and a penchant for stirring up trouble.

"That assistant principal with the big butt," he said. "She a butthead."

"Look, when there are rules you have to follow them," I told the children.

"Mr. Kravitz, you fresh," James said. "I mean, I know some people think you a cop but I don't believe that. Your class ain't boring. We learnin'. This is booty."

For James that was a positive and productive commentary, as he mostly "dissed" every kid in the class. He could insult three kids simultaneously. But his humor could be self-deprecating, like when another student said that James would end up in prison one day. He said, in a serious tone that included a rare two verbs, "Man, if I ever go to Rikers Island I will sew up my booty first."

My first taste of New York City Board of Ed-style observations came from the Guyanese lady. She wrote my lesson up as unsatisfactory because I'd only called on 20 out of 24 students. Also in the middle of the lesson, James called this kid Redrick a "fat shaky bowl of jelly."

I admonished him but the Guyanese woman wrote that I had no control of my class for allowing James to insult his peers, which perhaps was accurate.

Those children needed adult guidance with so many issues, especially nutrition. Not that I was the greatest eater, as wrestling had given me crazy eating habits. I would fast for hours and then binge eat. That wasn't good. But I knew enough to help my students.

James never ate vegetables or fruit. He had Captain Crunch for breakfast, McDonalds with soda for dinner, then stuffed his miniscule dessert belly with candy bars.

"You eat too much sugar, James," I said.

"I can't eat no good food, Mr. Kravitz," he said.

"If you could give up the sugar for a few days, you'd be able to enjoy other foods," I said.

"Dag, I wish I could do that."

"And it would calm you down a little and you wouldn't be bouncing around my classroom. You'd learn more and do better in school."

"Maybe you ain't no cop, Mr. Kravitz. You know, it's an old term, but you my homeboy."

First-year teachers are observed repeatedly and I was also observed by the business assistant principal, who we called Dr. Bob. He was short, fat, forty-ish. He walked around in a smock. I wasn't sure why, because he wasn't in science or shop or anything. He was gay. Then he saw me in jeans one day and wrote me a memo saying that jeans make a teacher less effective. I was baffled that he would call out my nice jeans while he billowed around in a stained smock.

His memo began with a poem, "To a Louse." I immediately responded with a retort featuring a few lines from Henry Miller's *Tropic of Cancer*: "I am living at the Villa Borghese. There is not a crumb of dirt anywhere, nor a chair misplaced. We are all alone here and we are dead. Last night Boris discovered that he was lousy."

However, I toned my memo down and concluded with: "I'm in no position to question your experience and success. I will try wearing nicer pants and even a button-down shirt and tie. I appreciate your effort to make me a better teacher."

The only reason I wore the jeans was because they were the only pants I had tight enough to put my wallet in my back pocket and not worry that some little thief may try to steal it. Though the kids all liked me and I felt that, even if one of the more disturbed ones tried to pickpocket me (a few of them might have been skilled little Oliver Twists), the others would tell me.

Now, there was an English teacher who I really liked, who didn't wear a smock, who actually wore jeans. Unlike Dr. Bob, Steve Neville was nice and cool. His bracelets and keys jingled as he walked. He was gay, too. And when I told him about Dr. Bob's memo he said, "He's an evil bitch."

I also had to deal with the Board of Education. In those pre-internet days, I had to physically go there to fill out paperwork in the endless pursuit of the elusive permanent New York State teaching license. The simplest question about the simplest form meant five different conversations with five different people on five different floors. The Soviet Ministry of Agriculture would have been easier to deal with than that nest of entrenched bureaucrats.

How would I survive at teaching? I began to look at the want ads in the newspaper. As the first semester wore down, and I with it, I tried to think of the positives. The kids seemed to like me.

However, Mickens had a staffing problem. He had to cut teachers for the second semester. While Mickens had come to like me and see that I cared about the kids and was trying to teach them, he had a school with nearly 4,000 African American students. He wanted African American teachers to instruct them. In addition, I was a long way from a provisional New York State teaching license, let alone the permanent one. My TPD license sank me to the depths of seniority. So, I was informed that I was out of a job at Boys and Girls for the second semester.

I wasn't that upset about it. I knew I'd land somewhere if I went after another teaching job. But I liked the school and many of the teachers. And I would miss the kids.

One student, Brian Freeman, returned to school for the first time in two months. "What happened to you Brian?" I said.

"I got into some trouble," he said.

After school I talked to him about it and he said, "I went upstate to make some money. They put me in a big house and I sold cocaine. After three days the cops busted me. I was in jail for a week, then my bosses bailed me out. They put up $2,000. When I got out the bosses got me some new clothes. They paid me for a week and I didn't have to do nothing."

He was a bright 14-year-old. I wished I could do something more for him than just listen. He had no positive adult guidance in his life.

One of my absolute best kids, John White, who was very quiet, told me he felt bad that I would lose my job because he thought I was a good teacher.

A few days later, Mickens came over the PA in the waning minutes of John's ninth-and-last-period class and said, "There are five students in this school who are on their way out. Would you all like to hear their names?" I couldn't believe he would name the students on the PA system. He did and the last name on Mickens shit list was John White.

The kids snickered. The bell rang and I asked John to stay for a minute.

"Why is Mickens so angry at you?" I said.

He shrugged. He was a quiet but bright kid, probably the best-behaved kid in that class. He listened. Always respectful, he tried his best.

"Well, I shot my friend."

I was shocked. I'd met people who'd shot their *enemy* in war, gangbangers who shot the opposing gang members, but never anyone who had shot his friend.

He saw that I looked upset as I struggled to respond.

"Don't worry Mr. Kravitz, I didn't kill him," he said.

The kid had read my mind. We talked for a while and then he went off to see Mickens. I would miss John White. I believed I could help him. I never gave up on a kid, but I had a feeling Mickens would bounce him from Boys and Girls the same way he had excessed me.

I thought this might be my chance to write my novel. I had some fertile material from that semester. But there was no way my wife would give me the time and space to write. She always seemed to be telling me to work. And not only did we have a dog, but Jennifer was pregnant with our first child, who was due in July. And she kept working hard servicing nursing homes and selling nutritional supplements to them—as our first child grew in her belly.

Instead of riding my bicycle to look for another teaching job, I walked down the street to James T. Stranahan Junior High School 142, a large brick building by the Brooklyn-Queens Expressway—Brooklyn Battery Tunnel (now the Hugh L. Carey Tunnel) merge. It was two blocks from our apartment. I figured I'd start there, rather than go to the Board of Education, where the bureaucrats might have assigned me to a school somewhere, anywhere in the city like the Bronx or an hour drive through traffic to Queens.

Today the building that housed JHS 142 is the Brooklyn New School, an elementary school, and the Brooklyn Collaborative, a small outward-bound school, grades six through 12. As a junior high in 1989, JHS 142 had about 25 teachers and 250 kids per grade.

The principal, Walter Sadowski, welcomed me into his office. I told him how I'd taught English at Boys and Girls the first semester but lost that job due to staffing cuts.

"I don't have any English positions," Sadowski said. "But would you teach Earth science?"

"Uh, Earth science?" I said. "I'm not a science teacher."

"I don't care," he said, not even bothering to look at my resume on his desk. "Look, I'm not looking for a science teacher. I'm looking for someone who won't quit on me. I had five teachers last semester for eighth grade Earth science. Five teachers! I just want someone who will do their best and won't quit. So, I don't care if you don't know science. The job is yours if you promise me not to quit."

I didn't really have to think about it. I could walk back to our apartment and tell Jennifer I had another job. I failed to analyze why five teachers had quit—because if I had, for a minute, or if I asked Sadowski why those teachers had quit, I might have searched for another English position. But after being locked in a mental hospital and fighting my way out and battling to regain my sanity, I felt like I could overcome anything. I saw this as a challenge, and it was another full-time, full-pay NYC teaching position, just a two-block commute from my apartment. My pregnant wife would be happy.

"Sure, I'll do it," I said.

Little did I know what I was in for.

Unlike Boys and Girls, this school was integrated. About one third of the kids were African-American, many of whom lived in the projects in nearby Red Hook. One third were Latino from different socio-economic levels. The remaining third were White and Asian.

I had six classes, for a total of nearly 180 students, pretty much all of the non-honors eighth grade science students. That's a lot of students. My classes were regular classes, but they featured a mix of academic ability. Some of the kids were very bright and would apply to top city high schools at the end of the year, in the same way high school seniors applied to colleges. Some of the kids never did any work and failed classes year after year and were significantly older than the typical eighth grader.

I taught out of a science textbook. There was no lab to teach, just six classes of eighth grade Earth science, one prep, a homeroom, plus a duty.

The classrooms had these closets in the back of the rooms with sliding doors on them. My first day, my first class, I finished my lesson, after being interrupted about 100 times, and the bell rang. Four kids emerged from the closets in the back. They had spent the period in the closets. It was not a good sign.

While walking to work two blocks was great, my students quickly figured out where I lived. Another very important rule about teaching is that you never want your students to know where you live—and all of these kids knew exactly where I lived.

However, a third-floor walk-up was not going to work with a baby arriving in the summer. We moved two blocks away, to Second Street and Hoyt Street. I don't know who named the streets in the neighborhood. West of Smith Street was First Place, Second Place. And then east of Smith Street you had First Street, Second Street.

Though it wasn't as confusing as sections of Queens, like Bayside, where Street, Road, Place and Avenue all competed with each other and you never knew where the hell you were.

Our new Second Street apartment only had a single, short flight of stairs to walk up. My commute doubled. And of course the kids quickly figured out where I lived.

Their knowledge of my apartment's exact location right away got me into trouble. And it wasn't with an assistant principal from Guyana. To explain this, I will rather immodestly say that I was a good-looking 28 year old. I was tall and lean and had straight blond hair.

So, these crazy little girls, children, but some of them looked like women, were always around my classroom.

And I talked to them and joked around. I should have created distance with them, but it seemed pretty harmless. I mean, they were children. But I failed to understand the inherent risks of being a young male teacher around hormone-baked, post-puberty girls.

It didn't take long for one of them to rumor me. And it was a whopper. She told everybody that I had invited her, and a few other girls to my apartment. Now, this was totally preposterous. But this girl, Leontina, ends up in the principal's office with another girl, JoLynn.

Leontina told the principal that she was in my apartment (of course she knew exactly where it was—something I warn you future teachers about again) and I showed her porn films. JoLynn interrupted this cheesy fiction and said, "That's bullshit." JoLynn was 14 going on 24. And unlike Leontina, she was a beautiful, well-adjusted young girl.

Leontina continued her fiction, making up even crazier details. JoLynn disputed it and said she was lying. Finally, Leontina broke down and said she made the whole thing up.

"Why?" asked the principal.

Through giant tears she said, "Because I have a crush on Mr. Kravitz."

During the principal's investigation he called me into his office and screamed at me. At the time I had no idea what I had done.

"You know, I don't need any reason to fire you," he said. "I could fire you anytime. In fact, you're fired!"

"Buy why? Why are you firing me?"

"It doesn't matter. I just don't want you here anymore." Of course, he asked me to finish the day and so I went back to teaching my classes. The firing didn't seem real. I told the kids Sadowski had fired me, and they told me about the false accusation against me. Later in the day, the principal called me back into his office.

"I'm not going to forget this," he said. "But you are doing a good job. You kept your word and didn't quit on me. I don't want those kids to lose another teacher so I'm giving you another chance."

Another chance? Really? When I hadn't done anything? I wanted to yell at him, or better yet, lateral drop him on his head. But I shut my mouth, swallowed my pride and actually thanked him for unfiring me.

The next day in my class, Leontina argued with another girl, Shanay, right in the middle of my instruction. Shanay knocked

Leontina to the floor and picked up a chair and aimed it at Leontina's head. This wasn't unusual in JHS 142. Maybe Shanay was sticking up for me, but probably not. More likely the fight was over something trivial. While part of me saw this as justice I couldn't let the kid have her head smashed so I quickly grabbed the chair from Shanay. As soon as I put it down Shanay picked up another chair. I grabbed that one, ushered her out of the classroom and got help.

That was just another day at JHS 142. I had yet to understand another golden rule of teaching, especially in New York City: Never break up a fight between girls or with a girl involved.

I wanted to quit so badly. It was turning into another type of a mental hospital. But I'd promised that I wouldn't quit. Even though Sadowski had seemingly presumed my guilt with no evidence whatsoever, I had given my word. Hopefully I would make it to June.

Walking the dog, KC, was a bit of a respite from long days of teaching. Jennifer was very pregnant and while that was difficult for her, it was for me, too.

Perhaps the lone positive aspect to working at JHS 142 was a teacher-student faculty basketball game. The kids were very good. Though the definition of a wrestler is someone who could never play basketball, I had a little bit of game. I played in half-court Carroll Gardens games. I had athleticism, speed. I could drive the basket, though my shot needed a makeover.

My students baited me the week of the game saying, "Kravitz ain't no good. He's just got a jumper." Clearly they hadn't scouted me at teacher practices. Would the students or the teachers win? We spent class time debating. Though five of the best student players were declared academically ineligible.

Colleagues teased me that I was taking this too seriously. "Well, I'm trying not to but we can't lose to those kids," I said.

Probably the best eligible student, Lawrence "Pookie" Claiborne, who was in my homeroom, spent the week leading up to the game saying he would kick my butt. It was a close game. I took one shot and missed. But I had several assists, steals and a solid defensive effort in a close teachers' win.

I still had great difficulty with administrators. One assistant principal observed my class and said it was unsatisfactory. I mean, hadn't the principal told me he didn't care what I did as long as I didn't quit? And this was a class of obnoxious maniacs, who I had totally quiet, learning and raising their hands answering questions about an Alaskan oil spill. Nobody came out of the closets at the end of class.

In addition to teaching about 180 kids every day, there were the coverages. Most weren't too terrible, babysitting basically. One day, a typical coverage found me overseeing 30 kids, seventh graders I didn't know. The study hall seemed split between African-American kids and White kids. Some of the boys were out of their seats and yelling at each other. I attempted to get them in their seats. Since I didn't know them, I struggled. Chaos reigned and it erupted into a mini race riot with the kids throwing paper at each other. Then a kid shrieked: "EWWWWW!"

And there in the back of the classroom was a rather large bowel movement stinking up the room. It's amazing how quickly the shitty odor of one doody can overwhelm a room. I opened the windows and got a custodian. That custodian was not happy. And I never upset a custodian—another important rule. Perhaps I should have cleaned up the human waste rather than disturb a custodian. He dumped a bucket of ammonia on the giant turd and the fumes filled the classroom. I ushered the kids outside so no one was overcome by the fumes.

Would I be fired for permitting a kid to crap in a classroom? It wasn't like a kid said he had to go badly and I didn't let him go to the bathroom. I assumed it was a male because I couldn't see any of the girls squatting and crapping. That's more a male maneuver. I don't know how I didn't see it, but it probably happened as I was trying to quell the race riot. Maybe the race riot was a planned diversion. Could these children be that calculated?

There was a lot of crap to deal with at JHS 142.

As the spring wore on, I realized that this was the most difficult job I'd ever had. It definitely topped working in a doughnut shop, driving an ice cream truck (neither of which worked out as I gained a lot of weight at both), and it was perhaps even worse than working at my grandfather's packaging company one summer.

Sure, it wasn't the near-impossible obstacle of regaining my sanity and escaping the cuckoo's nest, but I'd walk home every day, exhausted, and convince myself that teaching was too hard. I needed to find a new profession. I'd given it my best.

While I quickly learned that the teacher-administrator relationship is an adversarial one, at least in New York City, I liked the seventh grade supervisor, Murray Blyn. One day he said to me, "You get better every year at teaching. You learn what works and what doesn't. But it takes about five years, for even the best teacher, to begin to understand how to do it." It was nice that an administrator was actually trying to help make me a better teacher instead of just criticizing me.

However, I couldn't battle these kids six periods a day anymore. There was no chance I could go four more years after this one. My homelife wasn't helping. My beautiful pregnant wife wasn't a source of refuge. Our adorable little cocker spaniel puppy vomited and pooped everywhere. She also peed on the floor to get me out of bed to clean it so she could lay on my pillow. I was struggling to control my classes and my dog.

I couldn't imagine what my life was going to be like with a child.

Then the better weather of spring brightened my mood. I decided there was no way I would stay at JHS 142. But maybe I would stay with teaching if I could find a decent English teaching job. After all, as long as I didn't quit or get fired, I'd have my healthcare all summer—pretty important with a child on the way. And I'd get paid until September. There were definitely some positives to a full-time teaching gig, but it was so exhausting. And I was a little too easygoing when it came to controlling my classes. Perhaps I could get better at that. At least I liked the kids. One of my best students, Hee Byung Chai, would often thank me for teaching him science unlike my five predecessors. He was applying to very good city high schools like Stuyvesant and Hunter and would no doubt be successful.

One student, Chris Melita, thanked me for teaching him. Tricia Peart, or T Baby, who looked like she was 20, wrote in my yearbook:

"You've been a great teacher. I enjoyed having you even though it was such a short while. You were the best science teacher this year. You really taught me a lot. A certain person said you were cute. Enjoy your summer. I will miss you."

I would miss great kids like Tricia.

With only a few days left of my JHS 142 semester from hell, there was a knock at my door. My wife and I were having a late dinner. I went down the stairs to open it and there was JoLynn, the adorable little girl who had saved me months before by countering crazy Leontina in the principal's office.

"JoLynn, what are you doing here?" I said. She was with a friend.

Instead of answering me she just tried to push by me and come in.

"JoLynn, you can't come in," I said blocking her entrance.

And then I smelled alcohol on her breath. The sweet, adorable 14-year-old was drunk—trashed. I was shocked.

"JoLynn, you have to go home."

"Just let us in Mr. Kravitz."

"JoLynn, you have to go home."

My wife screamed from upstairs: "What's going on?"

"Nothing," I yelled.

"Is that your wife," she slurred. "I want to meet her."

"JoLynn you have to leave."

Of course, in yet another insane situation I lacked decisive toughness. There was nothing to discuss. I finally got her out the door and headed to wherever. If I were to keep teaching, I had to get tougher.

June took its time but finally arrived and the JHS 142 nightmare was over. I had made it somehow. My first year as a teacher had come to an end. Even though I'd been fired a couple of times, but then unfired, I had survived my first year of teaching.

In my yearbook, the Junior High 142 Stranahan Trumpeter, one student wrote, "I hope you don't get fired next year. I bet it's a boy."

Denise Moore wrote: "Thanks for being such a nice teacher." That was going to change if I kept teaching. "Thanks for teaching us more than any of our other science teachers and giving us tests, quizzes and all. I hope your wife has her baby on July 17. That's my birthday. I hope you become a Language Arts teacher next year. P.S. Your the cutest, too."

I wasn't her English teacher. If I got to teach English I would make sure all of my students knew the difference between "your" and "you're."

Summer off: one of the great perks of teaching. Though, Jennifer was very pregnant.

While I drank pints of Brooklyn Lager in yuppie pubs and flirted with pretty women, she remained sober. I stuffed my face with pork fried rice, the best pizza in the world, gelato, burgers, Thai food, pasta, Reese's Cups. She ate healthy, shopped and bought a crib, a dressing table, lined up a pediatrician, and set up childcare so we both could work.

"You're having too much fun," she said of my basketball and trips out to Long Island to play golf with her cousins. "Can you please look for another teaching job right now? You have to make sure you have a job in September. Maybe you could work part time now?"

She continued working, though she was only weeks away from giving birth. I was scared of parenting and taking care of a child. I thought back to all the traveling Jennifer and I had done and wished we could travel again. When would we get to travel? Not for a while. I had spent the 1980s exploring the world. How could I survive now without travel, without planning trips and jetting off to some remote mountain valley?

Our fighting raged. Then on a very hot July 20 the fighting stopped. Dana Rose was born. I fell so in love with that infant that I stopped thinking about travel or anything except taking care of her and keeping her safe. It was the best day of my life. Though it was strange for a guy from the suburbs of Philly to have a first child born in Brooklyn. Would this beautiful girl have a Brooklyn accent? I cured Jennifer of her Long Island accent. My daughter would pronounce the letter 'r.' She wouldn't say "memba." She would say 'Re-mem-beR.'

Dana Rose was born with blonde hair and blue eyes. I called my mom in Philly and said she had a granddaughter. After three sons and a 29-year wait, there was a little girl for my mom. She shrieked with joy.

From the July 20 front page of the *New York Times*: a plane crashed in Iowa killing 150 of the 290 passengers (unlike today's plane crashes where there are never survivors); the Sandinistas marked their tenth anniversary in power in Nicaragua; 21-year-old actress Rebecca Shaeffer was shot to death by a stalker outside of her Los Angeles apartment.

Dana was coming into a dangerous world but I would protect her.

As for 1989, the Berlin Wall would fall in a few months and freedom would deluge Eastern Europe. The U.S.S.R. would break up into scores of unpronounceable nations, like the stans—Kazakhstan, Kyrgyzstan, Turkmenistan, Uzbekistan, Tajikistan; additional nations included Moldova, Azerbaijan, Ukraine, Georgia, Belarus, Estonia, Latvia, Lithuania, Armenia and of course Russia. The Iron Curtain would fall, freeing Eastern Europe.

After I left the hospital, I went to a bar with my dog and my good friend Dan Shannon, who looked exactly like the actor Michael C. Hall. He was in Manhattan getting his Masters at NYU and would go on to star as Dexter, in the HBO series by the same name. Dan and Hall could have been identical twins.

Dan also lived in Carroll Gardens, had taught at Boys and Girls with me and was also excised after one semester. He'd landed an English-teaching job at Tilden High School. He said I could probably get a job there. He would talk to the English AP.

"But let me warn you," Dan said. "He's kind of a dick."

"Really? Why?"

"Well for starters his name is Joel Dick."

"No way."

But how could Tilden High School be worse than JHS 142? I didn't think that was possible. However, as wacky as some of the Brooklyn administrators were, I hadn't met Joel Dick yet.

Dan and I celebrated Dana Rose's arrival in the world with several beers. And if Dan was right, and I could teach English at Tilden, Jennifer would be appeased and stop harassing me and I could enjoy the rest of the summer.

Dan and I drank a couple of more beers with a Mafioso-type who said he was of Irish descent. Dan actually tried to buy the mob guy a beer but the bartender nervously pushed Dan's money back and said, "He's buying you beers. Just accept please."

Then the mob guy tried to buy my dog. No matter how important of a mobster he was, I couldn't acquiesce on this demand.

"I can't sell her," I said, not thinking that my family now consisted of two females and this canine bitch, making three females and me.

"I'll give ya a hundred bucks," he said.

"Are you kidding me? Do you know how much my wife has spent on this animal? And forget about what the dog cost to purchase?"

"Five hundred bucks."

With a potential job creating a truce with Jennifer there was no way I could sell the dog. Though for $500 I was tempted. That was a lot of money in 1989.

Carroll Gardens was inundated with mob guys. Dana's first babysitter warned me to stay away from the bagel store on Smith Street near Carroll Street. "Those are mob guys there," she urgently warned. "Don't go there."

I didn't believe her. And the place had good bagels. Then one day I saw feds sitting in an unmarked car watching the bagel store. John Gotti's driver, who had grown up on our Second Street block, was whacked. And my landlord Carmine further inundated me in the depths of Second Street mob connections.

"Yeah, 'dat guy Joe B, he's a bookkeeper for the mob. And you know 'dat guy who always stands in the middle of the block by the rail?"

"Yeah."

"He was a big soldier. And Benny-"

"Little fat Benny?"

"Yeah, he was the meanest guy you ever seen."

"Was Joe the Killer in the mob?"

"Nah. He didn't mean to kill that kid. That was an accident. But you know-"

"That's enough. Don't tell me anymore. I don't want to know nothing, I mean anything, more."

CHAPTER 4

East Flatbush, New York—September 1989

Samuel J. Tilden High School was named for a New York governor who battled corruption and opposed slavery prior to the Civil War. Tilden lost the 1876 presidential election to Rutherford B. Hayes, though he won the popular vote.

Tilden High School opened in 1930. By the 1960's the school had 5,000 students, of whom nearly 98 percent were White, mostly Jewish and Italian.

When Joel Dick hired me to teach there in 1989, the school was 99.8 percent minority, with the vast majority of students or their parents from the Caribbean region. The neighborhood around the school had become somewhat dangerous, especially compared to 30 years before, but the school still attracted good minority students from around the city—as New York City students were not limited to their neighborhood secondary school. The faculty had a good reputation and the school was reasonably safe. Kids learned.

Whereas Boys and Girls High was dominated by the oversized, omniscient presence of Frank Mickens, for Dan, me and scores of teachers and students, Tilden was dominated by the undersized presence of Joel Dick.

Joel and the principal, Everett Kerner, were in a relationship. They lived together. Sadly, in those days (long before gay marriages were legalized) they could not be married. Ironically, they might not have been permitted to work in the same school were they married.

With Kerner running the school, Joel cobbled together several departments—English, speech, reading, ESL, drama—into a fiefdom of 33 teachers. The younger women in the department were tortured daily by Joel.

Based on memory, I recalled that most of Joel's teachers were tall, young, good-looking men. But according to the Tilden yearbook,

Joel's Communication Arts Department actually had 18 men and 15 women. However, only four were Black, whereas out of Tilden's approximately 140 teachers, one-third were Black.

Joel was your classic New York City administrator. He rarely praised you but frequently criticized you. He'd been a speech and English teacher and no doubt he was criticized. Instead of ending such a negative vibe of poor leadership, he continued it. He wasn't evil. He didn't sexually harass any of the men in his department. He was, for the most part, professional.

Instead, he harassed us unmercifully—about every little nitpicky thing he could think of. He was, in his warped way, trying to make us better teachers. He wanted his massive department to be outstanding. He wanted to be a principal.

He was short, with what I thought were two toupees. Dan believed he had more than two hairpieces. He would swap them to make it appear he had a haircut or his hair had grown. The students thought the changing of the toupees was hilarious. Once, Tilden students had respected and admired Joel Dick—many of them thougt he was a good teacher, whether it was English, speech or drama. But the students in Tilden in 1989 saw him as a comic figure. He didn't interact with them very much. He mostly stayed tucked away in his tiny office. Some of his interactions with students were shockingly callous. For example, another teacher had been in Joel's office with a student and the student told them that his father had just died. Joel showed no empathy, offered a terse and insincere condolence and carried on with his meeting.

Perhaps a poorly treated adolescent case of acne had left his face pocked. His skin was very dry and his hands were chaffed and often bled. He wore large 1970s style glasses.

A woman who escaped his wrath because she taught math, Pauline Dunn, who became my good friend at Tilden, said of Joel and Everett: "I don't understand what Everett sees in Joel. Everett is a good-looking man. He could do better than Joel. Joel is so unattractive. He's got those short legs and that funny walk."

Yet Joel had this incredible drive. I believe it emanated from Brooklyn's Erasmus Hall High School, where he'd graduated in the early 1950s. Something about that school must have motivated Joel and many graduates. Erasmus Hall produced greatness in the arts, athletics, science, medicine—name any field. While other New York City public high schools also produced rosters of successful graduates, the "who's who" out of Erasmus Hall in the 20th century might have been the best.

Just a few of those who attended and graduated: actress Mae West, writer Barnard Malamud (author of *The Natural*), writer Roger Kahn, Chicago Bears hall of fame quarterback Sid Luckman, pro football owner and hall of famer Al Davis, actress Barbara Stanwyck, painter Elaine de Kooning, journalist Dorothy Kilgallen, opera singer Beverly Sills, singer Neil Diamond. Moses Horowitz, who dropped of school after two months and is known to all as Moe Howard of the Three Stooges, and world chess champion Bobby Fisher, another dropout, were two of the most renowned non-graduates.

The list goes on and on.

And there was Joel Dick, amid such genius and talent. The Erasmus Hall student he most envied? Barbra Streisand. Joel wanted to be like Streisand: talented, admired and beautiful. However, he didn't really have a great talent, he was no longer admired and, as Pauline said, he was ugly. Though, I thought he made himself look as good as possible.

As Dan, who would spend two-and-a-half tortured years working for Joel, said of him, he had this certain toughness. Dan grew up near Watertown in upstate New York. To be tough there, kids needed physical toughness. But Dan said city toughness was different.

"Toughness was more mental for somebody like Joel," Dan said. The mentality was that "you could beat the shit out of me but I won't back down."

Joel interviewed me in his tiny office and hired me. I was full-time again. But I still needed more classes to obtain the provisional New York State teaching license and then apply to graduate school to get started on a master's degree. Joel seemed to like me and so I hoped that maybe I wouldn't have to go through the fired/hired NYC crap during my first semester with him.

As soon as I started working at Tilden, there was an incident. The librarian was walking to the school after parking her car when a van pulled up. The driver aimed a shotgun at her and robbed her. She wasn't injured. I maintained a high state of alertness walking into the school.

Once in the school I felt safe. In crowded halls packed with hundreds of kids I was often the only White person. I'd smile, greet kids, and never feel threatened in any way—though some kids were armed with well-hidden knives and guns.

Yet, while walking in my Brooklyn neighborhood, if an African-American man walked by me I felt discomfort, a nervousness. Minorities for the most part stayed clear of the streets of Carroll Gardens because it wasn't safe for them. A lone Black man was a target for mobs of teenagers. They might harass or attack him for no reason. Those kids even went after certain White people.

One evening as I walked my cocker spaniel, a kid screamed, "Kike, fucking kike."

The derogatory word for a Jewish person was shouted at a single male Hasid (the group of ultra-religious Jews from a large Brooklyn community of Hasidim). It came from a group of 15 neighborhood kids, many of whom I knew well. The small Hasid walked, head down, quickly up my block and the boys began to follow him. I cut across the street, towards the action, with my dog barking. If the kids went after him, I would intervene and protect the poor guy.

Those kids often annoyed me. But other than pounding on each other and a lot of name-calling, I'd never seen them actually threaten anybody. The Hasid made it to the subway entrance, his feet quickly scooting down the stairs. The boys gave up their pursuit. I didn't attempt to be a teacher on the street—and admonish them for this insanity. That never worked and would result in an altercation. Though their parents would support me if the boys disrespected me, they probably wouldn't for their anti-Semitism.

I had quickly moved to protect the small Jewish man and would have done the same if I saw the boys pursuing an African American. So why did I feel so comfortable at Tilden and uncomfortable on the streets of this neighborhood, if a Black man walked by me?

I was in year two of teaching minority children. I supported and advised them so I didn't see myself as racist. Traveling the world in the 1980s, a decade that began very badly for me but was now ending well, I often found myself as the only White person far away from the U.S. It made me aware of what it could feel like to be the minority, whether I was in North Africa or India.

The incident with the Hasid led me to believe that White Americans had an irrational fear of those who were different. And fear easily slipped into hatred.

I had hoped to get my African American English students to read African American authors and, surprisingly, Joel Dick let me order a class set of the Alice Walker novel, *The Color Purple*. Walker's novel won the 1983 Pulitzer Prize for Fiction and was adapted into a Stephen Speilberg-directed 1985 film that launched the careers of Whoopie Goldberg and Oprah Winfrey.

It took several weeks before the two boxes of books arrived in my classroom one day. I wanted the kids to immediately read the novel. And most of my students were excited to read it after all of my hype. But there was a problem. It was wrapped so well I couldn't open the boxes. And there were no scissors in that room. I was frustrated.

"Oh well," I told the kids. "I guess we'll have to start reading tomorrow."

Then I noticed something being passed up from the back of the room. A girl placed a switchblade in my hand.

Now, I just discussed how kids had weapons in school and how it could always be an unseen threat. Clearly this knife was a dangerous weapon. What should I do? I knew the answer but I was so focused on opening the damn boxes and sending the books around the room. Should I open the boxes with the knife?

Of course, the answer was no. Nonetheless, I tried to open the switchblade and couldn't even do that. The kids laughed. Then a girl came up and showed me how to open it. I figured I had gone this far and I might as well get the books going around the room and start reading. I cut into the tape sealing the books. Now, of course, I should have confiscated the weapon. The experienced teacher would have done that and made it a lesson. No weapons in school, that's the rule.

But, I suppose, I wanted to show the kids I wasn't their enemy so I passed the knife back.

"I won't look where it's going," I said. And I kept my word.

However, I strongly recommend to any young teachers out there, if you ever are handed a weapon in your classroom, please do not return the weapon to its owner.

Yet, the books and my strange behavior had endeared me to the kids. I might not have known what I was doing in the classroom, as Joel Dick made clear to me at every opportunity, but the kids at Tilden now labeled me as a "cool" teacher.

Unfortunately, my friend Dan, who had gotten me this job and kept my teaching career alive, struggled with staying calm under the frequent duress. While Dan was brilliant and a very good teacher, his temper hurt him with the kids.

"Dan, you are the Sean Penn of this department," Joel said, comparing him to the actor, whose role in the 1980s film *Fast Times at Ridgemont High* forever endeared him to U.S. high school students. However, Penn often found himself in trouble in the late '80s—like the time he was sentenced to 60 days in jail for punching an extra on a movie set.

I never yelled at the kids, though I probably should have. There were many great teachers at Tilden, the main reason why minority students from around the city endured long subway and bus rides to go there.

Dave Cullen was a tall, skinny bearded evangelical Christian who was the most energetic and brilliant teacher I had seen at that point. He commuted to the school from New Jersey, often picking up Dan on the way in. Cullen had a tremendous sense of humor. I'd walk by Cullen's English classes and hear hysterical laughter from his students. He also had tremendous energy, despite his Jersey commute. Though unlike me he didn't have a wife, infant and dog. The kids loved him.

Rachel Sanchez and Anthony Castelli were also excellent English teachers. My friend Pauline, who flirted incessantly with some of the young male teachers like me, taught math well. She was born in Poland but spoke perfect English with a Long Island accent. Married, she raised triplets in the Five Towns section of Nassau County.

She was small and athletic, obsessed with tennis, attractive, thirty something, Jewish and completely shocked when I confided to her that I was Jewish, too.

"Both parents?" she said.

I nodded.

"Does Joel know?" she said. "He'll have an orgasm. I swore you were a WASP. You're from the Main Line in Pennsylvania and you look like a WASP. How can you be Jewish?"

Tilden also had a great faculty room, unlike Boys and Girls or JHS 142. Teachers would eat lunch together—a sign of a tight faculty as opposed to a school where the teachers eat in their rooms alone or in little cliques.

I learned more about teaching from great teachers like Castelli and Cullen than from Joel, who observed me constantly—each time pushing the Dick-teaching technique on me. And while he would always tell you when he was coming, it created stress and pressure to have an administrator come into your classroom and critique your technique, especially when you didn't have tenure, especially when it was Joel Dick—and at Tilden it was always Dick. And, while I hadn't been fired yet, I was one "Unsatisfactory" observation away from being bounced out of Tilden for any trivial reason. Though, I sensed that Joel liked having me around too much to dump me and then deal with the hassle of hiring a new teacher.

He chatted with me whenever he could. Perhaps as Pauline flirted with me (and I flirted back with her), Joel was flirting with me too, in his bizarre, subtle way.

"There are rumors going around that you are looking for a job in the suburbs," he said to me.

Why, however, would I commute all the way out to the suburbs? I didn't even know if I wanted to make teaching a career. Comments like that hinted that he wouldn't get rid of me so quickly and I'd nearly made it to Thanksgiving.

As far as my observations, I wanted them to go well. It was a competitive thing. You believe you are doing a good job of teaching kids and want your supervisor to concur.

Though Joel insisted we not alert the kids about an observation, you had to be a fool not to. You had to get them ready. "We are having a visitor tomorrow," I'd say.

Before one such observation, one of my many challenging students, Rohan Blackstock, said, "Who is our visitor?"

"Don't worry about it," I said. "Rohan, just get here on time."

"Mr. Kravitz," said Rohan in his sing-song Caribbean accent, "you were late the other day."

'Rohan, that was my first lateness," I said. "Forty more and I'll be even with you and it's only November."

Another boy, Jamu, who had a slight lisp said, "Our visitor is not going to be Mr. Dick?"

"Don't worry about it," I said to the class. "Forget I said anything. Maybe we won't have a visitor."

"Because me and Mr. Dick don't get along," said a worried Jamu. "If it's Mr. Dick I might not come to class tomorrow." Considering that Joel had mostly been a speech teacher I could only imagine the torture Joel had already inflicted on Jamu for his lisp. Joel constantly corrected my speech and I spoke clearly with no discernible accent—neither from Philly nor New York. If Joel heard Jamu speak he might pull him out of this class and change his schedule.

I thought the lesson went terrifically. My students were well behaved. They raised their hands and called me sir. Almost all of them listened, even Rohan Blackstock, who was actually on time, which shocked me. Kids learned.

Joel started his post-observation with, no exaggeration, "You had 30 students in class and you only called on 29 of them. You didn't call on a boy named, let me see, Jamu, I believe."

He looked at me as if I had just committed an act of educational gross negligence for that horrid transgression.

"Yeah, you're right Mr. Dick (I had to call him Mr. Dick at all times even when it was the two of us alone in his little office)," I said. "I should have caught that."

Of course I didn't call on Jamu intentionally because I didn't want Joel to hear his lisp.

"You had your homework in the wrong order. It should come before your takeaway, your big takeaway," he practically sang—slightly off key.

Was he serious?

"You said, 'Will somebody raise their hand?' That doesn't agree. What should it be?"

"Will somebody raise his hand?" I said.

"Very good."

"But that's sexist," I said. "What about the ladies?"

He let out a very shrill "ooohh" and said, "Don't let the principal hear you say that."

"You used 'gonna' three times," he continued while looking at a long list of inexcusable *faux pas*, mostly mispronunciation or slang.

At this point I stared at his hands. They weren't bleeding—for a change. The little capillaries were purple and kinda popping. But at least he didn't say my lesson was unsatisfactory, then fire me. It felt like it would take forever just to get my provisional state license. I hadn't even finished all of my undergraduate English and Education classes.

More torture from Joel could drive me out of teaching to another profession but interesting teachers and a lot of great kids made Tilden more bearable than my difficult first year. As I prepared to go to school in the morning, I looked forward to seeing some of the teachers, and teaching some of my classes. The year before I had dreaded walking into JHS 142.

Rachel Sanchez, who advised the school newspaper *Tilden Topics* and was trying to get me involved since I had been a newspaper reporter, told me about a friend of hers who died from AIDS. She said they all sat in the funeral home for an hour and cried. They waited two months before having a service. The young man's mom didn't know he was gay. That was pretty typical back in those days. Gay men and women were closeted and discriminated against, sadly.

Pauline also fascinated me. She kept asking me to play tennis. She seemed pretty athletic and I thought about it. It would probably be competitive. My game was fair but I could compete with better players. She talked up her tennis game so she must have been pretty good.

"Well, if you won't play tennis with me, maybe you want to be my friend's afternoon lover?" she said.

"What?" I said. "Are you a madam now?"

"Interested?" she said laughing. "Though my husband says she's plastic looking. Whaddya you think?"

"No Pauline," I said. "I'm happily married with a child and a dog."

"When you're not happy anymore let me know," she said.

Annie Greco, 30-something, taught science. Attractive and intelligent, she had a spicy, fun personality. She'd grown up in a big Brooklyn Italian family but had lost her brother the year before. He had been found dead, in the trunk of his car, full of bullets. Annie was very upset with the police investigation. She believed the cops didn't care about her brother's murder because he was involved with shady characters. He was a bookie and one of his friends owed him a lot of money, and owed money to other bookies. She believed it was that friend who lured him to his death so he wouldn't have to pay him back.

"My brother was the kind of guy who wouldn't back off," she said. "He would say fuck you when he should have apologized."

I felt bad for her. "I used to be lighthearted but I can't be happy 'til this is resolved," she said. "I know if I were murdered he would do everything to bring my killer to justice."

Greco was single and trying hard to find a guy. The guys she dated had a strong sex drive. She had a strong drive to start a family. She'd even tried dating a married man for a bit, but quickly dumped him.

"If he's cheating on his wife, I know he'll cheat on me," she said.

Interesting discourse and the stories of Tilden teachers kept me going. More importantly, helping kids created great satisfaction.

In my ninth period remedial reading class we were talking about addictions, specifically drug addictions. As always, I warned the kids how dangerous drugs were and how easy it was to get addicted and ruin your life.

This one 14-year-old Jamaican boy, Jason, who spoke in a lyrical Carribean accent, said, "There's other things you can be addicted to."

Jason was tall, good looking, witty, and a bit of a clown with a voice that cracked when he talked or laughed. He was intelligent and not always serious. He looked at his classmates, a rowdy band of rag-a-muffins, and said, "I'm addicted to eating dirt."

There was silence. I wasn't sure how to react.

"Eating dirt?" I said. "Are you joking?"

"No, no," he said. "It's true. I love to eat dirt. I keep a little plastic bag in my room of the best dirt and every night I scoop some into my mouth." He pantomimed the utter joy of a mouthful of delicious dirt. "I love my dirt."

I looked at the paraprofessional teacher in the room. She gave me a skeptical look.

"There's nothing like some nice dirt after a good meal," he said. "I started eating dirt in Jamaica. They had the best dirt there. They had this white dirt that was, ohhh, the best. It's hard to find good dirt here but I know this one place where they have nice soft, dry, very tasty dirt."

I looked at the other kids and said, "Do you guys believe this?"

A bony, hyper girl said, "I used to eat dirt in Jamaica."

"Really?" I said.

"It was very good," she said. "But then my mom beat that dirt eating out of me."

Well, maybe if two kids were dirt eaters this was legit. Though, the girl and Jason were pretty out-there kids, so a hint of skepticism remained for me.

Then one of the most normal kids in the class said, "I used to eat that white dirt in Jamaica."

No way these kids had set this up as a goof on me. I was a believer in dirt eating. They were making it sound so tasty I wanted to dig into this white dirt somehow.

The paraprofessional, an African-American lady, who remained skeptical said, "Jason, bring in your dirt tomorrow and prove all of this and eat some in class."

Jason looked at her with supreme distrust and said, "Oh noooo. You will take my dirt and throw it out and I'll have to get more. It's a long hard walk to the best dirt."

"Jason, who would throw out dirt?" I said. "That's silly. No one will take your special dirt."

The more this unusual discussion went on I began to think that if Jason really was addicted to eating dirt, it wouldn't be healthy. His dirt could be full of nasty stuff. So after class I went to the school's drug-program coordinator and told him about our dirt-eating discussion.

"That is a legitimate disorder," he said. "You see it more in younger children. But teenagers, especially on the islands with poor diets, might actually do it for nutrients they lack like iron, zinc, calcium."

The coordinator got to work with Jason. A month later Jason said to me, "Thank you Mr. Kravitz. I feel better without my dirt. I'm healthier."

And helping kids like that get clean, created this wonderful feeling that made ignoring Joel Dick's incessant nit-picking seem worthwhile. Perhaps I would remain a teacher. But Dick hung around, torturing me by demanding I turn in Aims forms every week, which I didn't always do. He wanted me to do a showcase window display. I stalled. The showcase looked fine. And there were other petty Dick demands that had nothing to do with teaching, motivating or supporting the children.

We rolled through Thanksgiving, a short December and the holiday vacation. And suddenly the 1980s were over. It was January 1, 1990.

I sat in the backyard of our Brooklyn apartment, looking at frozen snow melting in the 47-degree fog. Lights shone through the fog. The 1980s started for me hopelessly lost in a mental hospital. But since I had met Jennifer in college we'd spent eight happy years together, married since 1987. I was the father of a beautiful five-month-old girl, who brought meaning and purpose to my life. In my 29th year, I stared down 30, which loomed as a scary divide from carefree life to responsibility. It wasn't just about me, or me and Jennifer. There was this blue-eyed, blonde-haired girl who needed us.

I reflected on two of my favorite writers, Hemingway and Henry Miller. Miller had roamed some of the same Brooklyn streets that I had. Hemingway had experienced the horrors of World War I as a teenager in Italy, where he drove an ambulance. He'd survived and then had gone into journalism as I had. But he'd become a success with his writing. Miller's early novels went unpublished.

I compared myself to the two of them. Miller wouldn't write his first great novel, *Tropic of Cancer*, until he was in his mid 40s. It was published only in France and banned in the United States for nearly three decades until it was finally published in the U.S. in 1961. Miller wouldn't enjoy the worldwide success of *Tropic of Cancer* until he was 70. Hemingway published the novel *The Sun Also Rises* in his mid 20s. By 30, Hemingway's tight prose, sans adjectives and adverbs, vaulted him to literary superstardom.

What would the 1990s bring for me? Would it bring me writing success? I hoped so.

Though right away the new decade brought more challenging students, whom I struggled to teach. I wanted to succeed with every type of student. The good ones were easy to teach. I wanted to help all of them.

In a class discussion about the problems at the school a kid asked, "Should we have metal detectors here like a lot of schools?"

I tried to let the kids answer rather than give my opinion. At least I had quickly figured that out. Don't just blurt out what you think in a class discussion. Lead a debate of their opinions.

"I brought a gun to school once," Cyril Garmon said.

Every other kid in the class lit into him. They called him a hood, a criminal. They were all angry that he would put students and faculty at risk.

"You know, guns often don't protect you," I said, unable to hold back. "Kids with guns accidentally shoot each other more than they protect themselves."

The date was January 19, the last day of the first semester. And Cyril said it was his last day at Tilden. He would not return for the second semester.

"Well, you made a mistake bringing a gun here, but I wish you luck wherever you go," I said.

A girl angrily said, "I know where you are going, Cyril. You are going to prison."

What do you say when a kid says he'd brought a gun to school? At least that child would no longer be in the school.

Another difficult student who I struggled with was a small, skinny boy named Michael Pacheco. He was maybe 100 pounds. He was illiterate, perhaps reading on a first-grade level. He was also in remedial reading, but he was so hyper that neither the reading teacher nor I made any progress with him.

He'd spent the first semester disrupting my English class by talking, walking around the room—anything for attention.

I knew that perhaps contacting his parents was an answer but I'd tried that with a few kids and it hadn't gone well. One kid said his father beat him after my phone call. Was that the truth? Perhaps. Joel Dick said always call the parents. However, I didn't believe Joel cared about these kids' lives.

I didn't call Michael Pacheco's parents. I dealt with his constant disruptions as best as I could.

Later in the semester, I proctored a state test, as a relief proctor. I entered the classroom in the middle of the test. Usually the kids took state tests very seriously. In the back of the room there was a very overweight girl who was talking. She might have weighed 230 pounds. She had a good 50 pounds on me. I told her not to talk. I considered getting security and having her removed. But she would stop temporarily after I admonished her and I wanted her to finish the test. She wasn't cheating. I hoped to avoid a disruption.

I first realized that Michael Pacheco was taking the test near the girl in the back of the room when he told her to shut up. He was so small I hadn't seen him at first.

"Don't say nothing to me Michael Pacheco," the girl said. "I will kill you, you little, skinny dumbass."

I walked back there and told both of them that they would fail the test if they said another word. They stopped.

"Why you even in this test Michael Pacheco?" the girl said. "You can't read. You gonna fail anyway."

"Why you taking this test?" Pacheco countered. "You too fat to be taking this test."

"You say one more thing I gonna crack your head like a walnut," the girl said.

"You won't do nothing, you fat-ass bitch," he said.

"What did you call me?" the girl said.

I screamed at them to stop. But with surprising speed the girl lunged at Michael Pacheco and locked up his little head in an impressive and tight headlock.

"Let him go," I screamed and rushed toward the altercation.

Squeezing her headlock tighter, the girl smashed his face into the desk. Now, only a year before in a similar situation I had saved Leontina from having her head whacked by a chair. But this girl was bigger and stronger than that other attacker. And while Leontina had nearly ruined my life, I had felt bad for her. I didn't feel bad for Michael Pacheco. I mean, I wish I could have taught him to read, but he'd made class unteachable and had made me miserable every day.

I hesitated, stopping a few feet from them. The girl smashed his face into the desk hard—again.

Rather than try to grab her I yelled at a kid sitting near the door to quickly find a security guard while continuing to yell at the girl, who I didn't know, to release Michael Pacheco. She smacked his forehead into the desk again before a security guard, along with Dave Cullen—like a superhero teacher—bolted into the room and freed Michael Pacheco. And it took both of them to do it. Both Pacheco and the girl were removed.

"Okay, everybody, sorry about that," I said. "Please finish your tests."

"Mr. Kravitz, why didn't you break that up?" said a boy.

I should have made something up. Perhaps one reason I didn't try to separate them, which I didn't say, was that someone had finally found a way to shut up Michael Pacheco. And while I didn't want to see Michael Pacheco get hurt, I also didn't want to grab that girl and risk hurting her, having her make a crazy accusation against me or end up with her injuring me.

"I don't know why I didn't break it up," I told the kids. I thought about saying I didn't want to get hurt but quickly realized that I couldn't express weakness.

In the end, I did the right thing for the wrong reason. Always get security rather than break up a fight, especially one involving a girl. Cullen and the security guard struggled to release Michael Pacheco. Even with the two of them, both strong guys, prying apart her headlock took a minute, which seemed longer. And while I had been a collegiate wrestler, could I have freed the head of Michael Pacheco alone? At least I recognized that she had his arm in the head-lock, so she wasn't choking him. She smashed his face into the desk hard but he returned to school the same Michael Pacheco. It didn't appear that he'd suffered a head injury or a concussion—though in those days we didn't realize the dangers of a concussion. We called it getting your bell rung.

The spring semester had several interesting moments. As I tried to figure out how to handle all of them, my brain was smashed by something that no professor had discussed in an Education class.

The principal was in the hallway trying to clear the halls. It was late February, and I'd only seen Kerner in the halls talking to students once or twice. One of my students, Michelle Francis, a terrific kid, ran out of the bathroom crying hysterically.

I asked Rachel Sanchez, "What's going on?"

"One of our students was murdered this weekend," she said.

"Who?"

Now remember, there were thousands of kids in the school so the chances of me knowing the murdered child were slim.

"Shondella Webster," she said.

"Oh my God," I said. "I have her in eighth period." I realized that Michelle Francis was Shondella's best friend.

As the kids came into eighth period and sat down, most of them somber, I said, "We lost Shondella this weekend."

There was no lesson that period as I kept looking at Shondella's empty seat. I couldn't believe that she would never sit in it again. She was a happy kid, who tried her best.

I learned from that discussion that Shondella, 15, was stabbed 21 times by two girls, a 17-year-old and her 14-year-old sister. Apparently, she'd had a three-year feud with the girls. Michelle Francis had known Shondella since second grade and was in shock, devastated. I told her to go to her guidance counselor but she wanted to stay in class and talk about her best friend.

The murder took place at a Flatbush social club at 4:48 a.m. Sunday morning. Shondella's mother had told her she couldn't go out that night but she snuck out. The police charged Tricia and Patricia Lukien with murder and assault.

Some of the kids were upset that Tilden's administration had done little to support students over Shondella's murder. I thought that if this were a suburban school kids would have had easier access to guidance counselors, school psychologists and social workers.

I found out that Joel Dick had defended the principal's handling of the school's response by saying, "This is an inner-city school and the kids are used to this."

I couldn't believe he had said that. While I learned of these awful comments second-hand, it was a typical Dick thing to say.

A few days later I got Dan Shannon to go with me to Shondella's wake. The funeral home was on Church Avenue, right near where Ebbets Field once stood. We were the only White people at the evening viewing. As we walked into the funeral home, I heard people murmur, "They are teachers from Tilden."

Michelle Francis was there and was so happy to see me and Dan. She thanked us for coming. No other Tilden teachers went there that night, though some may have gone at a different time.

We learned that her killers were Jamaican. Shondella's family was from Guyana. Apparently, not long after we left, Shondella's mother loudly blamed Jamaicans for her daughter's death. Soon a group of Jamaicans arrived and fired their guns in the air outside the funeral home. And the cousin of the girls who murdered Shondella walked by the casket and said, loudly, "You got what you deserved bitch."

About a month later, we were talking about drugs. A boy in that class, Liston Craig, said, "Dying is hype now. Drug dealers don't care if they die. They want to die."

Michelle screamed at him and ran out of the room. I had no words for her, only shared sadness and grief.

Though I also felt for Liston. He had done time in Rikers Island prison. His older sister came to his parent-teacher conferences and told me that both of their parents were dead. Liston was intelligent. He had no adult guidance. I wasn't surprised at his callous words— with the best friend of a murdered 15-year-old a few feet away.

I decided to read Frederick Douglass's *Narrative of an American Slave* with Shondella's class. Could it help with the kids' grief and Liston's situation?

They all liked the book. One kid said it made her realize that her life wasn't so bad. Another girl, Ann Buchanon, told the class, "Those slaves died trying to read. And here we are, with all of these teachers working hard to teach us, flushing our opportunity to get an education for what? To sell drugs." She stared at Liston. "We need to educate ourselves like Frederick Douglass."

Douglass was 12 years old and living in Baltimore in the 1830s. His owners were a husband and wife. The wife began to teach him to read. Her husband found out and "forbade Mrs. Auld to instruct me further, telling her, among other things that it was unlawful ... to teach a slave to read ... Though conscious of the difficulty of learning without a teacher, I set out ... whatever the cost to learn how to read.

"The more I read, the more I was led to abhor and detest my enslavers. I could regard them in no other light than a band of successful robbers, who had left their homes, and gone to Africa and stolen us from our homes and in a strange land reduced us to slavery."

My days reading the words of Frederick Douglass to these children made me feel like I was doing something right. At least Joel didn't criticize me, though he was hibernating in his office, and not aware of everything I taught in all of my classes. I made sure to turn in my Aims forms. That week I only wrote "non-fiction" for that class and he never looked into it.

I thought of all the slaves who were beaten to death, murdered, tossed off of ships. I wanted to get closer to these kids but the incident from the previous spring led me to create distance. Shondella's murder made me want to reduce the distance and get to know all of them in order to protect them from the evil of the world.

But how could I protect these kids? Shondella's mom couldn't even keep her home that fateful evening.

I left Shondella's seat empty for the entire semester. Every day during eighth period I looked at that empty seat and thought about this nice kid whose life had ended so senselessly.

As I write this 30 years later, I can still see Shondella's empty seat. At the time, I hoped that I would never lose a student like that again.

But there was more death waiting for me.

I was teaching a class when another teacher entered my room and said to call Jennifer. I thought the worst. Could something have happened to my daughter? I worried a lot—still do. The teacher stayed in the class while I ran to a phone. My grandmother had died, just short of her 80th birthday, when her heart gave out.

I grieved for her even though she was selfish, insulting and cheap—despite being wealthy. She had, however, always been nice to me. And she had a good sense of humor. I would miss her.

At her funeral a few days later, though I tried to suppress my feelings, I was overcome by emotion when the rabbi mentioned her great granddaughter, her only great grandchild. He said Grandma Mae graduated from Rice University—which she actually bragged about, though it wasn't true. Had she even been to Houston? She lied a lot. She'd been born in Philly, my only grandparent born in the U.S. The other three were born in Russia, Poland and Azerbaijan. She grew up poor.

But as an adult, who'd grown wealthy, she traveled. She and my grandfather loved the Philadelphia Phillies. They had seats in a box on the field and knew many of the players. My brothers and I went to many games. After the Phillies blew a big lead in the final weeks of the 1964 season, handing the pennant to the St. Louis Cardinals in one of the all-time great sports collapses, she and my grandfather traveled to Morocco to escape the pain of that meltdown. I remember asking her what Morocco was like in the 1960s and she said, "It was terrible. The French left and took all of their chefs with them."

Angelo Bruno was her childhood friend. Bruno ran the Philly mob until the back of his head was blown off in a 1980 hit that started a Philly mob war. In the film *The Irishman* (2019) he was played by Harvey Keitel.

I thought about how my grandmother would tell stories about young Angelo, which I think were actually true. She'd always finish with, "He was such a nice man."

I carried her casket to her grave and she was lowered into the frozen ground. She had been my last living grandparent. Her death wasn't tragic like Shondella's had been. But aren't all deaths tragic? I recalled the last time I'd seen her alive. She'd been full of energy and was insulting various people. She hadn't been a very good parent or spouse; however she'd been a good grandparent.

Joel Dick told me that he was sorry for my loss and then quickly segued into: "Please get your weekly Aims form in. Is this becoming a frequent occurrence? Get it to me before the end of the day. You want to work here next year, don't you?"

"Yes, I want to work here," I said. I wanted to add that I'd just buried my grandmother but he knew that. Talk about suppressing emotion. Joel brilliantly suppressed his humanity.

March turned into April and school was going well. We had our April vacation. We stuck around the city and took Dana to the Central Park Zoo, her first zoo trip. She leaned on the glass in front of the polar bears and studied them. She sang loudly and a monkey turned to see what the sound was, as she had the most beautiful little voice for an eight month old.

The week off refreshed me. I looked forward to hearing about the students' week off and to seeing them and my teacher friends. Tilden was a good work environment, except for hidden weapons, murdered children, and, of course, Joel Dick.

Soon it was the last day of classes—an indescribable and amazing feeling. I had a few days to get my grades in. Joel told me to have them to him by 8:20 a.m. June 20.

The appointed day and time arrived and I was wrapping up my grades, not being an experienced grader. I was nearly done when I heard Joel page me over the school PA, several times. I finished at 8:30 a.m., 10 minutes beyond Joel's deadline, but instead of taking them to Joel, I followed my usual strategy of avoiding him. I gave them to Joel's unofficial assistant, another English teacher, John Devine.

Joel emerged from his office and tracked me down in the teacher's lounge where I laughed and swapped stories with Cullen, Shannon and Greco. He furiously motioned me into the hallway and said, "Well, what do you have to say?"

"I'm sorry."

"That's not good enough. Don't you have an excuse?"

"No, I have no excuse."

I had nearly made it through the year but I believed he would fire me right there. He didn't need me anymore. My grades were in. He had two months to replace me. Shockingly, he just admonished me and walked away. Miraculously, I still had my Tilden job.

Joel kept me around because he wanted me to take over the school newspaper from Rachel Sanchez the following year. He liked that I'd been a newspaper reporter. It had been my reporting background that had led Mickens's secretary to hire me the year before—after Mickens screamed that he wasn't hiring me. So, all of those years of print reporting had been good for something. And I'd learned to type extremely fast.

Though running the journalism club seemed like way too much work. Even though we'd only have to put out two print issues per year. The club met once a week. I had gone to some meetings and had taken two kids to a field trip for a student press conference for the New York City schools Chancellor Joseph A. Fernandez.

Fernandez had taught college classes at Penn and Georgetown, earned his Ph.D. from the University of Miami, and arrived in New York to reform the city public school system of 940,000 students.

We saw Fernandez in Brooklyn Heights. Pasha Durr was an African-American senior: very bright, lean, intense. He believed that the Caribbean kids oppressed the African-American kids like him. In a terrific editorial in *Tilden Topics* he wrote: "Why is [African American] culture put down [by African Caribbeans]? Why is our music considered inferior to Reggae or Calypso? How can some African-Caribbeans proclaim themselves as better than African-Americans? ... We share the same history but a different shipping route. One African-American Tilden student said, 'I don't like the fact that we are disunited ... we as young people should work together to fight racism in all forms.'"

Michelle Lance was the *Tilden Topics* editor. Each four-page issue featured several of her articles; she took a journalism class on Saturdays.

At the press conference, Pasha scooted to a microphone and in a loud, clear voice asked Chancellor Fernandez, known as an education reformer, about the inequities between the funding of schools in White neighborhoods and Black neighborhoods. He described Tilden to other students in attendance, most of whom were White.

Most of the questions up to that point had been softballs. Fernandez said he didn't know what the exact differences in funding were but that he would look into the breakdown of what schools got.

"I'll give you kids a scoop," he said. And then he added that he would make public the breakdown of how much each school received.

After Pasha left the microphone I told him he'd done a great job. Then a *New York Newsday* reporter, Sylvia Moreno, grabbed him and asked him about Tilden, and about his question. He'd become a hit— an older gentleman asked Pasha if he knew Joel Dick. Not wanting Pasha to say anything negative in front of the *Newsday* reporter, I pulled him away before he could answer. You never knew what anyone would say about Joel Dick, but "he's a dick" was the most common response.

I took the kids to the Promenade. It was a bright, sunny March day. The view of downtown Manhattan from the Promenade was spectacular, dominated by the World Trade Center towers. Both kids had never walked the Promenade, which was built over the Brooklyn-Queens Expressway and back then had a clear view of downtown and the harbor, featuring the Statue of Liberty. Pasha said that it looked like one of the World Trade Center towers was taller than the other one. We went to eat at a burger joint. Pasha planned to go to Bowling Green University. Michelle hoped to go to the University of New Mexico.

Joel confirmed his intentions about my taking over as newspaper advisor in his closing letter to me, dated June 26, 1990. On the Samuel J. Tilden High School stationary Joel wrote: "Let not the 'year' end without my thanking you for all that you did to contribute to the success of the department. I know that this was a difficult year for you, but, hopefully, you have come through it unscathed. I am hopeful that when you assume the advisory position for our school newspaper, *Tilden Topics*, you will have another area in which you can prove yourself. I hope that you and your family have a very rewarding summer."

His signature begins with a massive and sweeping 'J.'

So that cemented it. I'd have to learn how to run the school newspaper club. I wasn't thrilled but it meant that once again I would get paid for the summer, keep my health care and have a job in September.

At a department lunch on the final day of school, Joel spoke briefly. I shook his hand—and afterwards subtly looked at my hand to make sure there was no blood on it. I told Joel to have a good summer and he said things looked good for me. He wasn't so nice to some other teachers. Bert Bloom was a small nerd, one of Joel's main veteran teachers. Yet Joel once threatened to "cut Bert's balls off" over some trivial transgression.

But nobody was abused more than an obese teacher, with a scary moustache, named Serge Schultz. Almost all of us felt Joel's constant wrath. But Joel really gave it to Schultz, who incessantly wrote poetry and consumed doughnuts washed down with chocolate milk. Joel did not like Schultz's poetry and told him to find a shrink, and even suggested one, insisting he spend his summer improving his mental health.

Meanwhile, Schultz countered Joel's assessment of him by attacking Joel's homosexuality. His nickname for Joel was "Tinkerbell." Though he never said it to Joel's face. Schultz called homosexuality "a perversion," common for those days.

Another teacher who was probably tortured by Joel was a 50-year-old from Michigan named Don Bowerman. I would often give Bowerman a ride home, as he lived near me. After that last day Bowerman said that Schultz warned him not to say anything to me about Dick because I would run right to him and tell him.

"That's so ridiculous," I said. "Schultz does that. I spent this entire year trying to avoid Joel and talking to him as little as possible."

Bowerman said that if Joel and the principal were in a relationship and lived together and worked in the same high school in Michigan it would be a scandal. While Joel and Everett weren't blatantly open about their relationship, every teacher and plenty of kids in the school knew about it. Nobody cared. Nobody ever complained to any higher ups in the city education bureaucracy as far as I knew, and no doubt some of those administrators knew about it. Had that information been received by some powerful administrators, Dick and Kerner wouldn't have gotten away with it. But the thick webs of bureaucracy protected them. After all, who had time to care about that?

I had survived year two as a teacher in New York City. I had a whole summer to have fun. Of course, my wife would try to make me work.

Life seemed wonderful since I didn't have to get up at five a.m., get ready for school and think about what I was teaching. We had a share of a house on Long Beach Island, a narrow South Jersey barrier island. I sailed on the bay with my younger brother John Enoch—named after our great uncle Enoch, who I believed had perished in the 1919 Spanish flu but who John Enoch insisted had died from complications from surgery.

We trapped delicious crabs and washed them down with several beers, and unlike today I didn't have to urinate every ten minutes. My weight ballooned to an all-time high of 205 pounds—well over my lean 180 pounds from college seven years before.

I finished a draft of a novel that summer. It was my second complete manuscript, and much better than my awful first one but still not even in the same league as Henry Miller's early works, which weren't great. My protagonist was a teacher in Bedford-Stuyvesant.

I still had my Raleigh three-speed and pedaled it over the Brooklyn Bridge into Manhattan and headed to Village bookstores. In the Strand Bookstore I stumbled on a first edition, hard copy of Wildfred Thesiger's *Marsh Arabs*. It cost me $7.50. I still have it. I consumed non-fiction, fiction and carbohydrates at a prodigious pace. Could youth combined with summer off be the best thing about teaching?

My good friend Gil Spencer came up to New York from Delaware County, Pennsylvania, where he was a columnist for the *Delaware County Daily Times*. We had worked together there in Delco, just outside Philly, in the 1980s. I often headed down to Delco, so it was fun running around Manhattan with Gil. We closed a bar in the Village. We stayed at the apartment of his dad, F. Gilman Spencer, who had won a Pulitzer and had been the editor of the *New York Daily News* from 1984-89. He'd just taken over as editor of the *Denver Post* but still had his place in the Village.

When I first arrived in New York I went to his dad's office at the *Daily News* to see if I could land a reporting job there. While in his office, he introduced me to one of his star columnists, Mike McAlary. McAlary went on to capture a Pulitzer for exposing New York City police torture of a Haitian immigrant in a Brooklyn police station in 1997. But McAlary would die of colon cancer at 41 a year later.

Gil Sr. liked me but spelled out the labor issues at the *Daily News*. A promising job as a reporter at the *Philadelphia Inquirer* had been derailed for me by a 46-day newspaper strike. I didn't want to deal with newspaper labor strife. And even if he somehow squeezed a position out of his tight budget, I'd have to start at the bottom again. And I'd already worked my way up from writing obituaries once. My last day at the *Daily Times*, young Gil had made a satirical-goodbye front page for me with the headline, "Times Obit Writer Quits, Editor Pissed—Page? Who Cares?" I didn't want to battle upwards through one of the largest newspapers in the country.

My terrific summer continued as I played basketball, golf and softball. I was at my athletic peak. I helped lead my fast-pitch softball team to the championship. There is no better feeling than cracking a homerun in a championship softball game.

There were interesting people and conversations everywhere. I walked the dog by my previous Second Place apartment, where my former landlord, Don Clarke, invited me to join him for a cup of coffee in his backyard.

After my second cup Don's cat appeared with a bird in its mouth. I thought the bird was dead. Don opened the cat's mouth and the bird flew out. It was like a magic trick.

Don had dropped out of school in ninth grade. But he owned buildings and liquor stores, and even managed boxers, back before MMA, when boxing was still the king of the fight game. He took young Black kids out of poverty and turned them into fighters. His most successful was Tyrone "The Harlem Butcher" Jackson.

At one point in his early career Jackson was 22-0, fighting in the Felt Forum in its heyday on cards with Buddy McGirt, Hector Camacho and a young Brooklyn heavyweight named Mike Tyson. Jackson got a couple of title shots, including one in May 1990 at the Inglewood Forum in California against Manuel Medina for the super featherweight title.

"He went the distance and he won that fight," said his trainer Teddy Atlas in a 2019 Maxboxing.com interview. "They gave it to Medina by one point but Tyrone won that fight."

Don said that when he first met Tyrone, he didn't like White people. Don told Tyrone that his 96-year-old grandmother was raped by three Black guys who had broken into her apartment.

"So Tyrone, should I hate all Blacks because of that?" Don said.

It gave Tyrone a different perspective.

After more boxing stories (a few crazy ones about Tyson) Don brought up the real estate developer Donald Trump. He said he had once sold a building to Trump's father. He said Donald Trump got into the casino business, was clueless about it, and got killed financially. "He should have stuck to the only thing he knew anything about, real estate," Don said of Donald.

I read a terrific autobiography of Somerset Maugham that said he'd once hung out with Oscar Wilde when young and didn't write *The Razor's Edge* until age 70. Reading about Maugham's India travels took me back to my Himalayan adventures from five years before. Sadly, I banished the Himalayas from my thoughts and focused on year two of working for Joel Dick.

The final days of summer quickly melted away and I attended Joel's first meeting for my third year as a teacher. A dapper Joel Dick opened the meeting with: "Did anyone go anywhere interesting this summer?"

Before anybody could answer he launched into a long drawn out, unnecessarily detailed, description of his summer trip to the Southwest. At times it was actually funny. Joel's storytelling ability surprised me. And his tales showed a little humanity.

Joel had even hired four new teachers, despite a city-wide budget crunch, including one minority, an Asian guy. The other three were tall good-looking White guys, Joel's preference. In a school with thousands of Black students he hadn't managed to hire a Black person.

I enjoyed seeing everybody. David Cullen told a story, much better than Joel's summer vacation one. After I said I graduated from the University of Delaware, Cullen said he would go there, to the Deer Park Tavern, where he met a Long Island Jewish coed. They started long-distance dating. He even met her folks and the girl introduced him as David.

"What's your last name?" the mom said.

"Cullen," he said.

"David Cohen," the mom said, all excited her daughter had met a nice Jewish boy.

"No," he said. "Cullen."

"What kind of name is that?" the mom asked.

"Irish."

And that was the end of the relationship.

Pauline wore a very sexy dress. She gave me a long hug. She wouldn't let me go. "Are we about to have sex?" I joked. She immediately let go, laughing.

After a couple days of completely useless meetings, we had our first day of classes. My first two classes went well. Then Joel sent a teacher to inform me to report immediately to his office.

Crammed into that compact space, I stood and he struggled to look me in the eyes. "I'm going to have to let you go," he said.

"What?" I said.

He struggled to speak and I wondered what the fuck was going on.

"You are firing me?" I said. "Why?"

He swallowed his words and they didn't come out with his usual speech-teacher clarity: "There was a new teacher meeting and I paged you several times."

"A new teacher meeting?"

"Yes. And I kept paging you because you were supposed to attend."

"But I'm not a new teacher. This is my second year here and my third year of teaching." I was furious and about to scream at him. But I stayed composed. "Why would I possibly think to go to a new teacher meeting?"

"I paged you and you didn't respond. This has happened before."

"You know Joel, I mean Mr. Dick, you can't always hear the ancient PA system here."

"You've said that before and, um—" He seemed nervous and that angered me more and made me bolder. "I don't believe you. I think you could be lying. But please finish the day."

I was about to say I wouldn't finish the day and just walk away from Tilden and let him cover my classes. But he kept talking. He even asked me if I had a better excuse.

"Better excuse?" I said. "Mr. Dick, I'm not a new teacher so why would I go to a new teacher meeting?"

"Well, I was running the meeting," he said.

"But you never told me to go to that meeting," I said. "If you had I would have gone."

"But I paged you."

"You know what, go find someone who relates to the kids like I do," I said. "You won't find anyone as good as me at this point. By doing this you are proving you don't care about these children."

"That is absolutely not true," he said. "I care about Tilden students."

I wanted to say that maybe he once had but he didn't care about these students today. But I didn't say that. He seemed to be getting defensive.

"You came here a bright-eyed young man," he said. "Whatever happened to that pleasant man."

"I'm still pleasant, Mr. Dick," I said. "Alright, I will go and finish my classes for the day." I rushed out of his office and called Jennifer and told her what had happened and that I was going to finish the day and then I was done at Tilden.

"You can't quit," she said. "We need your job. You aren't quitting. At the end of the day you go and ask him for your job back."

"I'm not begging that asshole for this stupid job back," I said.

"Well you'd better figure out a way to keep it," she said.

At lunch I talked to Cullen and Greco about my termination.

"He'll give you another chance," Cullen said.

"Go see him at the end of the day," Greco said. "Tell him you are sorry, offer some excuse-"

"What's with Joel and excuses?" I said.

"Whatever," she said. "Just kiss his ass."

"I'm tired of doing that with him," I said.

"You'll be fine," she said. "He likes you too much to fire you."

"Then why did he fire me?" I said.

I taught my classes. So many kids were happy to see that I was back. The kids' happiness at seeing me swayed me. I went and apologized to Joel and told him I'd never miss another new teacher meeting. He unfired me.

Yet a week later he observed me and ripped apart my lesson. I showed Greco, whom I hung out with in the teachers' lounge period five, what Joel wrote about my lesson. She couldn't believe it. (I was doing a double teacher's lounge, fifth and also eighth period when Pauline would sometimes be there. Though I don't recommend that non-tenured teachers do a double teacher's lounge. Limit your time there.)

However, Greco quickly moved beyond my problems with Dick and talked about something much more pressing—her dating problems.

"I like these guys I date but they are young and just don't satisfy me intellectually like you guys," she said, pointing to Castelli and me. "What am I going to do? Take this guy I went out with last night. He wants to cook for me and do my laundry! How crazy is that. But he doesn't have it up here. (She pointed to her head.) And the guy I'm seeing out by my Hamptons place is 24 years old. He's a cobbler. But I need something more. All the mature good guys are married."

Meanwhile, Joel injected himself in my teaching in a variety of annoying ways. He disrupted my classes with speech diagnostic tests. Sure, he had unfired me, but his invasions of my classroom drove me crazy. I had avoided him for long stretches the year before but he made sure I could not escape him this year.

He tested my students one at a time while I gave the other kids work.

My best student, Sarah Mustafa, who had gotten the best report card of any Tilden student I'd ever taught, was reading sentences for Joel. He stopped her and said, "Where were you born?"

"Jerusalem," she said.

"Oh, how exotic," Joel said.

Then he tested Balquis, a girl from Yemen. She read the sentences and Joel pulled me aside and whispered, "Tomorrow tell this girl to remove that scarf from her head."

"But Mr. Dick," I said quietly as Balquis read, "she's from Yemen."

"What does that mean?"

"She's Moslem," I said.

"Oh," he said. "Oh, Okay. I guess then that she can cover her head—if it's a religious thing."

After Joel left that class, a few minutes before the bell rang, one of my more troubled students, Freddie Moore, told a story to the class about his weekend.

Apparently he and his boys had had a little altercation with a posse from another project. They captured one of the other gang's kids and took his hand and spread it out and said, "This little piggie goes to market and this little piggie-" And then one of Freddie's boys hacked the kid's pinkie off with a meat cleaver. Freddie laughed hysterically, as did a number of other boys, at this mutilation.

Freddie behaved perfectly during Joel's testing. Meanwhile one of my better students, Nikki, said something to Joel. He made me write a pink card for her. What would he have done if he heard Freddie narrate the awful gang assault? I didn't know what to do other than tell Freddie that there was nothing funny about chopping off a person's pinkie, and he had to cease his gang activities, before he ended up missing a digit or worse. He laughed at my advice.

Despite Freddie Moore, my classes went well. My morning commute, however, had become problematic, as I often drove Bowerman to school. I was also driving Greco home some days. And while Bowerman could be entertaining, my afternoon drives with the flirtatious and attractive Greco were a better use of my free-Tilden-taxi service.

I told Bowerman about my latest Joel Dick issues and he said, "Joel told me that you never come to him for help, you only come to destroy."

"What does that mean?" I said, as I drove through East Flatbush one morning.

"Don't worry about it," Bowerman said. "You have to hear what happened to me this weekend. So, I go to the bank and get $100, cleaning out my bank account until the next paycheck. I see this kid walking behind me with a gym bag. Next thing I know the kid pulls a gun on me and tells me to give him my wallet. So I do that—but I tell him to take the cash out and give the wallet back. He goes through the wallet while holding the gun on me. If only I were a little younger and quicker, I might have gone for the gun. But no, I was just glad he didn't shoot me. The kid takes off and I chase him and flag down a fire truck. Some cops saw and joined the chase. The kid runs into the subway. The cops have their guns drawn and are yelling at me to get behind them so they don't shoot me. We are all chasing the kid. Me, cops, a couple of firemen."

"So what happened?" I said, trying to focus on my driving.

"Oh, the kid got away. But it was so exciting it was almost worth the $100. It was like being in an action movie."

"Crazy that you got robbed at gunpoint by a 13-year-old kid in Brooklyn Heights," I said.

"Yeah, I'm gonna tell my worst class today that they are losers being taught by a loser teacher."

"I don't think you are a loser," I said.

"Well, you might be the only one because I know your friends Cullen, Shannon and Castelli think I am."

I couldn't really dispute that.

As the fall semester sped by, I was doing well, even though I took two graduate classes in the evenings. After a long day I drove to Queens College. It was 13 miles and at that hour, battling traffic—on the Brooklyn Queens Expressway and then the Long Island Expressway—a slog of an hour to 90 minutes. For a shocking change, Joel Dick was happy with me. The journalism students were getting close to completing Issue No. 1 of the school newspaper. We had our front-page story, on how the Board of Ed was pumping $23 million into a two-year Tilden renovation.

Joel was so pleased with me that he said, "If I go to another school I will take you with me."

Of course, were that to happen I would never go with him. Jennifer and I looked at homes in Eastern Nassau and Western Suffolk Counties on Long Island on weekends. And if we bought a house I would find a teaching job on Long Island. But I didn't dare tell Joel.

Since I wasn't on Joel's shit list he had to badger someone else. Surprisingly, that someone was David Cullen. Apparently, Cullen foolishly thought he could tell the principal things about Joel in confidence. Of course Kerner would tell his partner everything Cullen said. And while Joel couldn't fire Cullen, he could make his life miserable.

Meanwhile, Bowerman made my life miserable. I drove him to work every day. Shannon had been driving him but he just couldn't take Bowerman so now I had the pleasure of listening to him ramble from the minute he got into the car until we walked through the front door of the school. His latest problem was that a parent had accused him of hitting her son. Kerner wasn't very supportive and reamed him out. Bowerman said he might quit.

Greco provided more entertaining discourse. In the faculty room one Friday she was about to plop into her favorite chair to take a nap when I raced her to the chair and knocked her out of it with a meek hip check.

"You're pretty strong," she said.

She sat on the window ledge and threatened to sit on my lap. Somehow that turned into boob boasting. "I have the best tits," she said.

"What cup size?" I said.

"C."

"Oh, my wife has C and hers are better than yours," I said.

"How do you know that?" she said. "You've never seen mine."

The next day, another English teacher, Sandy Lightcap, who had witnessed my banter with Greco, warned me to be careful with her.

"We are just joking around," I said.

"Maybe you are joking," Sandy said. "But she likes you."

"She's dating like five different guys," I said.

"Just don't get more involved with her," she said.

So, even though Greco was my friend—she had begun to ask me to drive her home more frequently—I cut down my period-five faculty-room time with her and logged more time in period eight with Pauline. She badgered me to play tennis with her so I finally agreed. We hit balls and I agreed to play a set.

"You know, this isn't official because I had a big fight with Mitchell (her husband) last night," she said.

"Well, I haven't played in months," I said.

I won 6-4. "You tried to hit the ball too hard," I said. "I know you can play better."

"When do we get to play again?" she asked. "I was distracted."

My classes went well outside of a couple of wacky incidents. In one class, the most goofy-looking, skinny boy—wearing ski goggles, a rooster ski cap and pants below his butt—stuck his head in the door window. The glass had been broken and removed. He had teeth going in every direction, like an Englishman. He looked around the room and said, "Jamal a pussy." He favored the verbless mode of speech. He paused, saw me and added, "And the teacher a pussy, too." Then he ran.

This girl, Oneeka Mack, fell out of her chair and spread out on the floor hysterically laughing. I ignored Oneeka and taught. Rooster hat returned and stuck his head back in the open window. I feinted towards the door; he took off again. I got to the door and saw him sprint down the long, empty hall. How did he run so fast with his pants falling down? I fought the urge to pursue him and instead talked to the class about how a lack of self-respect leads to disrespecting others.

In another class, with five minutes left, a student named Anthony Foster sauntered in and announced his presence. I looked at my Delaney book—an antediluvian method of keeping attendance with little cards in a spiral binder—to make sure Anthony was in that class. It was nearly December and Anthony hadn't been to class since the first day of school.

"Anthony, if you are going to come to school, come every day and come at the beginning of the class," I said in front of all the students.

His mom arrived the next day, with Anthony in tow. Distraught, she cried and asked me what she should do. I had no idea what to say to her. I felt bad for her. Who knew what had been going on?

"School isn't the answer for every kid," I said. "If he can't get to school maybe he should find a job."

Meanwhile, Dan Shannon had lost it on a kid and there had been a physical altercation and he was going to have an administrative hearing. Joel had defended Dan and was now his self-proclaimed champion. And while I was in Joel's cramped, tiny office for yet another Aims forms failure, I said to him, "How are you Mr. Dick?"

He looked exhausted. "Just wonderful," he said.

A new year arrived, 1991, and with it came the fateful evening of January 16 (technically January 17 in Kuwait) in the United States when Operation Desert Storm began. U.S. troops, along with soldiers from 35 other nations, unleashed an aerial assault to liberate Kuwait from Iraq. The Iraqi leader, Saddam Hussein, sent his army into Kuwait six months before. His master plan was to then invade Saudi Arabia and control the world's oil supply. Our troops, and the coalition troops, went into Saudi Arabia in August in Operation Desert Shield to protect the Saudis, and especially their oil, from Saddam's army—and liberate Kuwait from the Iraqi occupation.

Prime-time TV showcased the war. I flipped from CNN to ABC and watched as laser-guided bombs hit strategic targets in Iraq and Kuwait.

It was also the end of the first semester and I had grades to do but couldn't stop watching the war. President George H.W. Bush announced, "The liberation of Kuwait has begun."

I changed my 18-month-old daughter's diaper as President Bush said he prayed for the people of Iraq. The reporters called the tracer bullets, and flak flying through the desert, beautiful.

There was little teaching in school the next day. We talked about the war. Many of my students had siblings, cousins, uncles and aunts stationed in Saudi Arabia in the U.S. military. I didn't have a single friend or relative serving our country and fighting the Iraqis.

The students walked out of school in protest of the U.S. offensive. The protest was followed by a mini riot. In one of my classes, a student, Mark Jackson, stood up and shouted, "Death to the A-rabs."

Sitting right in front of him was my wonderful student Balquis of Yemen. She was terrified.

I explained to Mark that the Iraqi people were victims here. They had been oppressed by a brutal dictator. We were fighting him and his army, not the Iraqi people. I attempted to persuade the children not to blame Arabs.

"People everywhere are the same," I said. "It's poor government leaders who start wars, often in quest of more power, and it's the people, whether Arabs, Persians, Afghans, who suffer," I said. "Don't blame Arabs for this."

Then a few days later the Iraqis fired Scud missiles at Israel. There was fear that there would be poison gas in the missiles. The Israelis and all the U.S. and Coalition troops in Saudi Arabian bases had gas masks at the ready. I was pedaling my bicycle down Atlantic Avenue near Carroll Gardens and noted how many storefronts there had signs in Arabic script. It seemed ironic that we were in a war in Arab lands.

As January rolled on it appeared it would be a short war. This U.S. and its coalition partners' pounding of Iraq fired up many Tilden students. Yet I felt bad for Balquis. She was dealing with racism of the Black kids against the few Arab kids. I tried a geography lesson on where Yemen was. But the kids neither listened nor cared. Even Joel Dick had failed to grasp that Balquis was a Yemenite Moslem.

Speaking of Joel Dick, while the war had distracted me during an easy week of testing and no classes, he informed me that due to budget constraints I was out of a job—again. I couldn't believe it. But this time he wasn't randomly firing me. He said I'd done a great job with the school newspaper and he would figure out a way to keep me.

The next day he said he'd saved my job. Then he apologized and said he couldn't save it. So, a new New York City teaching "first"—I'd lost my job twice in a single day. Meanwhile, I didn't even really care. The Gulf War consumed my thoughts.

Again, Joel told me that he'd found a way to keep me full time. But I wouldn't be teaching a regular schedule of classes. I'd start out helping out in the library and then he'd try to plug me into any English position where the teacher had to go out on leave.

"However, you must work on not procrastinating," he said. "When you get a class I want your Aims forms every week and I want you to be absent less."

"Yes. Thank you, Mr. Dick. May I—"

He shushed me. "And please shave every day," he said.

"I promise I will," I said.

"And you have such nice hair, could you get a haircut?" he said.

"Of course," I said. "My hair is way too long."

I couldn't believe that the administrator who had fired me for missing a new teachers meeting had gone out of his way to find a creative way to save my job—twice. Maybe he wasn't a complete dick. Though I wasn't looking forward to keeping up with Aims forms, daily shaving and regular haircuts.

My second semester began in the library. And that was great. The two librarians, Suzanne Burach (Sue) and Renee Mizrahi, were in their 50s. When I introduced myself to them Renee said, "Oh, it's so nice to be working with a handsome young man."

While Renee and Sue went at each other, both liked me. I heard Renee scream at Sue: "You have a split personality. I can't talk to you. I don't want to talk to you anymore."

But she smiled at me.

Sue, the head librarian, told the school's No. 2 administrator, Mrs. Silton (Joel thought he was No. 2 but he wasn't): "He's great. Can we keep Peter the whole semester?"

"Don't count on it," Silton said.

And the best thing about working for the two librarians was that I wasn't working for Joel Dick anymore. No Aims forms or bulletin boards for the time being. I missed teaching. But I loved books so I didn't mind shelving them. Plus, one of my two grad classes was Victorian Literature and we had to read a lot of Dickens. I didn't have to buy the books; I took them out of the Tilden Library. Nobody had checked out *Little Dorrit* since 1962.

They also had me throwing out books. I was supposed to toss a 1951 Dodd, Mead and Company first edition of *Typee* by Melville, last checked out in 1979. I didn't toss it. I kept it, read it and 29 years later it's still alive on my bookshelf next to its neighbors: Larence Durrell's *Justine* and Bruce Chatwin's *In Patagonia*. In good condition that *Typee* edition lists on eBay for $800 in 2020. Though my Tilden copy isn't in good condition.

It was great to not have to grade and deal with Joel Dick. Meanwhile we bought our first house in Melville, Suffolk County. Getting everything together for a mortgage was time-consuming and stressful.

Jennifer had a new job that required travel. She journeyed to Evansville, Indiana. My days that week went as follows: Wake up and walk the dog; wake up Dana; dress Dana; take Dana down the street to the babysitter and then return to shower. Drive to school with Don Bowerman; work seven hours at school; drive home with Don Bowerman; pick up Dana; take Dana to the park—in a strangely warm late February; feed Dana; bathe Dana; entertain Dana; pay attention to the dog; get Dana to sleep and pass out. And that was on the days I didn't have a grad class in Queens.

Unfortunately my library gig didn't last too long and I found myself covering for a couple of different teachers. My gangbanger, Freddy Moore, was in one class and he told me how he was suspended for bringing a stun gun to school.

"How could young bring that to school, Freddy?" I said. "You are smarter than that."

He shrugged.

After five weeks the U.S. and coalition forces defeated Iraq. Dick Cheney said, "Saddam predicted the Mother of all Wars. But what we are seeing is the Mother of all Retreats." The Iraqis fled Kuwait. But President Bush, 41, didn't chase them all the way back to Baghdad. His son, President Bush, 43, would attack Baghdad 12 years later.

Life was tiring despite my easy semester. And since we were buying the house out on Long Island, my teaching days at Tilden were numbered. But I didn't dare let Joel Dick know that. I kept that very quiet. Joel had spies everywhere and I had to make sure none of them knew. After he'd saved my job, he would probably fire me if he knew I planned to look for a teaching job on Long Island. He'd always feared I'd leave him to teach in the 'burbs.

* * *

Death intruded again. This time it was my former editor at the *Delaware County Daily Times*, Stu Rose, who was 49. Rose had hired Gil Spencer and me during his nine-year-run at the *Daily Times*. At his funeral there were amazing eulogies by writers like Paul Mulshine, who had worked for Stu and would go on to become a nationally syndicated conservative columnist for *The Star Ledger* in New Jersey. Stu's widow said that Stu never believed in God nor an afterlife. So Stu's younger brother followed that by addressing the mourners and especially the minister of the Methodist Church: "I believe in God, I guess that makes me the black sheep of the family."

Mulshine introduced me to a *Philadelphia Daily News* journalist as "another of Stu's great finds." And even more sarcastically followed that by saying now I taught journalism in the ghetto of New York City.

I didn't dare let on that I taught nothing currently, neither journalism nor English. Though I was full-time and working every day, I was essentially a permanent sub, filling in for sick and injured teachers.

Then Spencer told a group of writers that I'd written a manuscript.

"I read it," he said. "It needs a complete overhaul but there are a few funny parts."

I didn't think my novel was that bad. Though, none of the agents and editors I'd sent it to had shown much interest. My Queens College writing workshop professor, Joseph McElroy, who had written seven novels at that point to critical acclaim, had liked much of that novel. Nonetheless, I suppose that Spencer, who back then was a wildly successful columnist and had had a screenplay of his made into a 1982 horror film called *Girls Nite Out*, was pretty much right.

As I walked away, I felt like Henry Miller, in a scene from the movie *Henry and June*, where Miller walks away from a bunch of writers and one says, "He will never get published."

Back at Tilden, Joel Dick was out for days. I hoped his illness wasn't serious. Yes, he'd tortured me for nearly two years but he had kept me employed full time. He had the flu. His nemesis, Schultz, said, "I hope he gets pneumonia."

I covered a typing class. At least nothing could go wrong. Or so I thought.

The kids typed away, on what I assumed was their assignment, so I read Charles Dickens for my graduate class. I didn't enjoy Dickens. He was no Henry Miller. The click-clack of typewriters relaxed me. I felt like I was back in a newsroom. The kids were occupied. Though one kid in the front of the room didn't type or study. That kid, Michael Nelson, said, "Mr. Kravitz, why is Sharon Young smirking back there? That ain't good. You'd better see what she's doing."

"She's just typing Michael," I said. "What could she be doing wrong?"

Just in case I walked behind Sharon and she laughed as I saw she typed a love letter to — ah—to me?

"Sharon, what are you doing?" I said. "I'm 30 years old. I'm old."

"I don't care," she said.

"I'm married."

"You can cheat on your wife."

I peeked at the paper the girl next to her typed. It was bad pornography.

"Alright," I screamed at the class. "I want everyone to take whatever letter you are typing, rip it to pieces, and come up here and deposit it in the trash can."

The kids, mostly girls, actually listened to me.

Good thing Joel wasn't in school. He could have popped into that class, to check if I had shaved and cut my hair and seen what those girls had done in my supervision.

I covered several different classes. One class had a lot of Haitians in it and they taught me Haitian Creole. I love how they say, "How are you?"

Instead of the French, "Comment allez-vous?" they say "Como ou ye?"

For some reason I never forgot how to say that. I'll meet a person who will say they are from Haiti and I'll say, "Como ou ye?" They will look at me in shock. But the only other Creole I remember is "Eske ou grangou?" That's "Are you hungry?"

The spring rolled in; the weather brightened. A kid in Dan Shannon's class got up and left without permission and punched out a window. Dan went after him and they wrestled on the floor. Joel, who had returned from his illness, was back to being a Dick. His role as Dan's savior had expired. I felt bad for Dan.

Spring fever overwhelmed the kids and teachers.

Greco caught the spring fever full on. In the faculty room, in front of several other teachers, she teased me about my married sex life. Bert Bloom had to leave the faculty room as he couldn't tolerate the carnal chatter. Greco went on about orgasms. She implied that I wanted her.

"I don't lust for you," I said.

"That's a lie," she said.

That forced me to avoid the faculty room when Greco was there.

But by then my Tilden days were numbered. In early May we moved to our new home in Melville, a town on the border of Suffolk and Nassau Counties in the middle of Long Island. I had to commute 35 miles in brutal Long Island traffic to Tilden for the last two months. Joel Dick knew that I would leave him. He wasn't happy. He vacillated between offering to write me a recommendation and trying to convince me to commute to Tilden.

"Plenty of teachers live out there and work in the city," he said.

I didn't trust him. One day I walked into his office. A veteran Business teacher, Sy Landsman, was crammed in there with Joel.

"Hi babe," Landsman said to me.

"Peter is looking very feminine today," Dick said. "Don't you think Sy?"

I was in a great mood because soon I'd no longer work for Joel—so I laughed. But what was he up to? Feminine? I didn't like that. The bottom line was that I couldn't trust him as I pursued a teaching job out on Long Island. I would get a recommendation from someone else at Tilden if I needed one. Luckily I didn't have to plan lessons or submit Aims forms.

I painted rooms, called plumbers and handymen to work on our house. I put together IKEA furniture and dreaded walking into that store. A single termite led Jennifer to freak out and call an exterminator. We celebrated our fourth wedding anniversary by ripping up carpet and matting in the living room.

Ironically, we lived on Bushwick Street in Melville. Bushwick was another rough Brooklyn neighborhood next to Bed-Stuy. We transitioned from a one-bedroom Brooklyn apartment to a four-bedroom suburban home, with a fenced-in backyard of tall trees. As the June sun set, the sound of sprinklers competed with the quiet. A worm scared my daughter. She was used to asphalt—not earth. The dog walked around sniffing everything hoping for something edible. The sun crept through the trees, which made sweet music with the wind and the birds.

I sent my resume to the English chairpersons at 65 Long Island high schools. One from Baldwin High School immediately contacted me. They needed an English teacher for summer school. I interviewed there and got the job. Jennifer was happy that I would work over the summer.

Would I find a full-time teaching job on Long Island? It would be difficult.

On the last day of classes at Tilden, there was a lot of action outside of the school. A kid threw a rock at a security guard and it hit an older teacher in the chest. He was taken to a hospital by ambulance. The football coach, a physical education teacher named Pete Waterman, tackled Freddy Moore, who had been booted out of school a few months before. I supposed he was a suspect in the assault.

As I left school that day I saw Freddy.

"I heard some things about you today," I said to him.

"I didn't do nothing," he said. "I didn't throw it. I was just laughing."

Freddy's response surprised me. He didn't curse me out, like he did almost every other teacher at the school. He didn't want me to think badly of him, probably because I was the only teacher who ever listened to him and didn't get in his face and scream at him for his many transgressions.

"Freddy, do me a favor," I said. "Stay out of trouble this summer. Stay alive."

A devious smile spread across his face and he said, "I'll stay out of trouble this summer but not today."

My last day at Tilden arrived. I took my yearbook around. Unlike JHS 142, where my yearbook was signed by students, no students signed my Tilden yearbook. Teachers signed it. Greco kissed it and her lipstick remains painted on the page. She wrote: "Thanx for all the oral—I mean verbal stimulation. Annie. Seriously—luck and love!" Don Bowerman wrote: "Best of luck to the future Hemingway." Dan Shannon: "You lucky bastard, escaping from J.D.'s sphere of influence is like breaking out of Alcatraz. From those of us still on the inside, good luck."

Dan would be one of only three students or teachers from three years and three Brooklyn schools whom I would ever see again.

I parted from Joel Dick on that last day and he seemed sad. I wasn't. Did he make me into a better educator? Not really. Perhaps I learned to try to call on every student—but certainly not in every lesson as he encouraged. He emphasized appearance—though that didn't resonate with me. Most of his teaching ideas seemed petty.

As for his life, he never became Barbara Streisand. So few of us achieve our wildest dreams. But, at least, looking back from this perch 30 years later, I'm happy that he was lucky with love.

He died at age 81 on March 17, 2015. I'm nearly certain that Everett Kerner was by his side, because exactly five months later to the day, at age 85, Everett Kerner died. Both would repose in the same Great Neck, Long Island funeral home before being laid to rest. A few of their former students wrote nice things about them on legacy.com. They had been good teachers once; they had cared about their students. And they cared about Tilden High School. They tried to make Tilden a good school when I taught there. And for many of its students, it was a good school.

From a hot morning on the chaotic streets of East Flatbush I segued to an afternoon in the forested hills of Melville. I rode my bicycle around my new neighborhood, passing the childhood home of Walt Whitman, the same structure built by his father, still intact. I pedaled up a steep hill, Jayne's Hill, to West Hills Park. It is the highest natural point on Long Island, at 401 feet. The woods smelled like honeysuckle.

After five years of urban life in Philadelphia and Brooklyn it was nice to return to the mellow, boring suburbs. But would I land a teaching job in the suburbs?

CHAPTER 5

Wantagh, Long Island—The Gateway
to Jones Beach

Wantagh High School English Department Chairperson Brian Donohue, Assistant Principal Terry O'Connor and a ten-year veteran English teacher, David Dubin, all interviewed me. Donohue liked that I spoke some Spanish and French. Dubin liked my journalism background and three years of teaching experience. I did so well that Donohue decided to stump me.

"Can you name a 19th century American playwright?" Donohue said.

Whoa. I had no idea. Was this Final Jeopardy? I barely knew 20th century American playwrights, though I could have named a few. Why didn't he ask me about 19th century Russian writers? I dug deep into my memory, which was good back then. What play did Lincoln watch at Ford's Theatre when he was assassinated by John Wilkes Booth? Did Booth write it? He was a successful actor. My mind spun as I tried to come up with an answer. Little did I know that the play *Our American Cousin* was written by English dramatist Tom Taylor.

Dubin interrupted my thinking, "You don't have to answer that."

Oh, Okay. Great.

The interview ended. They seemed happy with me. Donohue threw an application at me and said, "Fill this out quickly and bring it to the superintendent's office."

I stayed at Wantagh and rushed to fill out the application. I dropped it off at administration, which is in the same building as the high school and the middle school, on a dead-end street, across from a pet cemetery where Richard Nixon's dog Checkers was buried.

I got the job at Wantagh, though there was a lot of drama—as there always seemed to be with me and my educational job pursuits.

Apparently, I was far and away the best applicant for the job. But the district Superintendent of Schools Dr. George Besculides noticed that there was an item on the application that I didn't fill out fully. I believe it was a second emergency contact. I had put my in-laws' names in but I didn't know their phone number and address. So, because of that Dr. Besculides was going to hand the full-time, tenure track English position to a young woman who had just graduated from college, had no teaching experience and lived on her sailboat.

When David Dubin heard that he stormed Dr. Besculides' office. "How can you not hire this guy," he said, raising his voice to Besculides. "He taught for three years in Brooklyn. He's teaching summer school right now in Baldwin." (The summer school principal at Baldwin had written me a glowing recommendation, mercifully enabling me to avoid contacting Joel Dick for one.)

Dubin argued with Besculides and the Assistant Superintendent Dr. Carl Bonuso. "Maybe this failure with the application proves that he's bad at paperwork," Dr. Bonuso countered.

Dubin finally prevailed and I got the full-time job. The young woman would get a .9 English position which would turn into full-time the next year.

I had a job. Jennifer was ecstatic, more excited than me. I still peddled my second novel, which wasn't going well. That was far more important to me than another teaching job. But I didn't want to keep interviewing. I was in the interview process at Huntington High School and there was a chance for a job at Baldwin High School where I taught summer school. It was nice to withdraw my applications from both districts.

I was very appreciative of the lengths David Dubin had gone. But why had he battled so hard for me? Could there be any ulterior motive? He taught theater at Wantagh, directed the school plays and advised the school newspaper. He wanted to hand off the newspaper to me eventually. Wantagh had a journalism class and an extracurricular club for the school newspaper. They printed four papers per year and there was a nice stipend for it. Had my journalism background once again helped me land a teaching job?

Meanwhile, I had to drive to Albany to make sure my New York State Provisional license was complete in time for me to start at Wantagh. I woke up at 4 a.m. and hit the road to avoid traffic. The Palisades Parkway was foggy, wet and scary. The mountains mesmerized. It was great to see mountains. Long Island is a giant sandbar. Albany slanted down towards the muddy Hudson River.

Bureaucrats packed the New York State Board of Education, but it was much more efficient than the New York City Board of Education. I was in and out with my provisional license in hand. I'd finally gotten a New York State Education Department English grades 7-12 license. It had been hard work. I still needed my master's degree to get my permanent license but I had a few more years for that.

At the State University of New York at Albany, I foolishly searched for one of my favorite writers, William Kennedy, who at the time was in charge of a Writers Institute there.

Kennedy had won a Pulitzer for his novel *Ironweed*, one of several he wrote set in Albany. Kennedy wrote the screenplay for *Ironweed*, too. The film starred Jack Nicholson and Meryl Streep.

Ironweed had been rejected by 13 publishers. Prior to that Kennedy "had 30-odd short stories rejected by magazines all over America. He later explained that he'd only kept going because a rejection slip from *The Atlantic* had praised his style," according to an April 2018 article in *The Guardian* by Sam Jordison.

I didn't find Kennedy that day. And while I haven't read his work in years, *Legs*, *Ironweed* and *Billy Phelan's Greatest Game* reside on my bookshelf between Rimbaud and Carlo Levi's *Christ Stopped at Eboli*.

Wantagh is a mostly middle-class community, in the southeastern part of Nassau County, that runs along Wantagh Avenue south towards the bay, which separates Long Island from the barrier island, Jones Beach. The Wantagh Parkway becomes a causeway, slipping over small islands, ending up at Jones Beach Theater, right on the massive sandy beach fronting the Atlantic Ocean. The high school was dramatically different from Tilden or Boys and Girls. Instead of teaching minorities, I would teach White suburban kids. In my first few days I didn't see a single Black student.

At Tilden there were always rumors that a White kid was in the school. At Wantagh, supposedly, a few Black families lived on one street. There wasn't a Black teacher in the high school. Apparently, all along the South Shore of Nassau County, in Massapequa, Seaford, Wantagh and Bellmore-Merrick there were few Black folks—as a result of de facto segregation. But at least the school district Jennifer, Dana and I had moved to, South Huntington, was one of the few integrated districts on Long Island.

My first day at Wantagh, a veteran English teacher billowed into my room.

"Hi Paul," I said to him.

Paul Keryc had a fake English accent. He commuted from Connecticut to the south shore of Long Island each day, which took him about 2.5 hours each way.

Keryc, tall and overweight with jowls, scowled at me. "The budget cuts next year are going to be simply draconian in nature," he retorted to my pleasant greeting and then walked out of my room.

I told Dave Dubin about my Keryc moment.

"The way to get Paul Keryc to stop talking is to lift your leg and pee on him," he said.

Julie Euston, the teacher who almost got the job over me, shared a room with me. She was pleasant and engaged to an English teacher at another school. She thought David was very cynical.

"Do you think he's gay?" she asked.

"I don't know," I said.

My wife also asked me if I thought David was gay.

I said to Jennifer, "I don't know and I don't care. What does it matter what he is? He's very funny and he's been teaching for ten years and the kids love him. I'm hoping I can learn from him how to teach better."

I would get to teach four classes in my room and park right next to the school, which was right by the Wantagh Parkway. Unlike in the city, I could go to a photocopy machine and photocopy whatever I wanted. At Tilden I had to submit materials to be photocopied three days in advance.

Wantagh seemed like heaven, yet pitfalls lurked.

I was a young teacher, tall and lean, with straight blond hair. I liked the kids. They liked me. After school, several of them hung out in my room. It happened to me at JHS 142 and as a result I got into trouble. At Tilden I tried to get closer to the kids and had difficulty, as there were large cultural divides. But here the kids tried to get close to me, especially two girls.

Marylou Basso was a cheerleader, and in my first period class. She had been adopted and her adoptive parents had split up when she was young. She lived with her mother. She had no siblings. She was a junior with soft brown eyes. She also had braces—which reminded me that she was a child.

Taylor, like Marylou, was a pretty blonde junior. She was in a different class from Marylou. Taylor was an athlete, louder, more talkative and aggressive with a strange deviousness. If Marylou were the proverbial good girl, and certainly had that adorable look, Taylor, with her ice-cold blue eyes, was the bad girl.

In those first couple of weeks they often sought me out. I should have shooed them away. But, I guess, on some level, I liked the attention from these two pretty girls. Though they didn't like competing for my attention.

They weren't the only ones who sought my attention. Boys came in, too, like Pete Conlin, a very bright junior in Marylou's class, who wrote well but also drove me a little crazy with his behavior. Some kids came in for help with their classes. I taught regular 11th grade English classes and a 10th grade C-track (an academically weaker English class). In 11th grade English in New York the students took an English Regents test at the end of the year. I taught aspects of the test throughout the year so they would do well. Thirty years later the test is more difficult, more about writing. Generally, the 11th grade curriculum continues to prepare students for the Regents test. I added SAT prep, by building their anemic vocabularies. And there was literature. I assigned many essays and spent a lot of time grading them.

I told the kids stories, too. Some of my stories were about my previous three years in the city.

The kids asked what the city kids were like.

"They were very similar to you," I said. "Except that many of them did not have intact family structures. Most of them didn't live with their real father. But kids, whether in impoverished neighborhoods or out here in the middle class 'burbs, are similar. Some were bright and lazy. Some were bright and hard workers. Some were weaker students who tried and others who had given up."

Marylou asked why I stopped teaching in the city.

"Was it because you didn't want to teach Black kids anymore?" she said.

"That's ridiculous," I said. "I was tortured by my boss, Joel Dick." They all laughed at his name. "I had a long commute. And everything about teaching out here is better than it was in the city."

"Maybe you are racist," another kid said.

"I think we White people all suffer to some degree from being racist," I said. "Even those of us who are well intentioned. The key is to recognize that and try, in whatever way you can, to do something about racism in America. It's not as bad as it once was, but it's still pretty bad. The tennis star Arthur Ashe said, 'Growing up Black in America was tougher than having AIDS.' And he'll probably die from AIDS."

"Raise your hand and someone tell us when Blacks' right to vote was protected by the Constitution?"

"After the Civil War," one kid said.

"After Reconstruction," said another.

"It was in 1965," I said. "Thanks to Martin Luther King the Voting Rights Act was passed. The 15th Amendment to the Constitution gave Black people the right to vote in 1870. But many southern states got around that with sneaky racist ways to deny Black people their Constitutional right to vote. The Voting Rights Act eliminated much of that discrimination."

All of these White children listened to me. They learned. Moments like that overrode all of the nonsense and made teaching rewarding. I liked educating children about facts, but as an English teacher also about literature.

I narrated stories about my traveling to these mostly White middle-class kids. I had explored Europe and Morocco (on my own in 1984, except with a friend in North Africa) and then India in 1985. When I returned from my solo passage to India I met up with Jennifer in Greece. Jennifer and I honeymooned in Peru in 1987. Finally there was the 1988 trip with Jennifer that concluded in Paris, where I conceived of the idea to teach.

A raconteur, I spun true tales about strange cultures and places that these children knew nothing about. This was different from my three years in the city. At Tilden, many of the children came from a different culture. They were born in the Caribbean region and I tried to define American culture for them. I wanted them to be safer. I wanted them to understand the United States.

At Wantagh I had a different objective.

Teaching came naturally to me, but I still had much to learn. And, I was thrown into some situations I was unfamiliar with. I had ninth period detention room duty and I had no idea exactly how to handle that. I hadn't been instructed well in what to do—or possibly I was instructed and didn't listen carefully.

I was overseeing the detention room and Marylou showed up. She said she had to serve a detention but she wasn't on the list. She was talking to me when another kid, who was serving a detention, said, "There's no talking allowed in here you know."

"Oh, I didn't know that rule."

Marylou got mad and said, "We can talk."

Then Taylor came into the room. She had probably asked to go to the bathroom from another class.

Annoyed that Taylor intruded on her time with me, Marylou said, "Taylor you should not have came here."

"Marylou, that's grammatically incorrect," I said.

"What's wrong with it?" she said.

"It's correct to say should not have come here, not 'should not have came here.' 'Came' is past tense and 'come' is the irregular past participle."

"That doesn't seem right," said Marylou.

"Of course it's right," I said.

"I like that verb," Taylor said.

"Um, you know, we'd better not talk about this anymore," I said.

I was okay when teaching these girls in class but they seemed to always find me on an off period, in a duty, after school. Clearly, as a new teacher, I should have created distance. My JHS 142 experience should have served as a warning. David Dubin said, "Familiarity breeds contempt."

My English Chairperson Brian Donohue said, "Don't smile for two months. Be very tough with them in the beginning."

I heard these things but I smiled. I laughed, a sincere laugh, that I guess bred contempt. David said that I had a nervous laugh. I disagreed. Life could be preposterous, so I countered that with laughter. Most important, while I did recognize when the children attempted to take advantage of me, I failed to stomp it out.

I was on my way out of the school one day when Marylou and her friend Stefanie intercepted me.

"Mr. Kravitz, we want to apply for jobs at The Gap," said Marylou. "Could you give us a ride?"

"I don't think I'm allowed to do that," I said.

"It's okay," Stefanie said, "As long as it's after school."

I didn't want to give them a ride but they pestered me. I caved— pretty easily.

"Okay," I said.

"Shotgun," Marylou yelled.

Marylou was in her cheerleading outfit. "I can't believe I'm driving a cheerleader," I said.

"Don't you wish you were 17 again?" Stefanie said.

I didn't want to be 17 again. I was happy to be 31. But I wasn't happy to drive these girls. I told myself I'd never do that again. I had to check if the girls were correct, and they were allowed in a teacher's car after school.

But life was too hectic for me to remember to check on that rule. Jennifer was pregnant again. Child number two was seven months away. We were in a state of constant home improvement.

At least my teaching went well. I had ordered a class set of the novel *Ironweed*, and it arrived quickly. With another class I taught *Hamlet*. I knew very little about Shakespeare, but I enjoyed figuring out the bard with the kids.

Marylou talked to me about her problems with her boyfriend. I felt like her therapist. But she spent way too much time with me and some of the older teachers saw her in my room after school. Luckily, I had Frank Mickens's commandment to "Treat the children as if they were your own." I kept thinking, if this were my child, would I want her teacher to do what I'm doing. I convinced myself that I was helping her, though at times I had my doubts.

I also thought about Nabokov's novel *Lolita*. I tried reading it. The first line bothered me: "Lolita, light of my life, fire of my loins. My sin, my soul..."

Unlike Nabokov's narrator Humbert, I wanted to educate children. I liked them, but when I left school I didn't think about them. And since Marylou was adopted, with her father not a big presence in her life, I convinced myself that I was a father figure and that I helped her.

But then there was also Sting's song: "Young teacher, the subject of schoolgirl fantasy ... Don't stand so close to me."

I didn't think that Marylou had a crush on me.

And Marylou wouldn't stand close to me. Oh no, after school she plopped on my desk in front of me. I quickly stood up so as not to be eye level with her crotch.

"Marylou, you can't sit on my desk. Please sit *at* a desk." It seemed that that Sting song was always on the radio as I drove home from Wantagh.

All of this insanity was interrupted by death. It wasn't like the murder of Shondella in my first year at Tilden. Some of these crazy kids would get high by sucking on freon from the car air conditioner. One senior, Billy McCarthy, died after doing that in late September in a 7-Eleven parking lot. I couldn't believe it. One of my wilder students, a good-looking junior Frank Gallagher, swore off getting high on freon. There was nothing in the local newspaper, *The Wantagh-Seaford Citizen* or in *Newsday* about McCarthy's death. I wondered how it was squelched.

As I struggled to figure out how to deal with these children demanding attention constantly, I talked to a guidance counselor who also began his first year at Wantagh. Frank Muzio mentioned that he'd wrestled. That ended the discussion about the kids. Hearing that someone wrestled always excited me.

"Really," I said. "Where did you wrestle in college?"

"I didn't wrestle in college," he said. "Did you?"

"Yeah," I said. "And I was a head Division III collegiate coach."

"We need a coach here," he said. "You should become the head coach."

"I don't know if I want to coach wrestling at this point," I said. "I've got to figure out teaching first."

But Frank became the head wrestling coach at Wantagh and after Jennifer encouraged me, I plunged back into wrestling as his assistant coach. I had been completely out of wrestling for nearly five years.

Wantagh had had a tremendous program, with another current guidance counselor, Bernie Columbo, as head coach. In Columbo's last year the team had three Nassau County champs, including its star, three-time county champ, Tom Ryan, who in 1992 was a returning All-American for Dan Gable's national champion Iowa Hawkeyes.

But Columbo stopped coaching the high school team in 1987 and the program saw a coach a year for the next four years. By the time Frank and I took over in fall of 1991, the once-proud program—that had produced New York's first state champ—was in ruins and at risk of being dropped.

As if I didn't have enough to do, with a new job, a child, a pregnant wife working full-time and traveling—I was going to return to wrestling. Jennifer was happy, however, because it meant extra income. Coaching paid several thousand dollars extra. Of course, it was a tremendous time and energy commitment—especially if we were going to rebuild Wantagh's program.

I thought that might look good to the administration. And while they wanted young teachers to coach, and run clubs, it didn't really help you or protect your job if there were budget cuts.

The year rolled on and I was very happy at Wantagh. Still I struggled with some of the children's blanketing attention. One day, after Taylor's period five class had done a lot of talking during a lesson, I gave up with two minutes to go.

"Stay in your seats," I said. "Don't rush the door."

None of them listened and they crowded the door. I stood with my foot at the door so none could escape into the hallway. The bell rang and I was nearly stampeded. And there was my chairperson, Brian Donohue, just outside my room. Things had mostly gone well with Brian. I liked that I could call him Brian and not Mr. Donohue. Another plus about being out in the suburbs.

"You shouldn't let the kids crowd the door like that," he said. "Give them a task to do at the end of the period so they have to stay in their seats."

At least Brian was trying to help me and not just criticizing the final-minute door rush. Everything wasn't a "gotcha" moment for him, like it had been for Joel Dick.

"Unfortunately, things aren't looking great with our budget," he said. "Any sections with less than 15 kids will be dropped. So you really have to talk up English electives. You will be teaching creative writing next semester and next year you will start doing journalism. We need strong numbers in there to keep everybody's job."

I wasn't sure what was worse, possible budget cuts threatening my job or these girls pestering me and my inability to tell them to leave me alone.

But a couple of incidents in the spring semester clarified everything. The first one came in February when the school was abuzz with word that the cops were there. That could have meant anything. But supposedly they were there to arrest a teacher. In those pre-cellphone and internet days it's amazing how quickly word-of-mouth spread.

The teacher was a health teacher named Gary Soka. I hadn't known him well and had barely talked to him. He seemed friendly though a little odd.

Marylou had rushed to my room to tell me the news and right at that moment Soka walked down the hall, head down, staring somberly at his shackled hands in front of him. Marylou and I watched as the cops led him away.

Supposedly, he had had a male student in his room and he'd had the kid pull his pants down and paddled him. The alleged victim was not the most credible kid, as he was constantly in trouble. Soka had been alone in his room with the kid with the door shut and a wooden paddle was found in his closet. From that moment on, anytime a student entered my room and no one else was in there, I went right to the door and opened it.

As I drove home that day, a newscaster on the radio said, "A Wantagh High School teacher was arrested yesterday and charged with third-degree sexual abuse..."

I felt sick. I also began to stay out of my room so neither Marylou nor Taylor could find me when I wasn't teaching. I tried to avoid Marylou. I feared that a teacher or student could make something up about her being in my room all of the time. David Dubin wasn't convinced that Soka was guilty. Though Dubin said that for his nearly 20 years at Wantagh there were rumors about Soka. The teacher I'd replaced, a character named Ed Russell, had always predicted that one day Soka would exit Wantagh High School in handcuffs.

In the days after the Soka arrest, if I would spot Marylou in a crowded hallway, I would duck into a room or hide. Then she finally snuck up behind me and said, "Boo." I jumped; she'd scared me. But what had scared me more: The boo or the realization that I missed her?

Meanwhile, my struggles to control Taylor's class were becoming troublesome. It was a rowdy group. As the year went on it became more chaotic unless I gave them constant busy tasks. Not long after the Soka arrest, a boy in that class, who was not one of the main troublemakers, was disruptive. When I told him I would send him to the dean if he didn't stop talking, he screamed: "Suck my dick."

Every student froze and silently stared down the culprit, Mike Chiorazzi. I sent him to the dean's and wrote him up. I had written up very few kids at that point. (The *write up* was a form that went to the dean describing a serious offense that deserved detention.) I avoided using the dean's office. I tried to discipline the kids on my own. But the dean, Ron Lebel, told me I had done the right thing, as he sat in his office throwing a tennis ball against the wall.

"We'll make a man out of him," Lebel said.

Chiorazzi was externally suspended from school for a day and his parents were very angry at him. Most of Chiorazzi's classmates let me know that I was no longer cool.

"He didn't mean it," said one student in that class.

"You didn't have to tell Lebel what he said," said another.

"He wasn't joking around," I said to period five. "He said it in anger. And I'm not your friend."

Then Taylor, who looked stoned, said, "Wait, what did Chiorazzi say?"

"Don't anyone dare say out loud what he said," I said.

Somebody whispered to her what he said and Taylor stood up and said, "Mr. Kravitz, suck my tit."

Was this really happening to me? What was wrong with Taylor? Of course, I didn't handle her stoned outburst correctly. I should have written Taylor up and ripped into the whole class. This was my fourth year of teaching. I did not send Taylor to the dean's office. I gave her a stern warning.

"Next time Taylor, you are going to get suspended, too," I said. And I knew her parents would be furious. At least I was finding that the parents were supportive when a teacher said their child did something crazy.

Another day Taylor told the class that she hoped to marry a rich Jewish guy, buy a house on the water, then divorce her husband. She said she had no desire to go to a good college because she didn't want to waste time studying. At least she wasn't high as she shared her future dreams and aspirations.

While I continued to try to avoid Marylou she crept back into my world. She was in my room one day when Taylor and a boy, Josh Malone, a nice kid and a football star, stopped by. Marylou appeared to be annoyed at Taylor's presence.

Josh begged me to give him credit for detentions because he had been good in class and hadn't cursed me out. As kids accumulated detentions, we teachers could write them off if the kids came after school for extra help or helped us move books or even if they sat in our rooms and did work.

"Come on Josh, that's ridiculous," I said.

"Josh, you can't bother Mr. Kravitz," Taylor said. "He's with Marylou."

Marylou's cuteness morphed into rage. I'd never seen her so angry.

"Hey Taylor, why don't you and Josh get out of here so you can go blow him," Marylou said.

"Are you going to write her up for that?" Taylor said to me.

"Well, I didn't write you up Taylor when you told me to suck your—ah, you know," I said.

I'd never had to confront anything like this in my first three years in the city and I had no idea how to handle these kids. I knew the best thing to do would be to teach them and then not talk to them after school, during any of my duties. Just teach them, give them a lot of work. I tried. I avoided Marylou and Taylor when I wasn't teaching them. I hid out in the teachers' faculty room, where I didn't like to spend time. Unlike the fun Tilden faculty room—with Greco, Pauline, Cullen and Shannon—this one was mostly older teachers grading. A few talked to me but I just felt like I had nothing in common with most of them.

One day after school Marylou found me grading essays in my room.

"Mr. Kravitz, Stephanie is in the hospital, can you take me to visit her?" she said. "Please. I want to see how she is."

"Um, I don't think I'm allowed to drive you," I said.

"After school you can," she said.

Why couldn't I just say no to this kid? What power did she have over me? I didn't understand it. I wasn't going to drive her. I didn't want to. I would be strong.

Not long after I had proudly resisted her demands, she was next to me in my car. How had that happened?

"What hospital is she in?" I asked.

She knew the name of it but not where it was. I consulted my Nassau County map but couldn't find the hospital in it. I suggested maybe going to a gas station and asking someone. Marylou spiked that idea. Was a 16-year-old telling me what to do? I realized that everybody walked all over me, students, my pregnant wife, my dog. The only one who didn't was my two-year-old daughter. Hopefully Dana would never tell me what to do.

Marylou said to get off at Hempstead Turnpike, because she thought it was there. And she was right. We found the hospital and went in to see Stefanie. She thanked us for coming. We made her laugh. Marylou told her about Taylor's outburst. She loved that.

"Did you write her up?" she asked me.

"No," I said.

"Mr. Kravitz, you have to be tougher," Stefanie said. How ironic that a child told me to be tougher when I caved and drove her friend to see her against my better judgement. I recalled Don Bowerman from Tilden, who said he was a loser teaching losers. These kids weren't losers. I hadn't felt like a loser for a decade, since I was locked up in a mental hospital. I had no control in that situation, however I had lost control here. I had to regain it.

We walked out of Stephanie's room and I said, "Marylou, can you call your mom or a friend and get a ride home?"

"Can't you please just take me home?" she said.

"You can't get a ride?"

"What is the big deal?" she said. "Just take me home."

I thought about Gary Soka in handcuffs and definitely didn't want to ever be arrested, as I had never been arrested. I had always obeyed the law and done the right thing.

"Okay," I said. "I'll drive you home."

As we drove back to Wantagh, to her house, which was only about 15 minutes away, I said, "Marylou, I can't drive you anywhere anymore. This is the last time you can be in my car."

"Why?"

"I'm going to get into trouble," I said.

"We're not doing anything wrong," she said. "Don't be so paranoid."

"I'm not paranoid. This just isn't smart. Don't you see that?"

We returned to Wantagh and Marylou said, "Back in civilization."

We were in front of her house and she said, "I don't want to leave."

I looked at this child. Her braces had come off and she looked older.

"Well, you have to leave and this is the last time you can be in my car with me. I'm sorry."

"All you did was take me to see Stef at the hospital."

"Yeah, I know, but don't you see that it's wrong?"

"No. There's nothing wrong with it."

Finally she got out of the car and walked into her house. I felt like an idiot. I did nothing wrong. Though I still hadn't found out if teachers were allowed to drive students anywhere. And if it had been a boy in the car, one of my wrestlers, it would have seemed appropriate. Why couldn't I just say no to this child?

The next day I was in my ninth period duty in the suspension room when a secretary popped in and said, "Marylou Basso's mom is here and wants to talk to you."

There were 35 minutes left in ninth period. I was in there with a couple of kids and I felt like my head might explode. I tried to calm down and think. I knew where Marylou was that period and told one of the kids in the suspension room to go and get her and tell her to come see me immediately.

Five minutes later Marylou appeared. She seemed nervous. We went into the empty hallway.

"Please go ask your mom why she has to talk to me?" I said.

"My mom is here?"

"Yeah. You didn't know that? What did you say to her?"

"I didn't say anything," she said.

"Well, go ask her why she's here," I said, and I gave her a hallpass.

The ten minutes I waited for her to come back took forever. I felt like a criminal. I felt like Gary Soka, though I had done nothing wrong.

Marylou returned and said, "You are so paranoid. She just wants to talk to you about SATs."

Mrs. Basso was well spoken and in her late 40s. With just the two of us in an empty classroom she right away said, "Marylou told me you drove her to see Stef in the hospital."

I thought to defend myself for that but realized from her stern tone that I was in deep trouble. I just nodded.

"Don't you think that that was poor judgement permitting her to go into your car?" she said.

"Absolutely," I said. "It was terrible judgement."

I said that Marylou spent a lot of time with me and she told me about her problems and I tried to help her but also that I knew I wasn't her therapist and should not spend so much time with her.

"I think you've helped her this year," she said. "Every year she seems to pick out a teacher to lean on for support and you're that teacher this year. But you shouldn't let her into your car. No matter what she says to you. You have to be the one to say no."

"Mrs. Basso, you are totally correct. I've made a lot of mistakes this year. I'm learning. This was one of my worst mistakes."

"I have not told any administrators or my friends about this," she said. "And I won't tell anybody."

I realized right there that if she had told anyone or would tell anyone, I was finished at Wantagh. This was no Joel Dick firing me only to rehire me the same day. This was no Walter Sadowski firing me before he'd even talked to the child who made a false allegation against me. This could have finished my teaching career. Why had I let that child in my car?

"Thank you so much, Mrs. Basso," I said. "I promise you this will never happen again. I can't tell you how much I appreciate you not saying anything to anyone. It was foolish of me to drive her to see Stefanie."

In addition to profusely thanking Mrs. Basso, in my mind, I thanked Frank Mickens. His words replayed in my brain constantly, and though Marylou was adorable and without her braces looked like a 22-year-old, she was a child. I just kept thinking of her as my child. I reminded myself that I had a wife and I loved her. She was pregnant, a bit hormonal and driving me crazy, but soon I would have two children. Responsibility bore down on me and it was time that I grew up. I was not a teenager. I had to act like an adult.

As Mrs. Basso and I walked out of the school, we saw Marylou.

"I was looking for you everywhere," she said. Her eyes were red and teary.

I felt bad for her but I would avoid her now. It wasn't her fault. I couldn't let her bat her big brown eyes at me and talk me into driving her somewhere.

Meanwhile, Taylor kept appearing in the ninth period detention room. Nobody would be there and she'd park herself next to me and talk about kissing, guys, how much Marylou annoyed her, whatever popped into her brain.

"Taylor, what class do you have right now?" I said.

"Oh, we have a sub," she said.

I knew she was lying, as much of what Taylor said to adults was complete fabrication. But I let it go. Yet another fourth-year teacher faux pas.

She liked to talk about pot, too. I had a rap with the kids that "sure, when I was a dumb, stupid teenager I smoked pot but that I'd outgrown it and never smoked anymore." That was fiction. I still smoked occasionally but dared not admit that to any of the kids or even other teachers for that matter. Marijuana was illegal and not viewed as a mild recreational drug in those days.

Taylor, alone with me in the detention room, produced a joint.

"Hey Krav, nobody is at my house this afternoon, Want to come over and smoke this with me?"

"Taylor, put that away right now," I said.

"Do you want to smell it?"

"Put that away right now or I'm going to rip it out of your hands and give it to Lebel and you are going to be in massive trouble," I said.

She put it away but the smile never left her face.

"Don't ever do that again," I said. "I've told you that I don't smoke anymore."

"Are you going to write me up for having a joint in school?" she said.

"You know what, yeah, that's a good idea," I said. "What is wrong with you?"

"You won't tell Lebel," she said, daring me, taunting me.

I couldn't believe this child could bluff like that. What chutzpah.

"Come on Krav, you know kids get high," she said. "I thought you were cool with it."

"No, I'm not cool with it. It's illegal and if you ever show me weed here again, I will tell Lebel and you'll get suspended for a week. How cool is that?"

"You are no fun at all," she said. She got up and left, no doubt to torture someone else.

At least Taylor had no power over me. Though, I should have told the dean about what she had done. I did her no favor by continually warning her for her repeated transgressions and not pushing her into an external suspension and her parents' wrath—which I knew would be severe.

While my struggles with my English students continued, my mat return to wrestling went much better. I had been the head wrestling coach at Haverford College from 1983-85, and then helped out for the next two seasons.

At Wantagh, the wrestling team warmed up for a meet after the cheerleaders practiced on our mats. Marylou stretched on the mats as a cheerleader. It seemed that she or Taylor were ubiquitous. Wherever I was, one of them appeared.

Marylou thought the other team would crush us because they had better warm ups. Ours were lame. She was right, but not because of the warmups. We were awful.

Holy Trinity, a Catholic school, nearly shut us out. Only our 190-pounder Mike Camberdella won. After the loss I gave a good pep talk. I told the kids that wrestling made you a winner. That so many of the most successful leaders in business, politics, and every field had wrestling backgrounds. The kids listened intently. Our team was mostly freshmen. John Rossi, our heavyweight who was always in the detention room, didn't listen to one word of my speech. He laid on the mat, his massive belly spilling out, a true heavyweight in those days. He mumbled that I bored him.

In mid-December, a Wantagh grad came to the room with his older brother to work out with us and talk to the team. Not even Rossi was bored when Tom Ryan spoke.

Ryan was Dan Gable's 158-pounder at the University of Iowa during that 1991-92 wrestling season. Ryan was the defending Big 10 champ. The year before he had lost to Oklahoma State's Pat Smith in the NCAA final in the closing seconds, after being ahead by a point. Smith would go on to be the first NCAA Division I wrestler to win four NCAA titles.

I had always admired Gable and his Iowa wrestlers, as they were the nation's best, and while I had wrestled a few Big 10 opponents, only after my collegiate career in various tournaments, I had never wrestled an Iowa guy. Ryan and I wrestled. I had a good 30 pounds on him he, still he slaughtered me on my feet taking me down relentlessly. And I realized what Iowa's secret was as Ryan worked my head, pulling it, smacking it, cracking his forearm into it. He tired me out in 30 seconds and I was in decent shape.

But that day Ryan also taught me something that no wrestling coach ever had. It was a simple correction he made to my stance. I led with my right leg, in a staggered stance, and I sometimes tied up with my right arm.

"Never do that," Ryan said. "If you lead right, only tie up with your left. You want your right hand down protecting against a leg attack."

It was a simple, brilliant bit of coaching.

Ryan's coaching resume is long and impressive and it all started in the Wantagh wrestling room. He would be a two-time NCAA coach of the year and produce a four-time NCAA champ, Logan Stieber, and Olympic gold medalist Kyle Snyder. Though I wasn't in Ryan's class as a grappler, now that I knew what his tactics were I wanted another shot at him. I hoped I'd get it.

My first year at Wantagh wound down. I avoided Marylou. I finally stopped warning Taylor and sent her to the dean and wrote up the kids more regularly. I had forfeited all of my coolness. My tougher approach made it a little easier to teach. And I had success in the classroom. My juniors did well on their New York State English Regents tests. Their parents liked me; the kids told them I was a good teacher. I liked literature and helped them to understand it. My writing instruction succeeded, too.

Then, however, a high school senior did something crazier than anything I'd seen in four years of teaching. It might have been the craziest idiotic teenage maneuver I'd ever heard of. Fortunately, she didn't go to Wantagh. She went to John F. Kennedy High in Bellmore, an adjacent community.

Amy Fisher, who became known as the Long Island Lolita, was having a torrid sexual liaison with a married father, Joey Buttafuocco. When he tried to end the affair she knocked on the door of his house and shot his wife in the face. A lot of my students knew her. Frank Gallagher, the junior who gave up getting high on freon, said he had recently thrown her out of the deli he worked at and she cursed him out.

"She has the foulest mouth I've ever heard," said Gallagher, somewhat surprised that any teen could act that way, seemingly forgetting about his own insane teenage freon habit.

It became a huge national story. Amy Fisher met Buttafuoco, 38, at his auto repair shop when her dad took his car to be repaired there. When Buttafuoco tried to end the 18-month affair, she bought a gun from a 21-year-old ex-boyfriend, who then drove her to the Buttafuoco home in Massapequa. Mary Jo Buttafuoco recovered and for the next four months the tabloids blitzed the story.

Initially Fisher pleaded not guilty and the prosecution painted her as a prostitute who wore a beeper to school. Ultimately Fisher pleaded guilty to shooting Mary Jo and ended up serving seven years in prison. Joey Buttafuoco did five months of time for statutory rape.

Alyssa Milano and Drew Barrymore played Fisher in two of several made-for-TV movies in the early 1990s.

The first reports about the incident, three days after my fifth wedding anniversary, described how a housewife opened her front door and was shot by an unknown assailant. I thought that we'd left Brooklyn for a much more dangerous Long Island.

When I learned that a high school senior had done the shooting, I wondered if any of my crazy students could do something like that. But I was convinced that none of them were that crazy, not even Taylor.

The shooting kept coming up in class discussions. We talked about Fisher's parents, and if they were at all responsible for how she had behaved. The kids discussed who could talk to their parents and who couldn't. One well-adjusted kid, Kelly Russell, said that she could tell her mom anything and that all of her friends talked to her mom about their problems and not to their own parents. Most kids said they couldn't be open with their parents about their behavior.

A few days later Taylor told me that while driving with her mom she tried to explain that she'd had sex with her boyfriend. She tried to be open, I guess due to our class discussion.

"My mom slammed on the brakes in the middle of the Wantagh Parkway," Taylor said. "She screamed at me to get out of the car and then she tried to run me over."

Was it true? Was Taylor telling the truth? I believed her. I envisioned the frustration of parenting Taylor because I knew the futility of attempting to teach her.

Spring made the kids even crazier. John Rossi, my wrestling heavyweight, drove back to school drunk from a senior-cut-day keg party on a Friday in the woods, where many non-seniors had also cut school. He pulled up in front of the school colonnade with seven girls in his jeep. I was thinking these kids were crazier than the kids in the city. What was worse, my Tilden gangbanger Freddie Moore chopping off a kid's finger or a senior risking the lives of seven girls and himself in a drunken ride?

John Rossi landed in the detention room for days. And one day in anger he flipped over this huge table. It was a science room. I wrote up exactly what he did. He lied about it with great conviction. The principal appeared to believe whatever wacky tale he'd concocted more than my detailed write up. He'd done some serious damage to the room. I had tried to stop him. I couldn't understand how any administrator could believe Rossi over me. That's when I realized that I might be in serious trouble with Principal John Pisani.

Pisani was a strong, quiet leader. He'd been a science teacher in another district and the principal at Wantagh for the past five years; he was a good principal—unlike my previous two principals.

It was June 15th. Jennifer would give birth any day.

Pisani called me into his office, where he and my English chairperson Brian Donohue sat at the big table. Pisani began the meeting by saying that I had had problems with colleagues.

I hadn't been aware of problems with any colleagues. I hadn't really talked to too many of them. I had always been surrounded by kids.

I told him I thought I got along very well with other teachers.

"Well, there is a young Spanish teacher, Ms. Kelly," he said.

I was completely baffled. I talked to her. She was a nice young lady.

"The kids asked you how old she was and you told them," he said.

"Uh, well, I wasn't sure exactly how old she was," I said. "I guess I approximated."

"You can't do that," Pisani said.

Okay, was that it? I mean, that was nothing. I expected something about Marylou or Taylor. Then Pisani mentioned the recent incident where John Rossi damaged a science room under my supervision.

"Mr. Pisani, you are aware that John cut school, got drunk and then drove back to school with seven girls in his jeep?" I said. "That's why he was in the suspension room. I tried to stop him from destroying school property. He doesn't listen to anything or anyone."

Pisani seemed to ponder that. "What about absences?" Pisani said. He looked at my record and saw that I'd only been absent like three times.

"Well, that's pretty good," Brian said.

I felt that Brian liked me but that Pisani didn't. I kept waiting for them to bring up Marylou in my room after school every day. I had nothing to counter that and would just admit that I hadn't dealt well with her.

But neither Marylou nor Taylor came up. Brian told me that I needed to wear a tie the next year and not have any discussions in class about kids' problems. Pisani looked at me sternly. Was a tie always the route to better teaching?

"Luckily for you, Mr. Kravitz," Pisani said. "A lot of parents said you were a good teacher and a good coach. Continue being a good teacher and coach. But start creating more distance with the children."

I walked out of the office and knew I had been lucky. As that meeting dragged on, I was sure Pisani would fire me, which would not have gone over well with my very pregnant wife.

On June 19, my son Brett debuted in Winthrop Hospital in Nassau County. The epidural worked well and Jennifer felt no pain. And unlike Dana's birth there was no episiotomy. Jennifer suffered a slight tear of her vagina, which required only a stitch, much better than the five stitches from Dana's birth. I took photos of the birth. No blood. Brett looked exactly like Dana did at birth—another "gorgeous" baby. I had a "gentleman's" family. I had a son.

It's easy to watch a bris when the penis of your friend's son is flayed. What man calmly observes the removal of his own son's foreskin?

"Can you slow down Mr. Moyle," I whispered. "What is that tool?"

"Relax bubby," he said.

The moyle went for theatrics, especially blood and screaming. I pleaded for the pacifier dipped into wine to go into the kid's mouth but my son's screams drew a reaction from the crowd. Brett was fine, thank God.

The *New York Times* front-page headlines the day of Brett's birth were about Jesse Jackson's criticism of Arkansas Governor Bill Clinton's stance on racism and Russian President Boris Yeltsin's visit to Kansas.

I returned to school a few days later, on Monday, June 22. When I signed in Principal Pisani was waiting for me. He motioned for me to go into his office. I went in there thinking he'd congratulate me, give me a cigar or something. He was angry. It was just the two of us and he shut the door. What could be he angry about?

"You never called in sick on Friday," he said.

"My mother-in-law never called in for me?" I said. "I told her to because I couldn't."

"Why would she call in for you?" he asked.

"Well, ah, I was in the hospital all night."

"Oh, I didn't know. Is everything alright?"

"Yes. My son was born early in the morning."

"Oh, I didn't know that," he said. I waited for congratulations, but none came. Pisani stood there, sternly, a tall man with a bald head and a gray beard.

"You know, you are a good teacher," he said. "But you didn't handle these kids correctly this year. You need to create more distance with your students. If you hadn't done well in the classroom I don't know if you would be coming back next year."

I said nothing. He'd already told me this. I understood my short-comings and had told him I would improve. He was mad I didn't call in for being out? After I'd just told him I was up all night with my wife while she gave birth. Like, maybe he could have discussed this another time—especially if he had decided to not fire me.

Pisani was a good educator and a good principal but I didn't like him after that. At a softball game at the end-of-the-year teachers' picnic Pisani stumbled going for a ball. I cheered silently. Then he pitched to me. I could line a slow-pitch softball right back at him. I considered doing that. But I had not done well with Taylor and especially Marylou. I hadn't done anything wrong. I had learned from my mistakes and would change my approach and prove to him that I could handle the children correctly. I tried to see it from his perspective. He had written goals for me for the following year. Pisani was well respected. He was no Joel Dick. I didn't smack any of his lobs back at him.

I had a long talk with David Dubin, not about my Pisani issues—though they came up. It was about his relationship with his father. At some point during the year it became clear that David was gay. It didn't matter to me. His sexual preference was his own business. He'd gotten me the job, which I liked. He advised me and helped me through challenging situations. He was one of the few teachers I'd hung out with, frequently eating lunch with him.

I'd just had a son, who I hoped to have a good relationship with. David told me about his difficulties with his father. He first told his mother that he was gay in his 20s. He waited months to tell his father, and his mother said nothing. But David said that when he came out to his father he was understanding.

But now David was going to introduce his father to his boyfriend, Paul. He was terrified. I tried to calm him down. I told him that a lot of guys had strained relationships with their fathers. I had a difficult relationship with my father. I loved him, but he had smacked me around as a child. My dad was 6-feet-2-inches tall, 220-pounds, with a short temper. I vowed that I'd never strike Dana or Brett.

All year David advised me how to teach better. I tried to help him deal with his father.

Finals came and went and I got my grades in on time. My first year at Wantagh ended and I wasn't fired. I was almost fired. If Marylou's mom had breathed a word of me letting her daughter in my car, I would have been one and done at Wantagh.

I looked forward to a summer with my son and daughter. Jennifer wasn't harassing me to get a job, as my job would be to watch the kids with her. I had pretty much given up on placing my novel, *Sarah's Principal*, which racked up rejections when I was able to get it to an agent or a publisher.

I looked forward to coaching wrestling the next year. Frank Muzio and I had gotten a number of kids to join the team throughout the wrestling season, including senior Mark McGuigan, who qualified for the Nassau County championships with our senior captain Mike Camberdella. The community had good vibes about Frank and me. A former wrestler brought his younger brother to a few practices. That brother, Michael Ginsberg, was in sixth grade and he had a lot of talent. He played ice hockey and I tried to persuade him to give up hockey for wrestling. He beat all of our kids, three and four years older, at his weight.

What could be better than a Long Island summer off? Spending time with my children, going to pool parties, playing softball. I played softball with my brother-in-law and a few of Jen's first cousins on a team called the Bathits, in a modified fast pitch league.

We played on different fields in New York City and then after games we'd go out to bars. At one game in the Bronx, near 128th Street and the FDR Highway, there was a short, high fence in left field. During the game our guys all tried to hit the ball over the fence. No one could. I tried to hit the ball up the middle. Our other slugger, Noel Boyland, hit the fence three times for long singles. On the one swing I tried to hit it over I did. The ball went right over the foul pole but the ump called it foul. I quietly said to him, "You know how to hurt a guy in a slump."

The count was 1-1; the pitcher walked me intentionally. We won 15-3. We beat the Manhattan D.A.'s office 13-1.

I grew a garden with tomatoes, peppers and cucumbers, listened to the cicadas in the tall trees, and drove with the family a short 15 minutes to wide, sandy beaches.

Life was perfect—so of course I attempted to screw it up.

CHAPTER 6

Lower East Side Manhattan

Ten days after Jennifer's birthday, summer had wasted away and we had our final softball game. If we won, we made the playoffs. Jen had birthday plans that night with our friends Stephanie and her husband and me. She lined up a babysitter. She demanded that I miss the game.

"I can't do that to my team."

"Who cares? They don't need you."

"The Bathits need me," I said.

"It's my birthday," she said.

"Your birthday was days ago."

"I had this date on the calendar for weeks," she said.

She had me. If it was on the calendar, there was nothing I could do.

"The game was rescheduled," I said, hoping to refute her ironclad calendar argument. "Don't you care about the Bathits?"

"No!"

Baby Brett screamed and projectile vomited on Dana. The dog licked the vomit.

Jen: "Help me clean."

I wiped vomit off Dana who was calm. She would only cry in the future, during her math homework. Math would make her cry, even though she was good at it.

"How about a compromise?" I said. "We'll go to the game, and then leave and go to dinner."

"I'll think about it."

After hours of negotiations, we reached an agreement. Jen would come to the game with me—her first Bathit game. At 8:30, and not a minute later, I agreed to leave the game, no matter what, and we would drive to dinner.

The tense drive in on the Long Island Expressway featured mostly silence. We weren't in a fight, but anger and resentment filled our leaky little Subaru. Annoying traffic stalled the four-eastbound highway lanes due to an Eric Clapton concert at Shea Stadium.

We drove through the Midtown Tunnel and down the FDR Highway to the ballfields, on the East River, underneath the Williamsburg Bridge. What a lovely night for a ballgame.

We were late and I missed the first two innings. We were losing. "Come on guys," I screamed. "Let's take it. Let's get fired up. Wait for your pitch. Patience at the plate. Let's get on that ragarm."

The Bathits were smoking now. Jen talked to cousins. She seemed happy. My teammate, the aspiring actor Matthew Shale, drove in a run. I was smitten by his girlfriend, Annie. Who wasn't? We Bathits were all smitten by Annie. Other Bathits were smitten by Jen. Despite having so recently given birth she was thin. A blonde, blue-eyed beautiful woman, she snacked on popcorn and didn't gain weight.

The Bathits trailed, 4-1, going into the bottom half of the final inning. We had last licks. Oh, they would be, baby. I batted second. I stood in the on-deck circle confident that I would lead the Bathits to a miracle comeback win and a playoff berth.

Jen said, "It's 8:30."

"What?" I felt like Cinderella.

"Let's go," she said. Her eyes demanded my immediate departure, as she used non-verbal facial expressions for emphasis.

"Can't I just bat?" I said.

"You made a deal."

"One at bat? Please."

"How long will that take? We have to go to dinner."

"But we'll lose?"

Shale: "If he doesn't bat, it's an out."

"Come on Jen," I said. "We can be a few minutes late."

"You promised," she said.

Everybody from both teams watched the drama. Jen screamed at me. We'd never fought in public. This was a heavyweight championship bout. I took shots to the head, to the body. I didn't care. I wanted to bat. I knew I made a deal, but it was the last inning. Didn't she understand?

"If I get a hit, I'll get a pinch runner and we'll go," I said.

"I've seen you. You could foul off 20 pitches. One at bat could take an hour. You made a promise! Let's go!"

"You go!" I yelled.

"No."

"Batter up!" the ump screamed. The inning hadn't begun because our fight was more interesting. I was too angry to be embarrassed. I'd never been so angry with Jen. And she was angrier than me.

Jen's brother and cousins urged me to go. They were logical. They believed our marriage was more important than this game. Her cousins pushed me towards the car. I hacked my favorite aluminum bat into a stone wall, denting it.

We were in the car together. Jen drove; I attempted to leap out of the car at a light. She said she wanted a divorce. Shale later told me that he did not marry the erotic Annie because of this ugliness. That made me sad.

Jen and I drove in complete silence. Though, at dinner, in front of Stephanie and her husband John Cusack (not the actor, as I said before), we acted normal and maybe even laughed about the incident. Maybe I laughed. We checked into marriage counseling a couple of days later. I slept on the sofa. I had waited for sex through months of pregnancy and then for Jen to heal and now that Jen had healed and could do it, she wouldn't do it. I couldn't believe I would get divorced. Most divorces occurred over cheating or money or kids, or not doing enough together, or not having enough sex, or wanting too much sex.

We would divorce over a Bathit at bat. I was a loser, or as Taylor said, "A *loose'ah*."

CHAPTER 7

Wantagh High School—September

Upon my post-summer return to Wantagh my presence was requested at yet another meeting in the principal's office. I figured I'd hear about creating distance again—no matter how repetitive it got.

I sat at the big table, both doors to the principal's office shut, with John Pisani, Brian Donohue and Ron Lebel. Once again Pisani said that if I hadn't been "such a good teacher" I would have been fired. He loved telling me that.

And perhaps the main reason Pisani believed I was a good teacher was that several parents had written letters to him. One mom, Susan Falconetti, wrote Mr. Pisani: "I am pleased to say that my daughter Caroline is doing the best she's ever done in English this year ... Caroline also credits Mr. Kravitz for helping her score much better than she had expected on her PSATs."

Another parent, Paula Blum, wrote the principal: "My husband and I are pleased with how well Lara is doing in English this year ... The reason for this apparent increase in both interest and performance is entirely, I believe, attributable to her teacher, Mr. Kravitz ... My sincere thanks to you and to whoever else made the decision to hire Mr. Kravitz. He is a credit to the school and the district."

Despite how I'd made parents and students happy, Brian, who usually defended me, said in a very pleasant, therapist-like tone, "Did something happen in the city, Pete?"

Did something happen in the city? Should I have said that Leontina made up crazy shit about me because she had a crush on me? Should I have attempted to describe Joel Dick's relentless torture? I decided on a different tact. Lebel had been a music teacher in the city. He was a sweet guy, though a tough dean. I aimed my salvo at him.

"Ron taught in the city," I said. "He knows what it's like there. Here's what happened to me in the city." They all leaned towards me. I commanded their attention. "My students were murdered, they attacked teachers, they brought guns and knives to school (I didn't tell them how I passed a switchblade back to its owner once), they chopped off rival gang members' fingers—and bragged about it."

They all looked at me. None of them spoke at first. Then Brian said, "Pete, you have to watch what you say to the kids in class."

"I don't think I ever said anything outrageous last year," I said. "We discussed life, like every other teacher does."

"Did you ever tell them that your marriage was bad?" Pisani said.

"No," I said. "I might have made a joke about my wife being pregnant and a little cranky, but I never gave details. I never tried to define my marriage to a class—or to students—in any way."

Where the hell had they arrived at that conclusion? No way any of them knew about our Bathits-at-bat fight. And now that tale would never be heard by any Wantagh students. It was *verboten* to everybody at Wantagh, including teachers. And Jennifer and I were working things out. We'd escaped divorce.

"Hey guys," I said smiling. "My marriage is great. I've got two wonderful children and Jennifer and I are very happy together."

Pisani said, "Anything you say to your students will get blown out of proportion by them. Please be careful what you say to them and just do what you do well, which is teach them."

I smiled, stood and said, "Have a great day gentleman." I sprinted to David Dubin's room. After all, he was the one who was responsible for my hiring.

He was in there getting set up for the year with an art teacher, Greg Tsontakis-Mally, who I liked a lot. I whined about my latest meeting with the big boys. They were both very supportive and David said, "Just don't say anything to the kids. Work them to death."

"And be careful what you say to other teachers," Greg said.

"I barely talk to anyone outside of you guys, Julie and a few others," I said. "I have no teacher friends. Well, maybe Frank Muzio."

I asked both of them how their summers went. It's fun hearing about other teachers' summers, though after you hear about a few, some travel stories, you get sick of asking, "How was your summer?"

"Mine was wonderful," David said. I noticed he'd shaved his beard.

"I think you look great without your beard," I said. He devoured that compliment.

"Let's see," David continued, "I slept till noon, ate breakfast, took a nap, went out to dinner. And I even went to the gym."

"Really, you go to the gym?" I said, shocked that someone who eschewed all forms of activity and exercise would go to the gym.

"Only because they have a great snack bar," he said.

And while David taught English and drama exceptionally well, teaching journalism was not his forte. We taught journalism together that year and together advised the school newspaper.

Our journalism class had 27 students, two of whom were boys. David had taught journalism for a couple of years and he would show me how he taught it, and how to print the newspaper. I had my one-semester experience at Tilden, and more importantly I had my five years of newspaper reporting experience. I was surprised that David didn't have the kids type their articles and submit them to the printer on floppy computer disks. In the Dubin "error" of the *Warrior*, all articles were handwritten and the printer charged for typing. David didn't think much of computers.

"They will go away," he said.

I had relied on technology since the mid 1980s, when traveling across the country reporting on a Disneyland-to-Disneyworld antique car road rally for *The Delaware County Daily Times*. I typed my dispatches on my eight-line-screen, TRS-80 computer and then transmitted through phone lines by attaching the computer to a phone with a suction-cup device.

Unlike David, I envisioned bringing technology into the classroom at every opportunity.

I had students type their articles, which would save hundreds of dollars in printing costs. David couldn't type; I typed extremely fast.

It also shocked me how David submitted photos to the printer. He cut photos with scissors to size them.

In those long-ago days, we used film and had our photos developed at photo stores—in that ancient pre-digital world. Instead of cutting photos, I had the kids tape them on a piece of paper and then simply write on the paper the exact percentage to size the photos without damaging the prints.

"Do you see why I needed you here so badly?" he said, somewhat sarcastically.

Assuming that I got through the year unscathed, the plan was for me to take over the newspaper and the journalism class the following year.

I had recruited well for creative writing, too. As a popular, young teacher, I filled my English elective classes. None of the students wanted me to create distance and teach them bell to bell. They loved any story I told them, whether it was about teaching in the city or my travels.

Determined to change how I interacted with Marylou, I approached her on the first day of school.

"You didn't send me a card for my birthday this summer," she said. "You were supposed to do that."

"Sorry," I said. The Marylou spell was broken. She told me how she'd fought with her mom much of the summer and split up with her boyfriend.

"Sorry to hear that Marylou but I have to go to a meeting," I said, and quickly escaped from her.

Two more grad classes and I had my master's degree and then my permanent state license. Two more years and I had tenure. That was my focus for Marylou's senior year.

Taylor was around but I didn't have her in class her senior year which made my life easier. Her sometimes boyfriend Josh Malone appeared to be the lead front page story for our first newspaper. He was declared ineligible to play football his senior year. I showed Taylor a dummy of our first newspaper front page with a headline that said, "State Sidelines Wantagh Star."

"I want to be on the front page," Taylor said.

"Well, if you get yourself into trouble so you can't play sports maybe you could be the second front page," I said.

"Oh, that's no problem," she said.

I would teach Marylou second semester in creative writing, but not having her in class first semester cut down on my contact with her. I saw her mom on parent-teacher night and told her how I didn't see Marylou very much.

"I understand that, but if she needs help or wants to talk to you, I appreciate you being there for her," she said. "You helped her through a lot last year and I appreciate that."

And of course I had appreciated her not even telling her friends how I drove Marylou to the hospital to see Stefanie.

I enjoyed parent-teacher night. I had confidence. We talked to parents for seven minutes about our classes. I had fun with the parents and told them what I would teach. I tried to cut down on the distance with the parents and they liked me.

Some of the young teachers were very nervous talking to parents. Julie said she broke into a sweat after her first class of parents as did another young teacher, Jennifer deLyra, who was tall, brunette and beautiful. And while I was friendly with the young teachers at Wantagh, there was none of the banter that went on with Greco and Paulette at Tilden.

The fall went well. I created distance with the kids as instructed and enjoyed teaching journalism and creative writing. Instead of trying to publish my manuscript I focused on teaching. Then wrestling began. Wrestling consumed enormous chunks of time and energy. There was a match or tournament every Saturday. Early weigh-ins and returning to school on the bus made for a 6 a.m.-to-10 p.m. day. We had more kids come out and were going to have a much better team. Whereas our first season we had begun with about nine freshmen and two seniors and then had kids come out, we began with about 30 kids with a few quitting—typical of wrestling. You never have to cut a wrestler. They cut themselves.

One of our new wrestlers was a sophomore, Ed Garcia, who had moved from Massapequa, which had one of the best wrestling programs in the county and was famous for graduates like Jerry Seinfeld and the Baldwin brothers. Billy Baldwin had been a very good wrestler there. But Ed didn't come to Wantagh because he wanted a better school, nor did he for wrestling—his old school Massapequa was the perennial county power. He was allegedly thrown out of Massapequa for some crazy behavioral mishap.

In his first meet, he was way ahead when the buzzer went off to end the first period. Frustrated that he hadn't pinned his opponent, he slapped the mat and screamed, "Fuck!" The referee disqualified Ed. We lost the meet because of the disqualification. Ed would be a project, but Frank and I believed in him. He had great talent. I wrestled him every day to make him better. Plenty of older guys coach wrestling. But being young, and still wrestling at a high level, I helped my kids improve. I enjoyed wrestling the kids, the coaches, whoever.

Another great aspect to wrestling is the coach doesn't decide who starts on varsity. Picking starters should be completely objective. We had a senior named Randy Weinstein—a tall, thin, and nice kid. He and Ed wrestled off for varsity. Ed attacked him with animalistic fury and quickly bloodied his nose. Frank wanted to stop the wrestle off. But Weinstein wanted to continue so I talked Frank into letting him. Garcia destroyed him. He had the right mentality. In a meet versus Plainedge, Ed was the only varsity wrestler for us to win.

And over the holidays, Tom Ryan came by our wrestling room again and I got a rematch. Afterwards he paid me the greatest compliment of my wrestling career. He said that I was a tough mat wrestler and had a very strong grip.

"A Pennsylvania cowcatcher grip," he said.

Ed Garcia watched our wrestling closely and afterwards said to me, "Coach, you got your ass kicked."

"Well, yeah, Ed," I said. "That's a two-time Big 10 Champ and two-time DI All-American. He was third and second in the nation. And he was coached by Dan Gable. I was third and second in the East Coast Conference and I was coached by Paul Billy. You're a good workout partner for me but his workout partners are a little better."

Creative writing, my favorite class, went well. Marylou and Stefanie were in the class but neither had any interest in writing—or reading. We read daring fiction that I picked out and then read the fiction written by students. Marylou and Stefanie talked and did other work. A short story by Blanche McCrary Boyd called "The Black Hand Girl" grabbed the students' attention.

If you know the story, you might wonder why, when I was trying to avoid the principal's office, I would teach it to a high school creative writing class. I photocopied a class set of the story, meticulously censoring it, blacking out vast swaths.

I figured that no parent or administrator who chanced upon it would know the story or bother to figure out the title. Just to be sure I blacked out the title and the author and numbered the copies and made the kids give them back to me at the end of the period. While this story did not diminish the distance I'd built up all year, I needed my elective English students to see the scope and creativity that was possible in literature.

The following scene by McCrary Boyd, after being censored, read like this: "I had made several unsuccessful attempts to lose my ___ at Duke, and Harvard had begun to seem like a possible solution.

"My roommate ... had been coaching me on the loss of my ___. In high school I had read an article that said _____ could _____ right through your underpants."

Yes, this was crazy censorship, but it also drew the kids in. They begged me to read some of the blacked-out words and here and there I obliged. I'd let them guess what the words might be, a creative exercise. The story's premise was that the protagonist, a girl, kissed a boy named Don. When he tried to put his hand under her girdle she made a jerky move, injuring his hand. They referred to the injury as a sexual injury that had blackened his hand. The censorship created a puzzle that lured the kids in.

Even Marylou and Stefanie paid attention—sort of.

Short stories worked better than longer works or their excerpts. Buoyed by the success of "The Black Hand Girl" I tried excerpts from John Kennedy Toole's dark comedy masterpiece *A Confederacy of Dunces*. I didn't have to black out my photocopied excerpts, but that novel didn't go over as well. A cult 1980s classic, Toole failed to publish it and took his own life. His mother then tried to publish it. She took it to the author and critic Walker Percy.

Percy wrote in the foreword, "[Toole's mother] was persistent, and ... she stood in my office handing me the hefty manuscript. There was no getting out of it; only one hope remained—that I could read a few pages and they would be bad enough for me ... to read no further ... I read on. And on. First with the sinking feeling that it was not bad enough to quit, then with a prickle of interest, then a growing excitement, and finally an incredulity: surely it was not possible that it was so good."

One of my students, a senior, Colleen Rosen, loved it. Colleen was a pretty, blonde-haired girl who hadn't enrolled in the high school fashion show. She often wore sweatpants and did nothing with her hair. Sometimes she slept in my class, but *A Confederacy of Dunces* kept her awake.

Around this time, early March, I asked Principal Pisani how I was doing with distance.

"You are doing well," he said. It helped that except for talking to her in class, Marylou and I weren't talking outside of class. The parade of teachers passing my room after school saw no Marylou or swarming girls, no doubt helping Pisani's improved perception of me.

Then Marylou returned. Our reconciliation began with her asking if I'd missed her.

"Not really," I said.

"You're lying," she said.

"I'm not a teenager," I said. "I don't lie."

"You missed me," she said.

Marylou approached me for help with an *Oedipus* paper.

"Which *Oedipus* did you read?" I asked. "There are three plays."

"I don't know," she said.

"Do you know anything about *Oedipus*?" I said.

"No, that's what you are going to help me with," she said.

I worried about having Marylou in my room after school as I explained *Oedipus* to her. It's one thing to teach it to a class. The 2,400-year-old Greek trilogy by Sophocles could sound a little weird with just the two of us.

"Okay, *Oedipus* is abandoned by his parents on a mountain top and left to die there."

"Why?"

"Because an oracle said that—"

"What's an oracle?"

"In ancient Greek literature or theater, the oracles would predict the future. The oracle predicted that Oedipus would kill his father so his dad tried to get rid of him. But he survived and another oracle said that he will still kill his father and in addition marry his mother."

"Marry his mother?" she said. "Ewww. That's gross."

Could she have come to me with another ancient Greek bit of literature? *The Odyssey* perhaps.

Taylor kept me busy, too. At a wrestling meet, Ed Garcia had a bloody nose so Frank and I went out to clean his blood. I cleaned it off the mat and as I bent down, Taylor screamed from the crowded stands, "Nice ass Krav. Bend down some more."

I tried to ignore her. Luckily no administrators were in the stands. Our wrestling team had improved from the previous year. We would finish with a 6-8-1 team dual meet record, up from 2-10 in our first season. Also, junior Brian Smith won the first post-season tournament, the Nassau County Qualifier. He was Wantagh's first qualifying champ since Tom Ryan's senior year, six years before.

As if it wasn't enough to coach wrestling and wrestle any kid or coach, I also played ice hockey for fun and to keep from getting a fatty belly—as it's another great calorie burn.

I began playing in 1974. That was the year the Philadelphia Flyers won their first of back-to-back Stanley Cups. I had gone to a Flyers hockey camp at Radnor Rink and every Flyer was there promoting ice hockey to Philadelphians. Even the enigmatic coach Fred Shero told us crazy stories about fights he'd gotten into and how important fighting was to skating and balance.

The most remarkable hockey camp moment happened shortly after skating onto the ice the first time. Every kid wore a Flyers jersey. After all, only two months before the Flyers had stunned the big, bad Boston Bruins in six games to take the Cup. The only kid not clad in a Flyers jersey was me. Nonconformity was my thing. For some dopey reason I wore a Bruins jersey, even though I loved the Flyers. Their Cup win lifted an entire city that had known only losing sports teams for years.

Don "Big Bird" Saleski talked to us on the ice. The Flyers were a physical team nicknamed The Broad Street Bullies. Saleski was the No. 3 goon, behind Dave Schultz and Bob Kelly. He stood 6-foot-3-inches and hailed from Moose Jaw, Saskatchewan. I was 14 and about 120 pounds—with stick arms, completely lacking muscle. Saleski looked at my Bruins jersey, and his face morphed into rage. Perhaps he forgot I was a kid and thought I was Terry O'Reilly, a Boston player he'd battled in the Cup Final series, because he took his stick with two hands and smashed me in the Bruins logo. I slid about 30 feet.

As 80 stunned boys looked on he said, in his thick Western Canadian accent, "Don't lean on your stick, eh!"

Today a kid might sue for that attack. I wore the bruise on my chest with great pride. One of the Broad Street Bullies had checked me hard.

Further inspired by Bobby Clarke slashing my ankles as I skated by him and the fluid river skating of sniper Rick MacLeish, I played on a hockey team with five friends that fall—a year before I tried wrestling.

We woke up at four a.m. for long drives to rinks in Delaware and New Jersey. My friends quit the team one by one. One day the phone rang, leaving two kids on the team: Albert Simmons and me.

"Who was that?" asked my dad.

"Two kids left in hockey," I said.

"No," my dad said. "There is one left. Your hockey career is over."

My NHL dreams were crushed but I couldn't blame my dad for not driving me to hockey anymore. And while I played roller hockey, I didn't play on the ice again for 14 years, until I moved to New York, where I would play in a game every two months or so.

One such one a.m. February game at Skyrink in Manhattan featured the writer Larry "Ratso" Sloman, who wrote Howard Stern's first two books, *Private Parts* and *Miss America*, and another third-string celebrity who was on *Saturday Night Live* at the time and had just done well with his first film the year before. I didn't know that guy, as I hadn't watched *Saturday Night Live* in several years and I hadn't seen the movie, a silly comedy, *Wayne's World*.

There were some very good Russian players in that game and the only players I was better than were Ratso and the *Saturday Night Live* guy. I rode the elevator down with him after the game.

"I'm not good at hockey," he said to me. "But what do you expect? I'm a Canadian who learned to play in L.A."

That Canadian, Mike Myers, would achieve comedy genius in his three Austin Powers films and as the voice of Shrek in four films.

Afterwards I told Gil Spencer about playing ice hockey with Mike Myers and Gil said, "He's really funny."

"You are funnier," I told Gil. No doubt I was way off in that horrific assessment of humor. That establishes me as completely unqualified at any attempt at dark humor or white humor, which David Dubin reminded of on a near-daily basis.

Though rarely absent, one day David was out. I was on my own in journalism. David ran a loose journalism class. The two boys in there, Peter Brown and Steven Bergstein, were talking so I told them to leave and go find a good story somewhere in the school. That was how David taught journalism—sending students out into the halls to find article ideas. But now I found myself as the lone male in front of 25 young females. I attempted to teach the girls about writing good leads, avoiding cliches and writing concisely.

The Jurman twins came in late, after shooting a cheerleading photo. Marni Jurman complained that it had been very windy out, and she had to interlock her hair with Heather Burnson. Hair trumped writing, I realized. My lesson failed, miserably. I preferred having David teach journalism with me and wondered how I would fare without him the next year.

At least I woke up to my two beautiful little blond-haired children. I quickly typed my plan for the day and Dana and Brett sat on either side of me watching me type. Brett hugged my leg and wondered where my music came from. Dana sucked her thumb, hugged her doggie-doggie and asked me to let her type.

At school, another child sought my attention by visiting my sixth period lunch duty, where from my cafeteria table I tried to keep the children calm and quiet.

I'd avoided Marylou for eight months. But for the third day in a row she came to the cafeteria to talk to me. She asked me to help her with a paper and I told her I couldn't. I graded essays as she wrote her paper. I didn't help her or talk to her. My attempted distance from her seemed mean-spirited.

She arrived at the cafeteria for the sixth-straight day to talk to me and tell me about her latest boyfriend problems.

"Marylou, you can't keep coming here to talk to me," I said. "Please. You know I like you and you are a great kid but please find somewhere else to go."

She walked out and as if on cue Taylor walked in. "Hey Krav," she said. "What are you doing?"

"I'm very busy," I said. "I have a million papers to grade. I can't even talk to you for three seconds."

She didn't budge and said, "Krav, I hate Bill Clinton. I can't believe he's our president. Don't you hate him?"

I never talked politics with kids nor told them anything about my political views, like who I had voted for. They asked if I was Democrat or Republican and I said nothing. It was a good teaching strategy. While I always wanted to answer their questions, learning not to answer some of them was critical.

"Krav, who should I go to the prom with?" Taylor said, switching to a far more important subject. "Josh or Chris?"

"I don't know, Taylor," I said, as I kept my head in my papers and graded. Nobody likes grading but it could be useful. "You are going to have to figure that out."

"I'd like to be with both of them," she said. "But I don't want either of them to be with anyone else."

I looked up from my papers. "Taylor, please go and discuss this with your guidance counselor. I can't talk about this with you. Don't you understand that? Do you know where guidance is?"

That worked. Annoyed, she left me in the chaos of cafeteria duty. Students ate lunch, threw lunch, screamed, danced.

"No running in here," I screamed.

Classes ended for the year. I survived my second year at Wantagh. Taylor and Marylou would graduate and my job would be much easier. No visits to the principal's office. I wasn't fired or almost fired. I didn't want to quit. I liked Wantagh. I wanted to stay there and be a positive influence for my students and the community. If I could get through one more year, I'd have tenure.

Marylou ran to me during her graduation rehearsal in the hallway by my room.

"How's it going?" I said.

"Well, I failed my math Regents," she said. But she would graduate and go to college in Massachusetts.

"Just make sure you work hard in college and get that four-year degree," I said.

"You are coming to my graduation," she said. "Right?" We had to work at graduation every four years. But it wasn't my year to work it so I didn't plan to go.

"I don't think I can make it to graduation," I said.

"What? You have to. Please. I need you to be there."

One of her friends said, "She sat through your classes so you can sit through her graduation."

"Sat through my classes?" I said, raising my voice. "She slept through them. And she threw handouts on the floor."

But of course, one final time I caved to Marylou. I went to the graduation and after it was over, I told her that I was very proud of her. "Now, work much harder in college," I said.

In the 1993 Black and Gold Wantagh Yearbook there was a Likes and Dislikes section. As I look at it now, I can't believe what they allowed the kids to write. Some of Taylor's likes were "the boys, my waterbed, being loved, older guys, flirting, Mr. Sachs (the handsome young football and baseball coach), Mr. Kravitz."

Her goal: "Have three kids, own a Mercedes Benz, never clean, cook or work."

Marylou didn't mention me in her likes which was good. Her goal: "Have a good job, get married to a wonderful man, have 2.5 children."

Taylor didn't sign my yearbook but Marylou wrote: "Well, now that I'm outta here I can talk and hang out with you without getting in trouble. And if you get phone calls late at night it's only me having a breakdown from school. Thanks for being there for me. I don't know what I would have done without you. P.S. My mom does like you!"

I haven't seen Taylor in well over two decades. But I know that she's married with kids and is a guidance counselor at a Long Island middle school.

I saw Marylou a few times in the 1990s. She graduated from college, married a good man and had two beautiful children. She posts photos on Facebook and is a nurse. Our one get-together in the past 20 years was a chance meeting in Denver at the Pepsi Center during a Flyers-Avalanche ice hockey game. She introduced me to her husband and kids.

She was in her early 40s and looked exactly the same as she had in high school. Seeing her with her husband and her kids filled me with pride. Her beautiful children made me emotional. I thought of Frank Mickens because I had treated her like a daughter. I had been a positive in her life as a good teacher should be. My intentions had always been to benefit her. The girl who was adopted, who had no siblings, now had a wonderful family and a good job. My lack of initial distance hadn't harmed her. To the contrary, she achieved her dreams and her Wantagh Yearbook goals.

CHAPTER 8

Tenure Year

Jennifer turned 30 and I turned 33 over the summer. David Dubin invited me to visit him on Fire Island. While I enjoyed the Fire Island town of Ocean Beach, David preferred Cherry Grove. Jennifer and I packed up the kids and drove to the Poconos and Eastern Long Island, but I never made it to Fire Island.

I completed my Master of Arts degree in English that spring at Queens College. I now faced a tenure year. I had had no problems my second year at Wantagh and hoped that my third would also go smoothly.

The summer and my softball career wound down. Softball beat me up: I injured my elbow and shoulder. I played the game hard; it would be my last season as a Bathit. We reached the playoff semi-finals. Jennifer didn't attend the game. My teammates had a new nickname for me: Dinnerdate.

The opposition had a very good pitcher, who fired the ball. We didn't get many hits. I singled, drew a bad throw and scored early, but by the sixth inning we trailed 2-1.

I came up to bat and again ripped a single, and then reached second base. On a Noel Boylan hit I rounded third. Our third base coach, Jen's first cousin David Green, threw up a late stop sign. I had never been good at stopping at stop signs. Probably the only person whose stop sign halted my hard turn at third was my Harriton High School varsity baseball coach, Nick Settanni. Settanni would have screamed at me 'til his mouth foamed—as he had for much lesser offenses. I never ran through a Settanni stop sign but I raced right through cousin David's two hands held high and screams of "Stop."

To this day I believe I slid under the tag. But the throw beat me and the catcher's glove was there.

"YER OUT!" screamed the ump. We lost 2-1 and missed out on advancing to the championship.

That ended my competitive fast-pitch softball career. My sports endings were often ignominious. In my last collegiate wrestling match the ref stalled me out of the conference title bout with five seconds left. My high school wrestling career ended in the PIAA District I South wrestle-backs to a Conestoga wrestler I should have beaten.

And so I began my sixth year of teaching.

Teachers packed the auditorium for Superintendent Besculides' opening speech. Not much of a speaker, he didn't compare to Frank Mickens. No nuggets of educational wisdom slammed into young teachers' minds.

David said his summer highlight was watching an HBO Special about a gay New York City cop and then meeting the cop in a bar. I was jealous of David. Not because he'd met the gay cop, but because he was free. It would be my last *free* summer for several years. Jennifer insisted I work at day camps. Young Julie was now a married Julie Magnuson and she was very pregnant. Jenn deLyra was pregnant, too.

Assistant Principal Terry O'Connor, who every teacher absolutely loved—a rare feat for an administrator—was very friendly to me. Principal Pisani was not. What did that mean? Would he deny me tenure? David said not to worry—I'd get tenure as long as I continued to distance myself from the children.

I had drawn big numbers into journalism, which I would teach solo. Nearly 60 kids would take my Journalism I and Journalism II classes. My numbers helped keep me and pregnant Julie in full-time jobs, as my numbers were also up in my creative writing classes. About 48 wrestlers went out for the team.

And while I always gave most of the credit for saving the wrestling program at Wantagh to Frank, years later he would say this of me: "You gave those kids the notion that wrestling wasn't the only thing that was important, and that literature and academics were things to be passionate about also. You could reach the toughest kids. You could get on their level, get them to like you, and be a positive influence in their lives. Those kids will never, ever forget you."

Frank and I were an unusual wrestling coaching tandem—a guidance counselor and an English teacher. Most wrestling coaches were physical education teachers.

My first solo issue of the *Warrior* featured Dr. Roberto Canessa, who was in the United States promoting the release of the film *Alive*. For some reason his first stop was Wantagh, where he told us how he and his rugby teammates survived a plane crash high in the Andes Mountains in Argentina (very close to Chile) in 1972.

He spoke at Wantagh High School to students, teachers and members of the community. Prior to Canessa's talk, Principal Pisani warned the students not to ask him about how the 16 survivors, out of the 40 passengers and five crew members, ate the frozen flesh of their dead friends. But of course a student asked that question anyway.

Canessa said that as a medical student, he was the first to resort to cannibalism. The survivors were trapped for 72 days. Rescue planes flew over the crash site initially but failed to distinguish the white fuselage of the plane against the snow.

"[Canessa] lost 66 pounds," wrote student journalist Diana Zimmerman in her front-page article. "He said that the decision to consume the corpses of friends was carefully considered. He ... concluded that upon death, the soul leaves the body and the corpse is consumed by worms as a means of survival. So he decided that he should consume these corpses (lacking souls) so that he could survive."

It was quite a lead article for the *Warrior*, featuring Zimmerman's great reporting. Underneath it was a Homecoming article, the usual front-page fare.

I talked to Dr. Canessa in one of my least favorite places, the principal's office. I asked him if he still liked mountains. He said he did. Though when he was trapped on that remote mountain, he didn't understand how anybody could enjoy mountains. I fearlessly spoke to him in my bad Spanish, asking if he'd read Gabriel Garcia Marquez's nonfiction *The Story of a Shipwrecked Sailor*. I was curious if a survivor had read a great survival story. He said he hadn't read it, but he had read a recent Marquez novel.

Canessa ended up hiking for ten days with two others, scaling a 15,000-foot peak with no gear, and found some Chilean *arrieros*, which led to the rescue of the 16 survivors.

A pediatric cardiologist in Uruguay, Canessa even made an unsuccessful run for president of Uruguay in 1994.

During David's couple of years advising the *Warrior*, there was little sports coverage. I made sure that each varsity sports team had an article in a three-page sports section. Our soccer team would win its second-straight state championship. Our football team had struggled but new Coach Keith Sachs was building up the program into an eventual Long Island powerhouse. We also had an amazing cross-country program that had won a state title the year before and was led by another great coach, Bill Hedgecock.

In addition, the previous year David saw me clipping students' articles from our year together.

"What are you doing?" he said.

"There is this high school journalism contest at Syracuse University," I said. "I'm going to enter our kids' articles."

"Why bother?" he said.

We won two honorable mentions in the state-wide Empire State Scholastic Press Association contest, one for Best Columnist by Susie Goodman and another, thanks to Dr. Canessa, for Best Front Page. Maybe David had been right. I'd spent a lot of time submitting articles for those two honorable mentions.

But I'd probably give it another shot the next year. I taught my sportswriters what my tabloid editor Chic Riebel had taught me, most of your readers aren't *kvelling* over your great prose, they just want to see that all the names are spelled correctly. I had them lead with the best and most interesting information they had. And I encouraged columnists to find unique stories about the students, the school and the community and come up with an interesting angle—pretty basic stuff.

Our wrestling team continued to improve, led by junior Ed Garcia and a great group of his fellow juniors. One of those juniors was heavyweight Toby Katcher. I wrestled him every day, kicking his butt, which made him better.

One of our biggest dual meets came against next-door rival Seaford, which had produced college-basketball coaching great Jim Valvano, who had died the previous spring from cancer. Seaford was coached by Sal LoStrappo, who had been a standout heavyweight wrestler there over a decade before. His athletic director had been Valvano's father Rocco.

It was difficult to beat Sal's teams. Our exciting meet in a packed Seaford gym came down to the heavyweight bout and Seaford had a much less-experienced wrestler there who was intimated by Toby. As the Seaford heavyweight warmed up, he grabbed a bottle he thought was water. But it was an unmarked bottle that had bleach in it to clean blood off the mats. He spat out his mouthful of bleach and had to default to Toby, giving Wantagh the victory in the meet.

The year cruised by. I received tenure—sans drama. The Wantagh Board of Education approved my tenure appointment in its April meeting. The next day I received a letter from Dr. Besculides saying my tenure appointment would become effective September 1, 1994. He added, "I offer you my fullest cooperation and help so that the years ahead will be profitable for you and the Wantagh School District."

I realize that there are a lot of Americans who don't like teachers' tenure and unions. But after I had been repeatedly fired, unfired and nearly fired as I've chronicled, I'm a firm believer in tenure.

The numbers of kids wanting to take my English electives and going out for wrestling clearly showed that I had something to offer the children of Wantagh. I still had a lot to learn about teaching. I was a long way from understanding many nuances and doing a better job of controlling difficult classes. But gaining tenure gave me the opportunity to improve without having to worry about administrators arbitrarily firing me, as Joel Dick and Walter Sadowski had done.

Yes, tenure is expensive and it does protect a very small percentage of bad teachers. But the overwhelming majority of teachers care, work hard to improve every year, and give so much of their time and lives to help students learn. Most teachers give everything to their students. The additional educational costs are worth it. I had great teachers at Harriton High School and great professors at the University of Delaware and Queens College. And all of that great teaching molded my teaching technique.

I had gained tenure at Wantagh after three years, where I proved myself. Sure, I made mistakes in that first year but I committed myself to overcoming my shortcomings, to adjusting to my administrators' critiques. They could have dumped me but they saw something in me and now the community benefited from my dedication, energy and enthusiasm.

While many pundits on the right (and even on the left) oppose tenure for high school teachers, college professors and college adjuncts, often, conservative educators are the ones most in need of tenure.

"Even sorrier is the plight of 'adjuncts,' part-time and on-tenure track employees who make up over 50 percent of higher education faculty," wrote James Martin in "Why Conservatives Should Defend Tenure" on the Jamesgmartin.center website. "Most adjuncts can be dismissed at the end of any day. At Bucks County Community College in Pennsylvania, adjunct astronomy professor Dwight Anderson was fired for using the word 'God' in a letter to students."

While that refers to colleges, all teachers at every level, once they've been recognized as competent, need time to develop their teaching techniques while being protected from stressed-out administrators. The teacher-administrator relationship is often a contentious one. There are potentially great teachers who need that protection from administrators who would fire them for petty reasons.

* * *

The spring of 1994 brought an incredible sports moment to New York.

The New York Rangers won the Stanley Cup in game seven of the final over the Vancouver Canucks. I rooted for the Rangers in those playoffs—for friends and especially Jennifer's first cousin, Joel Joachim. I had not deserted my Philadelphia Flyers. Had I still lived in Philly, rooting for the Rangers, or the Rags as they are called there, would have been an unpardonable capital offense. When you lived in Philly you rooted against every New York team, but now I longed for the end of the Islanders' fans "1940" chant—which had referred to the most recent Rangers' Cup-winning year.

Joel was at game seven in Madison Square Garden. I watched it on TV with Canadian friends from Montreal, John and Jodie Harcourt. You've got to find some Canadians to watch historic hockey moments. As Canadians of course they rooted for the Canucks. Jennifer, who didn't like watching hockey, was in Chicago for work that fateful June 14th.

It was the Rangers first Cup win in 54 years. And here we are 27 years later and that Cup is their only one over the past 81 years.

The final minutes of the game were nerve wracking for Rangers fans. The Blueshirts clung to a 3-2 lead. The Canucks were denied by the great goaltending of Mike Richter, a Philly-area native and probably the best NHL player ever from the Delaware Valley. Vancouver hit two posts in the final minutes. In the last 37 seconds there were three faceoffs in the Rangers end and it seemed inevitable that New York would somehow blow it. The final faceoff was taken by the Rangers' Craig MacTavish, the last helmetless player in the NHL. MacTavish won the draw and the celebration began.

The game-winning Rangers goal was scored by, who else, Captain Mark Messier. It was Messier's sixth Stanley Cup win, the other five coming with the Edmonton Oilers. Messier is, as of 2021, the only player in NHL history to captain two different teams to Stanley Cup victories.

My son's second birthday would come a few days later. He would grow up to become a Rangers fan, not a Flyers fan like me. I let him choose his team. He was a Rangers and Islanders fan. But after taking him to an Islanders-Flyers game a few years later, he was put off by the Islanders fans chanting the entire game, "Rangers suck" when not even playing the Rangers.

At that game, just before 9/11, the scoreboard at the Nassau Coliseum showed a depiction of Madison Square Garden exploding in flames. My son saw that and has hated the Islanders ever since. Hopefully one day he will watch the Rangers win a Cup.

I also took my girls to hockey games. During the 1999-2000 season, we were at an Islanders-Red Wings game. The three kids and I (more on the third kid later) sat right behind the Red Wings bench—Jennifer wasn't there. Scotty Bowman, one of the greatest coaches ever in any sport, was right in front of us. Rebecca Mae, our youngest, walked up and smacked the glass a few times, actually getting a Red Wing player or two to turn around annoyed. But when those toothless Red Wings saw this adorable blonde crazy girl, also missing a few teeth and snarling at them, they smiled. Nonetheless, neither daughter grew up to be a professional fan.

* * *

I've repeatedly warned potential teachers never to break up a fight between girls. However, one day in 1994, just outside of my classroom, Nicole Carey, a senior, was pummeled by another girl. Nicole had been my student and was a nice kid. She was a very thin girl, *una flacca*. Her face was absorbing furious punches from Ann Marie Napoli, who had several older brothers. Ann Marie was short and very strong. I couldn't allow Nicole's face to soak up one more punch so I violated my golden rule and grabbed Ann Marie from behind and lifted her in the air and pulled her away from Nicole. As I held her in the air she kicked and threw air punches at a battered Nicole, who was in tears.

I had saved Nicole. A few months later Nicole sadly told me that she had broken up with her boyfriend.

"That's too bad," I said.

"Do you want to know why, Mr. Kravitz?"

"Ah, not really," I said.

"Well I'll tell you anyway," she said angrily. "He fooled around with some ninth grader."

"I can see why you broke up then," I said.

"And she gave him a blow job," she said.

"That's a little too much information, Nicole," I said.

Seven years later, they would find the body of Nicole's father in the World Trade Center rubble. He was one of the 343 heroic, fearless New York City firefighters who perished there. Many more Wantagh parents and relatives of students would also die there. Dennis Carey was 51 when he died. He'd been in the NYFD for nearly 20 years and was in Hazardous Material Company 1.

"He loved to travel with his wife and their two children, Nicole and Dennis, Jr," according to a legacy.com tribute to him.

Looking back, I'm glad I violated my girl-fight rule to save Nicole. But sadly, I went to look her up on Facebook to confirm my memories and saw that she died in 2019 at age 42 after losing a two-year battle to stomach cancer. She is survived by her mom and her brother. I wish I had realized that she had passed away. I would have gone to her funeral.

CHAPTER 9

The Sweat Hogs

finally had my New York State Permanent English 7-12 license—and tenure. I distanced from the children. I drew good numbers into my journalism and creative writing electives. Frank Muzio and I had a full wrestling room. This looked like a career.

My journalism, creative writing and 11th grade English classes were terrific. My 12th-grade English class, unfortunately, appeared to be unteachable. With 19 boys and two girls, that class had several disruptive students, foremost among them my standout wrestler Ed Garcia.

I had coached Ed for two years but never had the pleasure of teaching him. Ed was an amazing athlete; the student part of student/athlete was not his forte. A vicious football player, Ed hit hard with intense acceleration. He was happiest on the football field hurling his body at opponents. He began the year setting off a stink bomb in my class—a hilarious maneuver to him and the other boys. As wrestling season hadn't begun, I wrote it up and Dean Lebel punished him. He didn't like that. But he understood punishment for his transgressions.

One tall, tough boy, Michael DiTroia, said to me daily in his raspy voice, "Kravitz, you ain't nothing but a JV coach."

He felt this put me in my place, lest I had any lofty and arrogant views of my coaching position. I was well aware that my coaching career had descended, from head collegiate coach to JV high school coach, according to DiTroia—or assistant varsity wrestling coach, according to me.

Frank Muzio called this class the "sweat hogs" after the 1970s TV sitcom *Welcome Back, Kotter*, starring the comedian Gabe Kaplan as Mr. Kotter, who returns to Brooklyn to teach high school kids. Some of Kotter's lovely students were Vinnie Barbarino (John Travolta),

Juan Epstein (Robert Hegyes), Arnold Horshack (Ron Palilio) and Freddy "Boom Boom" Washington (Lawrence Hilton-Jacobs).

My crew definitely contended with those sweat hogs when it came to obnoxiousness, especially Steven Bergstein. Steven was a good-looking boy, with dark hair and acne. Girls liked him, despite the acne. The star of the basketball team, with a sweet shot, he had been in my journalism class as a sophomore. He didn't write much then.

One day, as I blocked the door while students crowded it a few minutes before the bell rang, Steven faked a punch at my balls. I flinched and pulled every muscle in my lower body. Steven and the boys laughed uproariously.

I had to make sure Steven, who was very clever, didn't weasel out of the faux assault. I went on the offensive and wrote a novel on the write-up slip, not just on that incident, but for all the mayhem he'd already created. The dean punished him severely.

There were four boys in the class who had discipline. They were quiet and afraid of the sweat hogs. One negative about teaching is that you don't remember the names of the nice kids. Though I recall three of them—Anthony Primiano, Shawn Eckert, Jason Astrup. They had notebooks and pens. The sweat hogs never brought pens. At this point in my teaching career I hadn't learned the simple trick of picking up every pen and pencil on the floor. You do that and in a week's time you fill a drawer with them. But you had to wash your hands continuously.

The sweat hogs raised their hands, at least.

"Yes, Steven, what is your question?"

"Krav, can I please go to the bathroom?" he said.

Well, he said please, which was a positive. "We are doing something important right now. Can you wait a little?" That was my stall. Wantagh students had already asked to go to the bathroom, conservatively, about 20,000 times in three years.

Steven now called out, "Krav, I'm gonna get an infection if I don't go."

The irony is that I really wanted Steven to leave the class and "take a lap" around the halls. But Dean Lebel didn't want my hogs wandering the halls ninth period.

Many of them had girlfriends. Most were good-looking boys who didn't care about school or were weak academically. They treated their girlfriends reasonably well but were not always nice to the two girls in the class, who sat in the front and did their work. One of the girls, Gerrianne Bennett, didn't take any crap from the sweat hogs. Gerrianne was attractive but also a tough athlete. If the boys said something to her she gave it right back to them. She also defended the other girl, Laurie Schuck, who was quiet and didn't have the best last name for a class of sweat hogs.

A nice kid, who was technically a sweat hog—he was friends with most of that group—was Michael Giannino. He rarely disrupted class, other than maybe joining the laughter or the nonsense. Then in the middle of the year his father died. I felt terrible for him. He had a nice family with an older brother and a younger sister. As a teacher, the grief is almost familial when your students lose a parent. You've often met the students' parents. You see the pain of loss in the child every day.

Another one of my wrestlers in that class was Tim Lopez. The kids called him Taco. Nearly every Latino kid in those days at a mostly White school was nicknamed Taco. Those kids weren't necessarily the most creative when it came to nicknames.

Tim was about 5-feet-4-inches tall, 5-feet-4-inches wide, and about 190 pounds. Not a very good wrestler, he usually lost by pin. He was a weak student, though he tried. I wish I could have helped him more but I was too busy dealing with the atrocious behavior to give him the academic help he needed. I wondered how he had made it to his senior year and passed all of his classes. But if a kid behaves and tries, they will usually pass. Lopez's heritage was Mexican. Neither he nor Garcia spoke a word of Spanish. In those years they were in a minority of Latino kids, though each year saw more and more of them at Wantagh.

After a month of fruitless attempts to read fiction or non-fiction or even *Goodnight Moon*, I went to the videotape. I showed a classic, *One Flew Over the Cuckoo's Nest*. The film, based on the novel of the same name by Ken Kesey, swept the Academy Awards in 1976—winning Best Picture, Best Director, Best Actor and Best Actress.

Jack Nicholson won the Best Actor award for his role as Randall P. McMurphy, who, while doing prison time for statutory rape, is transferred to a mental hospital. In that mental hospital he battles the evil Nurse Ratched, played by Louise Fletcher. The film also features Danny DeVito and Christopher Lloyd as patients and Scatman Crothers as a guard. Michael Douglas produced it.

Kesey actually wrote parts of the novel tripping on LSD while working at a mental hospital. He claimed to gain insight into patients' illnesses by talking to them while on LSD.

In addition to showing my sweat hogs *Cuckoo's Nest*, I photocopied small excerpts of the novel for them to read. The genius of the novel was using a supposed deaf and dumb, massive Native American, the Chief, as the narrator.

One day Steven made a brilliant observation: "The mental ward in this movie is a lot like this class."

I wanted to tell the sweat hogs about my experience in a real mental ward but I didn't dare. From their behavior it appeared several of them perhaps had mental health issues or had family members who had, nonetheless I said nothing about my own personal cuckoo's nest experience. I did tell them other stories.

I also struggled with the VCR. It would stop, turn off. I couldn't figure out what was going on. I suspected a problem with the VCR, but then it would work fine and so I didn't get another VCR or ask the AV guy to look at it. After several weeks of problems and then no problems I noticed giggles from the boys during these many glitches and I realized the remote had long vanished. I had worked the VCR manually. Tim Lopez fessed up that he had the remote. The sweat hogs were behind all of the VCR technical difficulties.

I definitely thought about pursuing justice and getting them all in trouble, but it was such a classic prank that I let it go. Also, the remote had disappeared. It was annoying that they had destroyed the evidence of their misdeed but I was excited we could watch the rest of the film without the interruptions and laughter. Those sweat hogs could be ingenious—at everything except reading and good behavior.

Of course, teachers today rarely use a VCR. But if you have a remote for a Smartboard or other device, I recommend that you lock it up at all times.

The only way to deal with the sweat hogs was to call their parents. But once wrestling started I didn't have the time after school to make an hour's worth of parent calls.

I was excited for our wrestling season because we had a lot of good seniors and because I planned to see if corporal punishment would work on Garcia. If I inflicted pain on him while wrestling him would he behave in class? After all, corporal punishment had been used for hundreds of years in schools. Some of my good friends had been smacked around by nuns in Catholic schools and they'd turned out okay.

Garcia was so hyper and fooled around no matter what I said or did. He was the kid you wished was absent but he never was. I also had the problem, as wrestling approached, that if I called his mom or sent him to Dean Lebel he might not be able to wrestle. I didn't want him suspended and missing a single competition.

However, it turned out Garcia had a high tolerance for pain. With a good 50 pounds on him, I'd throw legs in from the top position and torque his body one way and wrench his head the other. Yet he felt no pain. He seemed to like it. Meanwhile, he cracked me in the face so frequently I had to wear a mask when I wrestled him so he wouldn't break my nose. Corporal punishment had once again backfired.

On the way to a meet, we passed the Nassau County Prison in East Meadow and Ed said, "It's not bad you know."

"What's not bad?" I said.

"Prison," Ed said. "You get three square meals a day. You can lift weights. They have a great weight room."

Punishment of any kind was no deterrent to him. The rest of that bus ride I tried to convince Ed that freedom was way better than prison food and the prison weight room. I tried to direct Ed on a different path. I never gave up on a kid. There was a lot of good in Ed. He made mistakes—but 90 percent of kids do, as do 99 percent of adults. I gave my all to set him on a different life journey than the one he seemed headed towards.

My journalism students were doing a great job. Our January front page took on the issue of Native American nicknames and logos. Wantagh had been called Jerusalem and then was named after the

Sachem of the Montauk Native people. The school's teams featured the logo of a Native American.

My student writers quoted a Native American spokesperson as saying, "Native Americans find sports nicknames, mascots, logos and chants demeaning. They reinforce the negative stereotypes of the savage warmongering Indian nomad wandering the plains."

Wantagh's sports nickname was and still is "The Warriors." Its logo was a Native American image. In their article Eric Criscuolo and Ross Fialkov also called out the Washington Redskins as having one of the most offensive nicknames in sports. It took 25 years until Washington finally dumped the name "Redskins." My students were well ahead of their time.

My 1994-95 journalism team doubled the number of annual awards at the Syracuse contest. We won four: two by Steven Wolkoff, including our first Gold award, as best in the state for a piece he wrote about how a Wantagh boys' track star came back from an ACL tear.

Years later I learned that Steven was killed in a multi-car crash in California in 2008. He was 30 and an up-and-coming presence in the Silicon Valley Tech revolution. His life was stolen by a 21-year-old, high on drugs and alcohol, weaving his borrowed vehicle in and out of traffic on the Pacific Coast Highway. His vehicle slammed into the car driven by Steven's girlfriend at 85 mph. Steven languished and died slowly at the scene, as help was slow to arrive. His girlfriend Cindy survived with serious injuries. I can close my eyes and visualize him, sitting in the back of my journalism class, making clever comments and then showing his brilliance through his writing. His tragic death was the world's loss.

* * *

From death to life: On April 27 Jen gave birth to Rebecca Mae. She was named after my grandmother, Mae Flaxenburg. For years Jen thought that her middle name was spelled May, but I showed her the birth certificate. Jen wasn't thrilled with that spelling. Jen controls a lot in our lives, but I had filled out the paperwork.

Rebecca was the easiest of Jen's three births. She came right out with no painful pushing. I took photos of all three kids at birth. They all looked exactly alike so I knew they were mine. I wasn't good at loading the film in the camera, and Jen was good at it. Minutes after giving birth I said, "Jen, could you load the camera?"

She did it. Her doctor said he'd never seen anyone give birth and then load film into a camera. Rebecca entered the world screaming. It portended something, though at the time I didn't know what.

I came home and nearly three-year-old Brett was very angry at his mother because she was supposed to get him a Power Ranger and I had been a little busy to pick one up.

"But Brett," I said, "your mom got your new baby sister."

"I don't care," he said. "I want a Power Ranger."

I took Dana and Brett to the hospital the next day to meet their sister. After a few minutes they destroyed things. Dana ran down the hallway and I told her to stop running and she said, "I'm not running. I'm skipping."

"Brett, you stop running, too," I said.

"I'm not running, I'm skipping," he said.

Brett's dorky skip looked like something out of Monty Python's "The Ministry of Silly Walks." Then Dana skipped backwards and said, "I can skip backwards and Brett can't even skip forwards."

We had three children and we both had full time jobs. And while teaching was a great career if you had multiple kids, I knew I was in for some rough years. I suspected that my golf game, which was going downhill, was about to completely collapse. I said back then, "If your golf game is good and you have young kids that means your parenting game sucks."

There were no big news stories on the day of Rebecca's birth, other than the continued mourning for the 168 killed and 500 wounded eight days before in the Oklahoma City terrorist bombing.

Wrestling went well. We had a good team. Nonetheless our nemesis Bethpage hammered us. We were only down 15-12 early, but then two of our best wrestlers, Ed and senior Frank Cammarata, were battered by their studs, Troy Gorman and Sean Severin. The year before Severin physically pounded our wrestler, Danny Maimran, who was also a sweat hog, but not a disruptive one. Maimran grew up in Israel. His father rushed out of the stands. I intercepted him.

"Please go back and sit down, Mr. Maimran," I said.

"I was Israeli paratrooper," he screamed at me. "I will not allow that."

Luckily I was bigger than him because he was enraged and who knows what he might have done.

"Danny is okay," I said. "That kid is very physical. We should have just forfeited to him."

"Yes, you should have," he screamed. "But let him try that on me."

"You can't go on the mat, Mr. Maimran."

I had to miss my first dual meet in four years. Ed said I wasn't permitted to miss a match. "I'll call my mom and she'll babysit for you if that's what you need," Ed said.

"That's nice Ed but I promised my wife," I said. "Sometimes you have to make sacrifices."

But I was there for the rest of the meets. We beat some good teams. I took Dana to a meet but I had failed to get her dinner so the opposing coach's wife gave her half a burger and fries. Ed pinched some of Dana's fries.

"Don't take any more of her fries, Ed," I said.

Ed gave Dana a ride on his back. Then he dumped her on the mat so he could make out with his girlfriend, Janine Barr, an attractive gymnast.

"Hey Ed and Janine, can you not suck face in front of little kids," I yelled at the two of them. At least Janine felt bad. Ed didn't.

After our final competition of the season at Glen Cove, before the postseason, Frank was told that kids had broken into lockers and stolen equipment and uniforms. The Glen Cove coaches were very upset and asked us to question our kids if they had seen anything or knew anything—as several teams had competed. But questioning our kids was unnecessary, as the next practice Ed walked in wearing a freshly swiped Glen Cove warm up.

Really?

I couldn't believe it. Frank said that was it for Ed. His season was over. He was off the team. Dean Lebel agreed.

Now, I realize that what I'm about to say is probably not the correct way to approach this situation. But, let's remember, I wrestled with Ed practically every day for three years. Training with him punished my body. He crushed my psyche as I struggled to teach him in English. I had to find a way to get him to wrestle. I mean, he was immune to punishment. It had no impact on him. We'd worked too hard for him to miss out on the postseason his senior year.

I realize that walking into practice wearing a stolen Glen Cove warm up was not the most intelligent maneuver. But I went behind Frank's back and talked to Ed's mom and gave her a few suggestions. Twenty-five years later I feel terrible admitting this, and I don't recommend this route to young teachers and coaches, but Ed's mom showed up in the Dean's office with a lawyer.

* * *

As we all tried to figure out the best way to deal with Ed Garcia, Brian Donohue said at a department meeting that jobs were in jeopardy the following year. Sure, just when I felt somewhat bulletproof, after working my butt off for my master's and my teaching license, I might not have a job the next year.

The more senior teachers were the most secure regarding budget cuts. I was the penultimate department hire, with young Julie Magnuson being the last full-time hire. We were also in a labor dispute with the board of education. Our first *Warrior* front page featured the lead headline: "Board Withholds Increments, Teachers Protest."

Each year, up to year 20, like many teachers in Long Island districts, we got a salary (step) increase, which was around two percent. As our contract had expired the school board froze those annual step increases.

"... the board's decision to deny teachers our increments was designed to humiliate us and I'm saddened that they would see fit to treat us with that kind of disrespect," David Dubin said in a front-page *Warrior* article by Peter Brown.

The school board president Christopher Wendt said in that article, "We must take into consideration the escalating taxes and our current economic condition. We have a legitimate dispute on the financial value of the teacher's work."

Teachers protested in front of the school in the morning; we wore black armbands. In New York State teachers can't strike as a result of a 1967 labor law known as the Taylor Law, which "establishes impasse procedures for the resolution of collective bargaining disputes; and prohibits strikes by all of the state's public employees," according to the Governor's Office of Employee Relations website.

"We have excellent schools and excellent teachers," said our union president, Suzanne Lawrence. "We need a contract."

On Long Island, like most of the U.S., public schools receive funding from the federal government, the state government and by taxing homeowners who live in that district. Long Island has great public schools, but the homeowners in each school district pay for that with high taxes. New York City's school taxes are much lower than those in Nassau and Suffolk Counties. Homeowners don't like seeing their taxes go up every year. More recently annual tax increases for New York schools have been capped at two percent.

For Long Island schools, also more recently, the costs for programs such as regular instruction, special education, extracurricular activities, sports and busing, make up 77 percent of spending; capital costs make up 13 percent; and administrative costs such as salaries of superintendents, other administrators and school board expenses make up 10 percent, according to "Long Island schools: Where taxpayers' money goes," a 2019 *Newsday* article.

The high administrative costs combined with Long Island's many small districts have led critics to call for mergers. But that same *Newsday* article said, "district consolidations have proved a hard sell with voters in recent years."

Though, if the school district is good, those homes increase in value. In districts where the schools are less successful, the homes might depreciate in value. So, it seems in the financial interest of homeowners to support quality public education in their districts.

It's one of many issues dividing American taxpayers. Some will pay for good public schools and others don't want to, especially senior citizens whose children have long graduated from the public schools.

* * *

After Ed Garcia's mom's meeting with Ron Lebel, Ron called me into his office.

"Pete, I'm very sorry but we are going to have to let Garcia wrestle in the qualifiers," he said. "I know it's not teaching him the right thing but we have no choice."

"You did your best, Mr. Lebel," I said. I felt like an ass. But if you ever coached a kid for three years in a high school varsity sport, in a place like sports-crazed Long Island, you'd maybe understand. And I'm not saying that what I did was right. Was I thinking more about the kid or myself?

Our county qualifier tournament was at Massapequa. Top four finishers were guaranteed a spot at the counties. We advanced six kids to the semifinals. Five of them lost. Only Frankie Camarrata made the final. Maybe Frankie had succeeded because he didn't have to worry about an upcoming test in *Macbeth*, due to my explaining the play to him during the endless hours of waiting around. Wrestling tournaments require a lot of patience. Frank Muzio loved that I had helped Frankie with Shakespeare at a wrestling tournament. And he had needed it. He knew nothing about that tragedy, which was also a tragedy. Had he listened in class or read a single page? Probably not. That intense tutoring session, while helping Frankie on his test, failed to gain him the title. He lost by a point.

Our five losers (in what Frank and I called the semifinal holocaust) made the consolation final and advanced to counties. We had six shots at finally getting a county place-winner.

At the county tournament we advanced three kids to the quarterfinals, one win from being our first place-winners: Frankie Cammarata at 138, Gordon Madden at 126 and of course Ed Garcia at 145. All three had tough opponents but Gordon and Frank could win. Ed had the No. 1 seed from Levittown Division H.S., Bob Bennett.

He'd lost one match all year to some upstate stud. His father was the Levittown Division assistant coach. Ed didn't have much of a chance.

Frank and I had worked very hard, first to just get kids to qualify for the county tournament and now to place. While it was only high school wrestling, as a coach it consumes your soul. Your best kids' losses hurt more than your own haunting defeats.

Madden lost first, then Cammarata lost. They could still come back through wrestle-backs and place at counties. Then it was Ed's turn.

I studied Bennet as he warmed up. He looked nervous. I grabbed Ed.

"Ed, Bennet is nervous," I said. "Are you?"

"No," he said. And it was true, which I knew. Ed never got nervous. He just attacked. Very few wrestlers exuded such calmness before a big match, before any match.

"Get right on him," I said.

Now, I said that to probably every wrestler I ever coached. The match began and Bennet danced around. Ed smacked Bennet's head hard and pulled it down while shooting his outside-leg single. He caught a stunned Bennet and spun him to the mat, flat on his back. The ref slapped the mat. It was over—the upset of the tournament. Unseeded Ed Garcia had pinned the No. 1-seed in 33 seconds. Frank and I finally had our place-winner.

Ed had to wrestle Bennet again for third place. Bennet wrestled from the whistle with intensity and rage and beat Ed, 10-0. But Ed was our first Nassau County place-winner in fourth place. He would usher in a reign of unimaginable success for Wantagh wrestling.

And what became of Ed?

He lives in Florida, has a good job, two handsome young sons and a beautiful wife.

I recently asked him about the sweat hogs. He didn't remember much—unlike how the hogs' antics were imprinted on my brain—and instead wrote, "I am so appreciative to have had a teacher, coach and mentor like you. I still to this day talk about you and how you always inspired me to be great. I hope someday to see you soon and for you to meet my two boys."

The Ed Garcias are the reason why, as a teacher, you keep trying and keep believing, show kindness (the corporal punishment idea lasted about 1/3 of a wrestling practice), and never give up on a kid. If you plan to teach or coach, never ever give up on a kid.

* * *

The spring brought more tragedy to one of the sweat hogs.

My senior, Michael Giannino, who had just lost his father, now lost his older brother Joseph Giannino, a 1993 Wantagh graduate. Joseph had been at a bar near the school. He got into an argument with another Wantagh graduate, James Baldi, and they went outside. Baldi threw a punch and knocked Joseph backwards, head first into the asphalt. He fell into a coma. His family took him off his respirator on March 28th. He had died from a severe head injury.

"Giannino was a popular, well-respected student and athlete. Everyone who knew him was touched by his kindness," said a non-bylined *Warrior* article.

"Joe was a fabulous kid," said his guidance counselor and the former Wantagh wrestling coach Bernie Colombo. "He was always willing to do anything for anyone."

Giannino, 19, had been Marylou's first boyfriend and she called me from college in tears.

I drove to his wake on a gray day, north on Wantagh Avenue, past the bar Lily Flanagan's where a tower of flowers marked the spot he'd suffered the fatal punch. Joseph's body, clad in his Wantagh football jersey, lay in his casket at O'Shea Funeral Home. I hugged his brother, Michael, and told him how sorry I was. He introduced me to his mother. She had recently lost her husband and now had lost her handsome 19-year-old son—in the most freakish, unimaginable manner. Mrs. Giannino somehow remained composed.

I hoped, and perhaps even believed, that this would be the last one of these funerals or wakes I would attend. But I had this feeling that there would be more.

CHAPTER 10

The Big Three

At the end of each wrestling season, Frank and I spoke in the auditorium to parents and students at a winter sports awards evening with the other coaches. I often begin my short speech saying that wrestling was not a fun sport, which irritated Frank.

"Don't say that wrestling isn't fun," he said.

"Well, I'm just being honest," I said.

And I loved wrestling. Hey, I returned to college wrestling after herpes flayed my upper torso, and after my mental hospital incarceration.

But cutting weight for weigh-ins and waiting around all day at a wrestling tournament are not fun. Staring down a superior opponent, who was always ripped with muscles, wasn't fun. Losing at wrestling was the worst possible defeat. Now, losing in any sport, for a competitor, is agonizing. But in a team sport maybe your teammate screwed up. In wrestling, when you lose, it's all on you.

Winning was rapture. But when you get good at wrestling you expect to win.

Three sophomore wrestlers appeared to be the team's future: Sebby Muscarella, David Bloom and Mike Ginsberg. Four years before Ginsberg had come to a practice as a sixth grader and now he was hooked on the mat sport. He no longer played ice hockey. I did both and while wrestling is addictive, chasing a puck on a few inches of ice is definitely more fun—but not to Ginsberg.

Bloom and Ginsberg were difficult to coach. I hoped that neither of them would take my creative writing or journalism classes. Muscarella was a dream student-athlete: coachable, nice, mellow, hard-working.

Ironically, Bloom and Ginsberg came out of solid families. David Bloom's father, Mike, was a wrestling coach at Lawrence High School and a teacher in that district. His mom, Cheryl, worked in the Wantagh Administration office. His sister had been in my first class my first year and was well behaved and mature. She would eventually marry one of the star Wantagh soccer players from the back-to-back state championship teams, Tom Donohue. Like so many small towns in America, many of these Wantagh kids seemed to marry each other.

David's younger brother Todd was also a wrestler and a great kid. Meanwhile, David could have led the sweat hogs. Ginsberg wasn't as hard to coach as David, but he was challenging—in terms of listening, being on time, keeping up with his academics.

How do you deal with these undisciplined kids? I had been too lenient and forgiving with Ed Garcia, but it worked out. The tougher approach as a teacher, coach or parent seemed more effective. Jennifer was more of a disciplinarian as a parent than I was. Our kids needed that.

You'd think Sebby Muscarella, as the best of the three in terms of behavior, came out of a solid family. Life never works like you'd think, though, does it?

That summer Sebby's father was murdered. He'd been a mail carrier, became addicted to crack and was killed by his drug dealer in Freeport. Sebby had lived with his father and his stepmother, two younger brothers and two stepsisters.

His mother was a substance abuser, who was in and out of rehab and lived in New Jersey. After his father's death, his two younger brothers went to live with two different aunts in New Jersey. Sebby had been in the Wantagh district since third grade and the family decided that he would continue to live with his stepmother, Ellen. Ellen agreed to continue to parent him.

Dealing with his father's murder and substance abuse and his mother's chronic addictions, one would think Sebby would have been troubled. But he was rock solid. I hoped that he would take journalism and eventually encouraged him to do so.

While Sebby's real parents battled addiction, his stepmother was a school principal and an amazing parent; she was the solid foundation in his life. No question that her parenting steered Sebby's childhood on a straight course. Here in 2021, Ellen winds down her 15th and final year as the superintendent of the Islip School District in Suffolk County.

* * *

A scourge of deadly drugs hit the Wantagh Class of '96 hard. Two boys turned to heroin. I didn't have either boy in class, nor did I know John Zappulla and Eugene Dimmick, other than seeing them in the halls.

Dimmick would overdose and die in East New York, Brooklyn in 2000. Only a few blocks from that spot, Zappulla, high on heroin, drove his father's car into two young mothers pushing baby strollers across Atlantic Avenue in 2003.

The *New York Times*, in less-than-its-usual staid prose, described the scene in a February sixth article: "a chain of collisions beginning at 2:30 p.m. that left a trail of bodies, clothing and mangled vehicles along the six lanes of Atlantic Avenue in Cypress Hills."

Zappulla killed Yartza Santos, 19, her ten-month-old son Manuel Noriega Villot and Nery Mejia, 17. Mejia's 11-month-old son was critically injured. Two years later Zappulla accepted a plea deal and was sentenced to 12 years in prison. Eventually released from prison, he died in 2017.

Heroin use in Long Island public schools hit in waves. When it did, the results were tragic. The pharmaceutical epidemic of drugs like oxycodone, years later, would be even deadlier.

* * *

I did, however, have some good classes and mostly great kids to teach. The year before I had had a wonderful 11th grade English class. Several students stood out, among them, one with a great sense of humor—Rob Cesternino. Rob had also taken journalism and he was back in journalism for his senior year, where he was one of my top editors.

Rob had the lead story in our first issue about a somewhat quirky but incredible Economics teacher named Bill Bogatz, who only missed school one day a year, for which he took a personal day.

"Bogatz had amassed 2,162 consecutive days of teaching without taking a sick day," Rob wrote. "In an ironic twist only Rod Serling could imagine, Mr. Bogatz has the most extensive substitute teacher file, which is fabled to contain seating charts, student profiles and a picture I.D. of every student in each class photocopied from last year's yearbook."

In those years I probably averaged about six absences per year and I only had seating charts and a few generic plans in my file for a substitute.

Bogatz taught at Wantagh from 1974-78 and lost the job in an economic downturn. He returned in 1988, then retired from full-time teaching in 2015. He continued his streak of not taking a sick day and only one personal day per year, to attend a conference for his teaching job, up until his retirement.

As part of our contract we could bank the sick days we didn't use. We got 16 sick and personal days per year, so Bogatz retired with around 400 days in his sick-day bank. Of those, 194 days counted and enabled Bogatz or any Wantagh teacher to get a payout of nearly $24,000 when they retired. However, Bogatz's remaining 200 sick days in the end meant nothing other than an incredible testimony to his dedication. The sick-day payout was different in every Long Island district as it was negotiated. Some Long Island districts had no payout. A few had a full year's salary. Others had double Wantagh's payout.

To the many Americans working in non-union jobs, a sick-day bank and retirement payout perhaps seems outrageous. When I went into teaching, I knew nothing about the payout. I knew about banking sick days. I didn't like being absent because it was a lot of work to prepare for a sub, as I always tried to prepare a lesson that continued what we were doing, and I had different preps so I had to make up plans for each class. But I was no Bill Bogatz—not even close.

But look, there are incentives to a teaching career, especially in a non-pandemic world.

* * *

Two girls in that 11th grade glass became teachers—Michelle Wishnevky and Kristy Nallan. Kristy (nee Nallan) Cornella now teaches at Wantagh Middle School, still lives in Wantagh and is married to a Wantagh graduate, Dominic Cornella.

You can't get more Wantagh than that. She is one of many of my former students who ended up teaching at Wantagh and marrying a fellow Wantaghian.

Another student in that anti-sweat-hog class was Erin Barry. As her junior year began, Erin had poor study habits. Some of the techniques that I was developing worked well for her and helped turn her around academically. One simple little aspect of my teaching was homework.

Homework. Nothing good about it right?

However, I would assign a little bit of homework, 10-15 minutes at most, three or four days per week. As soon as the bell ran to begin class I quickly walked around the room and wrote a check on my seating chart if they did it, a zero if they didn't, and if they did a poor job a ½. Homework was not to be done once they walked in class. If I saw them scribbling out homework at their desk it was a zero. If they did every homework for a quarter (marking period) they got a nice bonus on their quarterly report card, as much as 2 points. Each quarter I'd change my seats and we'd start over, so if they had a bad quarter they could still get the bonus for the next quarter.

I would tweak my homework every year of my teaching. It was effective at organizing kids. All of this worked really well for Erin. She blossomed as a student.

She had always been a very popular teenager and in her senior year, she was voted Best Looking and Best Personality in the yearbook. She was a pleasant and adorable dark-haired young lady. That's why when our senior wrestling captain, Mike Russo, broke up with his girlfriend in December, I violated the Principal Pisani distance rule and said to Mike, "You should go out with Erin."

Now, I take no credit for what happened next, but today Mike and Erin are married and have two adorable children. Another pair of Wantagh kids who ended up together.

In my 1996 yearbook Erin wrote: "I am serious when I say that you are my favorite teacher. Last year when I had you for English—I didn't do anything in the beginning of the year. Not only did I turn myself around for me, but I did it for you. You were one of those teachers whose class students wouldn't cut. Thank you for helping me realize what I could achieve and for helping me with Mike."

I always encouraged students to work hard, to succeed, to do their best. With a class like the sweat hogs in 1995 that didn't always connect, but with Erin's 11th grade class it got through to many kids. And I had found a balance between the distance that the principal demanded and enough closeness to get kids to listen, which wasn't easy. Often they didn't listen.

Regarding Principal Pisani, he retired at the end of that year. While I had had my disagreements with him, my student journalists wrote glowing articles about his nine-year run as Wantagh principal. The high school was in its 41st year in '96, and no other principal had lasted that long.

In one front-page article Pisani said, "When I first came here the statistics were not as good as they are now. I'd like to think that I was part of that, but of course it was the students, the teachers and everyone else ... When I look at the statistics, I see that 94 percent of our students are going to two- or four-year colleges."

When I read these articles about Pisani, I realized that he was a good principal. He didn't fire me and he could have. Sadly, Pisani only enjoyed seven years of his retirement as he died in 2003.

When he retired from Wantagh, his assistant principal Terry O'Connor took the helm of high school. And for me and many of my Wantagh teaching colleagues, Terry would become the best principal, and administrator of any kind, we ever had.

In his front-page *Warrior* article, after O'Connor was named the next principal, my student writers wrote: "Over 60 applications were received and 16 or 17 applicants were called for interviews."

It was no surprise that Terry won out over that group. And the school board and the teachers' union agreed to a new four-year contract that included a raise. Writing conferences and my job were safe.

Coaching wrestling became more difficult, however, with three young children ages one, four, and seven, and Jennifer's hectic pharmaceutical sales job. But Frank and I got our first county finalist that year in Mike Russo, our captain and also the football captain.

Russo came from a wrestling family. His uncle Ron Russo was an NAIA national champion and two-time Division I All-American at Bloomsburg State College, now a university, in Pennsylvania. I wrestled with Russo at every practice that year. He was a terrific athlete and very good at takedowns. I had a lot of weight on him but he took me down regularly. I really enjoyed teaching great wrestlers like Russo by battling them in practice. The best way for wrestlers to improve is for them to train with a more-skilled wrestler. And the incredible daily workouts kept me fit.

That 1996 class was one of my favorites. There were so many nice kids. The journalism crew again won four awards at the Syracuse contest, including a Gold by Miriam Lampert and a Bronze by Jared Rosenblatt. I was disappointed that Rob Cesternino, my humorous journalism student and newspaper editor, didn't win an award. Though most of Rob's energy went into an April Fools' Issue. It was very funny and a big hit. Rob wrote half of its articles.

Rob's personality would gain national recognition as he became a reality TV star.

Rob reached the final three of *Survivor: The Amazon* in 2003. He would fare better than Heidi Strobel, who would place fifth in that sixth season of the popular reality TV show. Heidi eventually married Cole Hamels, who led my Philadelphia Phillies to their second World Series win in 2008.

Rob married a Wantagh High School graduate, Nicole Palmeri. Rob and Nicole have two boys and live in Southern California, where

Rob has a podcast series called *Rob Has a Podcast* (RHAP). Rob also appeared on *Survivor: All-Stars* in 2004, where he was voted out early in a blindside by "Boston" Rob Mariano.

Recently, Rob said to me: "I started doing podcasts about *Survivor* in 2010 and have created a podcast network covering reality TV shows. I like to think that I'm still putting my journalism training to good use so thank you for that!"

In my yearbook Rob wrote: "We had fun in journalism. I'm glad to be part of the team. Guys, guys, guys, did you know that ..." I used to say that a lot.

CHAPTER 11

To Coach or Not to Coach

As I prepared for September, I confronted a difficult decision. Should I continue coaching wrestling?

After 20 years of competing in and coaching the mat sport, except for my time in Brooklyn, I was done. But not because I'd lost my love for wrestling and didn't want to coach. With Rebecca Mae advancing out of the terrible twos and into the threes, which continued to be terrible, and with two other children, and Jennifer working full time and often traveling for work, I felt that I couldn't coach any more despite our amazing babysitter—Blanca Schaeffer, from Bogotá, Colombia. Blanca loved our children as much as we did. Despite Rebecca's tantrums, crying, and stubbornness, Blanca called her, "The girl who will change the world." She even taught Rebecca soccer and the adorable blue-eyed blondie was a savant with a soccer ball at her feet thanks to Blanca's Colombian coaching tactics.

Blanca had a family that she returned to every day and I had to race home from wrestling practice. Tournaments chewed up my Saturdays—from December to March.

And endless hours of whistles, and screaming coaches and parents, had blasted my brain.

Time to call it a wrestling career?

David Bloom and Mike Ginsberg had made all county as juniors. I'd helped two of the three now-senior captains reach their goal.

Despite my attempts to convince him not to take creative writing, David was in the class for the second semester. I considered begging guidance, his parents, anybody to remove him from my class. If he wouldn't listen to me in wrestling, I suspected his insane behavior would destroy my class. Mike Ginsberg mercifully didn't take either creative writing or journalism and Sebby had signed up for Journalism II—which I was happy about.

A reason to continue coaching: Sebby hadn't placed at counties. I feared that if I quit coaching I'd be another adult abandoning him. The more I thought about it, the more I realized how his mother and father had let him down. Addiction stole their souls. His mother was lost and his father was gone. I couldn't bail on him his senior year.

It was an extraordinarily difficult decision.

I only briefly discussed it with Jennifer. She couldn't understand the deep connection between coach and wrestler. She would support me if I continued coaching. But she wanted me around more. I didn't say anything to Frank. He'd be upset if I retired from coaching. Regardless, Frank would be there for Sebby. Frank would put many more years into building the program, no matter what I did. Also, I had just turned 37 and it was more difficult to wrestle with the kids. The more I agonized, however, the more I realized that I had to coach one more year—for Sebby.

I had over 100 students to teach, too.

My journalism program entered a new phase. That fall I traveled to Syracuse University, to the Newhouse School of Communications, for a day-long journalism seminar and also the ESSPA awards ceremony. We only won two awards from the previous year despite having some talented writers, like two of my wrestlers: Paul "Mr. Headlock" Baron and Mike Stencel, who would become a high school English teacher, wrestling coach and advise the New Hyde Park High School newspaper. Unfortunately, both were shut out of awards at Syracuse and at placing at the counties.

At the Syracuse conference, newspaper advisors from across New York State promoted desktop publishing and how it was a gamechanger for high school publications.

The internet was on its way, too. A Wantagh science teacher, Eric Cohen, and I were working with our technology department to get the internet, with full access for the kids, into computer labs in the high school. The internet in my classroom would be a research library at my journalism students' fingertips. My Journalism II class moved to a computer lab, making me the first teacher in the Wantagh school district to put a class, other than a typing class, in a computer lab. Little did I know in a few years other teachers would battle me for computer lab access. But in the fall of 1998, it was easy for me to schedule my journalism classes for the lab in Room 405.

The co-editor in chief of the newspaper, Jason Leff, who had an utterly brilliant year of writing and editing, spelled out the future in a great front-page article "Wantagh Enters New Age of Technology."

Leff wrote: "... a massive technological revolution under the support of the passage of last year's $3.8 million bond issue ... will put Wantagh among the upper echelon of Long Island high schools in terms of technology."

While David Dubin still hoped that the computer age would go away, or be zapped by a massive Y2K failure in the year 2000, Principal Dr. Terry O'Connor gushed about the future possibilities of technology.

"Through this technology we will eventually have the capability for the entire district to be networked," Dr. O'Connor said in Leff's article. The high school and middle school were completely rewired for the new computers and servers.

"Say goodbye to the quaint Wantagh High School from 1955 and give a warm welcome to the interactive high school of the 21st century," wrote Leff.

"You can't turn your back on technology," said Dr. O'Connor. "It is going to be a daily part of life. To do nothing is to condemn your students to an archaic lifestyle that won't exist in their adult world."

The technology department planned to eventually put desktop publishing software in Room 405. My students would lay out the newspaper on the computer, requiring less time to create longer newspapers. Though I was nervous about plunging into desktop publishing, other teachers who were doing it said once I laid out my first issue with it, I would never return to dummy sheets.

I had an army of kids, 56, in my Journalism I and II classes in the first semester. Picking the editors of the school newspaper was difficult. Two younger sisters of my graduated editors wanted top positions. First there was Allyson Rosenblatt. This was the fourth year Allyson had been in the journalism class—one of very few who took it freshman through senior year—and she was a hard worker. She badly wanted editor-in-chief. And she was used to getting her way. She badgered me. Strong females succeeded at bossing me around.

The other girl, Lisa Cesternino, was sweeter than Allyson and didn't demand. I knew she would be happy with whatever position I gave her. The kids had a couple of weeks to prove themselves before I picked the editorial staff.

I remembered when I had been made co-captain of my high school wrestling team by my coach, Bill Zimmerman (Z)—the best coach and teacher I ever had—it was one of the best days of my life up to that point. I tried to model my teaching and coaching after Z, who was very mellow and kind yet somehow motivated a chubby, weak sophomore to become obsessed with fitness and wrestling. That sophomore was me. When I first walked into the wrestling room as a sophomore Z whispered to the team's captain not to laugh at my stick arms, flabby belly and love handles. My adolescent body portended a failed career as a Pennsylvania wrestler. Somehow Z willed me to succeed. I used his tactics on my athletes and students.

Over those first couple of weeks, while Allyson worked hard and wrote and took amazing photos, her behavior was poor at times. I leaned towards not giving her the one of the editor-in-chief spots. It seemed like it would better serve her future if I didn't make her an editor-in-chief.

It was a tough decision. I put her in the No. 3 spot on the masthead as managing editor. Jason Leff, a junior, earned the top spot along with the senior Vanessa Pozzi, another brilliant writer. Lisa Certernino was just below Allyson as an entertainment editor and she was thrilled.

Allyson was furious. I endured her wrath. She pushed and pushed and nearly forced me to make her a third editor-in-chief, but in one of the rare shows of strength in those situations I held firm. She worked hard. Seven of the photos in the first issue were hers and were excellent—still I endured her anger. But kids get over things.

That staff was one of my most talented. It would finally break through at the Syracuse contest and win 14 awards, ten for writing, and Lisa and Allyson won three between them for photography. Jason Leff would win four by himself. Vanessa Pozzi would win one, and two of my wrestlers would work together and snag a pair of awards, a Silver and a Bronze for News Writing. That duo of wrestlers was Sebby and Matt Landman, whose father was the president of the school board and maybe the best school board president in all of my years at Wantagh. Only one other newspaper staff, well into the future, would win more awards at Syracuse than that group.

The 1997-98 year would be unforgettable for me for so many reasons. Another was that Wantagh would add two teachers who would become important colleagues—Chris Rafferty (Raf) and Kathy Delgais.

Raf, a fellow English teacher, would eventually share a room with me for many years, where we spent countless hours discussing students, teaching and our lives. I would often sit in the back of Room 129 doing work or grading while Raf taught. I absorbed many of his teaching techniques. Raf was, and still is, a great teacher and that collaboration improved my technique. I lifted countless ideas because Raf let me listen in while he taught. Not all teachers allow a colleague in their room while they teach, but Raf didn't mind and I didn't care if he was in the room while I taught.

Kathy Delgais, who had graduated from Wantagh before my arrival, would marry and become Kathy Butler. She was a special education teacher and, in the future, we would teach collaborative classes together. Collaboration became a strength of mine.

That year was the second that I had taught ninth grade. Each year in English we taught a different Shakespearian work. Ninth grade was *Romeo and Juliet*. While that might seem like one of the Bard's easier works, teaching it well required a thorough understanding. In those early years I was learning its nuances.

My teaching strategy was to read the play in class, switching up the parts each day. I also used the 1996 Buz Luhrmann film on video tape. Luhrmann used original dialogue but set the story in the 1990s. Leonardo DiCaprio and 17-year-old Clare Danes played the doomed lovers.

There were certain parts that I loved to read, like Mercutio's death scene and the scene where Juliet's father goes ballistic on Juliet, the nurse and Lady Capulet. I enjoyed *Romeo and Juliet*, so my students enjoyed it too. It became one of the best parts of my ninth grade instruction.

I also started an offbeat tradition, on the first day of school with my ninth graders, where I asked them geography questions. Freshman knew absolutely nothing about geography—even seniors were pretty unaware of the world. As a kid I had pored over maps for fun.

I wanted them to know about other countries. Somehow, I ended up asking every freshman class for as long as I taught, "What is the capital of Burkina Faso?" Of course, 99.9 percent of them had never heard of Burkina Faso. It led to a discussion about West Africa and the rest of Africa that was educational.

Early on in my Wantagh career, I asked my Burkina Faso question and a student, Matt Bresler, raised his hand.

"Yes, Matt," I said.

"Ouagadougou," he said.

"How did you know that?" I said, shocked, as I thought that no kid would ever get it.

"I like maps," he said.

I began asking him capitals of countries, ones that I knew. I had to stump him and couldn't do it. I named maybe 30 countries before getting him on Costa Rica. It was surprising that he didn't know its capital, San Jose.

No ninth grader legitimately ever got it right again. There were a couple of kids who'd been tipped off about the question. You'd think there would have been more. But that doesn't count. Only Matt knew it. He became the salutatorian of his class and today is Dr. Matthew L. Bresler, who teaches anesthesiology at the University of Rochester School of Medicine and Dentistry.

* * *

Sebby achieved a dream season his senior year. I was glad I had stuck around. He won the MacArthur Holiday tournament, beating an upstate Suffern wrestler 4-1 in the final. That wrestler, Frank Pregiato, would go on to place at states that year.

Sebby won two more tournaments and was off to a 10-0 start. That 1997-98 team was also notable for a heavyweight, Geoff Waugh, who was African-American, one of the very few I taught or coached at Wantagh. I'd always wondered how it was for Geoff to be an African-American student at a nearly all-White school.

"Well, what was interesting for me was that growing up in Wantagh wasn't that bad," Geoff told me years later on Facebook. "I don't know if it was the fact that I was bigger than everybody else. I don't know if I was relatable to everybody. [Or perhaps because] I played sports and I was friends with all the popular people. But I can honestly say that in Wantagh I never personally faced open racism."

Geoff added that his lone issue was that he found it impossible to date any girls.

"Back then I attributed it to the fact that I was overweight but looking back and thinking about it, [it was because] I was Black."

"I spoke to Alby Rojas at a concert last summer and he echoed my sentiment of dating being impossible in Wantagh due to the fact that he was Hispanic and I was Black," said Geoff, who today is a New York City teacher.

I was glad to hear that outside of the dating issue, he hadn't experienced overt racism. He was a gentle giant type of a kid, who wrestled and played football. He was a very respectful, intelligent and terrific young man.

Meanwhile, Ginsburg and Bloom, who were often disrespectful—and who were our first returning county place-winners—both struggled on the mat, especially Bloom.

Bloom's erratic behavior made him difficult to coach. He constantly fooled around at practice. His younger brother Todd, a freshman on that team, told me years later that David hazed him, and other younger wrestlers, before Frank and I got into the room. David once rubbed icy/hot balm all over Todd, setting his flesh on fire.

I arrived early to practice and spotted David simulating sex with the takedown dummy, humping it vigorously, to laughter. I pulled him away from this sexual assault of a takedown dummy—a life-sized doll to practice wrestling moves on.

He would tell me he hated wrestling and wanted to quit. Then he'd defeat an excellent opponent and bring me the video to analyze with him. I learned years later that many younger wrestlers on the team, surprisingly, looked up to David and Ginsburg.

One freshman on that team, Josh Kanowitz, said recently to me, "I was in awe of those seniors. They looked like men to me, with muscles in every part of their bodies. I got my butt kicked constantly for four years but loved every minute of it."

Josh doesn't recall being hazed by David and Ginsberg. Instead he recalls their kindness.

"Ginsberg and I took the late bus to the Mandalay section after every practice," Josh said. "He talked to me about wrestling for the 20-minute ride constantly. I just listened, awed that he would talk to me."

I wasn't awed by David and Ginsberg. I tried to get them to act maturely and not fool around, which was somewhat impossible.

"David to me was the coolest captain," Josh said. "We all looked up to him ... But he brought us down to earth with his hilarious personality. When he said hello to me at school ... it felt (like I was talking to) a God."

While Josh saw divine moments in David's behavior, as the second academic semester began in January, David acted like a demon in my creative writing class. I changed the seating, putting seats in a circle, which I never did, always preferring rows. Maybe that would calm David down.

Many teachers espoused the seating circle. And it excited David. I literally saw his mind churn towards some idiotic prank. His mind rarely functioned for anything related to academics. He refused to write a word for several weeks until I badgered a couple of paragraphs out of him.

The class was mostly girls.

David jumped into the middle of the circle. "David, sit down now!" I screamed.

Though it was cold out, and the heat wasn't great in Room 129, David whipped off his shirt and danced around. One girl, Wendy Matthews, put a $20 bill in his pants. That wasn't helping the situation. I worried that he would take his pants off, which appeared to be his next move.

I bearhugged him from behind. "Are you going to stop?" I said, squeezing him tight. Many of the girls cheered and clapped for him to keep stripping. He had a lean, ripped wrestler's body.

"Come on Krav," he said. "Let me go. I could make a lot of money here."

Male stripping in creative writing? Well, it was creative. No way he could continue. I carried him into the hall and locked the door so he couldn't come back in. Yes, I tossed his T-shirt out there.

Again, I should have written him up, and made sure Ron Lebel punished him severely. But it was wrestling season and so once again, like with Ed, I feared he could be thrown off the team. I did tell his parents.

And while at that point I only had two observations per year, Dr. O'Connor observed that creative writing class with David in it. He wrote that I "had become a valuable member of the English Department, and that my instruction of writing had made me a strong addition to the staff." He referred to David, however, when he added, "There was one student in the rear of the room who constantly made comments ... that were snide and disruptive. It is important to establish a pattern where you don't respond to these."

What would Dr. O'Connor have thought about another time when, frustrated with David's disruption—more destruction—of my class, I body-locked him in wrestling practice? I hit David with an upper body throw. Though he was about 140 pounds and I was about 205, I drove my weight into him as we hit the mat; not to hurt him but because that was the nature of the judo-like throw. We hit hard and he writhed in pain, as he had bruised or maybe cracked one of his ribs. I didn't feel bad about it, which was a little messed up. But I realized that I shouldn't body-lock smaller kids. I guess that David's incessant insanity in my classroom and in wrestling drove me to that overly aggressive maneuver. I fessed up to his dad and, as a wrestling coach, he said that maybe it would do David some good.

"Do that whenever you have to do," Mike Bloom said to me.

The previous year we had had eight wrestlers reach the counties and four place-winners. We hoped to improve on that. But our county qualifier tournament was very difficult with another excellent Paul Gillespie-coached Long Beach team and an even better team from Bellmore JFK.

Bloom and Ginsberg both finished a disappointing third in the qualifier but Sebby's dream season continued as he upped his record to 27-1 with a qualifier title thanks to a 13-1 victory in the final.

Only those three made the counties, where David fizzled out and didn't place. Was he complacent with his all-county finish the year before? He seemed a little out of it.

Ginsberg, unseeded, wrestled his way to the semis. Sebby had a quarterfinal bout against a very strong Freeport wrestler whose surname was Stringer. Sebby led 1-0 when Frank and I realized that the scoring table, using a flip scoreboard, had Stringer leading 1-0. We stopped the match. The ref was confused about who led and the guys working the table were confused. The Freeport assistant coach, Steve Whelan, who had been a heavyweight state champ, did something I'd rarely seen a wrestling coach do.

"Yeah, yeah our kid is winning," he said.

I got in his face and screamed, "What are you talking about Whelan? You know that your kid is losing." While Whelan was a huge guy, I refused to let him get away with swaying the table officials or the ref into believing that his kid was winning when he wasn't. In coaching wrestling, you could never let another coach get in the official's head and steal a bout from your kid—and this just wasn't any kid out there.

Despite Whelan's lack of sportsmanship, we straightened it out and Sebby rightfully won 1-0. But another bad official lurked in the semifinals, where Sebby had to face Division's top-seeded Bill Bennet, a two-time defending finalist, one-time champ, and the younger brother of Bob Bennet—who Ed Garcia had stunned a few years before. Bennet's father still was the assistant coach at Division along with Ray Downey, the head coach—a great coaching duo.

Bennett was a strong wrestler but Sebby got the only takedown of the 135-pound semifinal match and had an early lead. The referee,

Jack Fiorvanti, then hit Sebby with a stalling warning. Bennet used an underhook and blocked Sebby with his other arm and never attempted a takedown. By rule, if anyone was stalling it was Bennet—who just hooked and blocked. Late in a 3-3 match Fiovanti hit Sebby with another stall call for one point, gifting the match to Bennet, 4-3. He reached the final where he won the second of his eventual three county titles. Sebby battled through wrestle-backs to take third. Fiorvanti should never have made that last stalling call. He should have let the kids decide the match in overtime.

Ginsberg won his semifinal 4-3 over Geoffrey Hampton of Long Beach. It was one of the few times one of Frank and my wrestlers beat a Paul Gillespie-coached grappler. In the televised 171-pound final, Ginsberg quickly took a 4-1 lead with two takedowns over Gerard Daddino of Sewanhaka. But the referee, Jack Fiorvanti again, hit Ginsberg with several stalling calls. It was so loud in the arena that neither Ginsberg nor Fiorvanti could hear Frank's and my screams. In vain we exhorted Ginsberg to circle and to attack. We told Fiorvanti that the other kid was stalling, too. But he never made one call against the Sewanhaka wrestler. Ginsberg did stall a little but didn't deserve Fiorvanti's superfluous calls, which gifted Daddino four points and an 8-6 championship.

The match ended and I hugged Mike and told him how proud I was of him. Fiorvanti ran into the tunnel. I sprinted after him and cornered him in the tunnel and screamed, "Jack, you stole that match from my kid. You should have let the kids decide it."

"Pete, your guy was stalling," he said nervously. He was a small guy. I loomed over him, but not in a threatening way. I was just mad that he'd taken a second county title from our kids that day.

"Ask Frank," he said. "He knows Ginsberg was stalling."

That was the last wrestling bout I ever coached. Afterwards I told Frank I was done. He was upset. He thought it was because of Fiorvanti but I made it clear that it was about my children and Jennifer's demanding job. If anything, Fiorvanti made me want to keep coaching and help a kid achieve a county title.

As for Sebby, Mike and David: Sebby and Mike did very well. Sebby graduated from SUNY Albany and right out of college he got a job in finance with a big Wall Street firm and has been doing that since. He married a Wantagh girl of course, Marissa Saraceni. In the yearbook Marissa was voted Class Clown with Mike Ginsberg. Sebby and Marissa have two children.

In my yearbook Sebby wrote: "You didn't think I would be that good when I was a stinking freshman. But with your help through everything I turned out alright for my senior year. I can't thank you enough for all of the time and wrestling you put in with me. I wish you would reconsider about retiring from coaching but you did stay for me and I'll treasure that because it made me better ... We will keep in touch and thanks again."

And I have kept in touch with Sebby. I didn't keep in touch as well with Ginsberg. He went into the Navy after high school and did four years there, two tours in the Gulf. Then he did four years in the army, with one year in Iraq. He said the military straightened him out and enabled him to gain a free college education. He became a corrections officer and now he's a corrections nurse. He's married, not to a Wantagh girl, with three boys. He sees two of them as wrestlers.

Then there is David. He gave community college a shot but that didn't last long. He visited me in the spring of 1999, a year after he graduated from Wantagh. He sat in my classroom, Room 129 where he had stripped, and chronicled his many excesses with alcohol and drugs from an early age. His binge drinking at such a young age shocked me.

He apologized to me for all of his insanity. He was calm. I had always thought David was mentally ill. I mean, I understood mental illness. I wasn't a big drug guy. I almost got through the 1970s without touching weed until my freshman year of college when a brief relationship with a senior girl led me to try pot in 1979. I was such a straight kid that my senior year of high school I didn't touch a drop of alcohol from October until March, when wrestling season ended. But now David's behavior started to make sense.

He talked and talked. I mostly listened, not saying much. Should I have advised him strongly? Would he have listened? He said he got it now. He said he was much healthier. He talked about his future.

I wished David luck. I could have said more but I didn't. David's parents always said I had done a good job with him. They thanked me and said I had been a good role model. But had I?

As a teacher you come to love your students. If you follow the Frank Mickens mantra, you love them like you love your children— even the ones who drive you insane. It doesn't make sense that you could love the ones who make you miserable even more than the good ones.

What would teaching be with all well-behaved, attentive students? I rarely had a class like that. Maybe Americans are the world's greatest innovators because in our schools we don't smother and try to control every kid. How many of our great successes were terrible students?

As kids graduated they would always say, "Krav, are you going to miss me?"

"No," I'd lie to every one of them. But of course you miss them.

Amazingly, here in 2020, I can message a former student on Facebook, who I haven't spoken to in years, and we carry on like we'd never been separated. It's like with your childhood friends. The line between your former students and your friends blurs.

Only two years before that talk with David, in the spring of 1999, he had had one of the greatest moments of his life when he placed at the counties. But a month or so after that afternoon chat, he was dead. His parents said he had a heart attack.

I went to his funeral. It wasn't at O'Shea's on Wantagh Avenue where I'd been to other student wakes and funerals. It was at I.J. Morris in Dix Hills.

What was with these kids dying? I was a teacher. What the fuck?

I'm sorry. I rarely cursed in front of the children but recalling all of this I'm angry. Each death of a student or former student angered me because it shouldn't have happened. They were kids. They should have lived long lives. But those kids are long gone from this world and I'm still here, all of these years later, remembering—just enough to haunt me.

I shouldn't have been going to these damn funerals. I no longer hoped that maybe David's would be the last one. I knew there were more coming. In the beginning of this teaching life I just wanted to hang on to my job, get my state certification and get tenure.

Now I just didn't want to see any more kids die. I wanted to protect them, teach them how to survive, like my dad taught me. But life is very much about death. I'm writing this in a pandemic where over the past year over 500,000 Americans have died, and that number goes up every day. This pandemic is not killing in the numbers of other plagues throughout human history, but death and sickness are everywhere.

David Bloom has been gone for 21 years. When I close my eyes I see him clearly, a good-looking boy with a round face and a light-brown crew cut. He laughed a lot. I vividly see him winning the bout that made him all county. I see him proudly wearing that green Nassau All-County wrestling jacket. But when I open my eyes, he's gone. Gone for one third of my life.

CHAPTER 12

An Unlucky Chapter Despite a State Title

The last *Warrior* issue of 1998 featured an article by Jason Leff titled "We Win." I lifted that from Gil Spencer's dad's *Philadelphia Daily News* headline when the Phillies won the 1980 World Series. Wantagh's baseball team had won a best-out-of-three Nassau County Class B title series over the Division Blue Dragons ending a run of four-straight county titles for Division.

Wantagh's star was a left-handed senior pitcher named Chris Smith. With the county final best-of-three series knotted at 1-1, in a tense third game, Smith "tomahawked a gargantuan grand slam to straight away center creating a six-run lead," wrote Leff. "As Smith rounded the bases and pointed to the stands, it appeared as though a higher force was propelled through the noise of the deafening crowd."

Smith then earned the save in a 14-11 win. A few days later the six-foot, 205-pound Smith, who was 14-0 on the mound that season, pitched all nine innings in a 3-2 win in the state quarterfinal. His bat and arm led Wantagh to two more wins and the New York Class B state title that year; and he earned a baseball scholarship to Florida State. The coach who engineered the baseball state title was Wantagh physical education teacher Keith Sachs. Sachs had turned around the football program as head coach as well.

While we watched, cheered and celebrated the Wantagh baseball team in June of 1998, we were pulverized by more tragedy. My managing editor Allyson Rosenblatt, who I didn't make editor-in-chief, died after a single-car accident when, heading home from an evening of waitressing, she lost control of her Nissan Infiniti and crashed into a house. There were no other injuries. She lay in a coma in the Nassau County Medical Center on June sixth, while across the street the boys somehow focused on a playoff baseball game.

She had done an incredible job with the school newspaper. She put countless hours into our college list that year and it included 198 names, a huge improvement over previous years, setting the standard for the future.

Allyson was 17 and had earned a full scholarship to Towson State University in Maryland. I gave one of the eulogies at her funeral in Gutterman's Funeral Home in Rockville Centre. My words elicited laughter and then tears from a massive crowd. Afterwards I wondered why I had tried to teach her a lesson for the future. Why try to be so tough? I should have just made her an editor-in-chief.

After Allyson, I frequently told students to make good decisions. Not that Allyson had made a bad decision to cause her accident. She wasn't drinking or doing drugs. I insisted my students drive carefully. My dad had repeatedly lectured me, "Drive a little slower. You'll get where you're going a few minutes later." Did those children listen to me? How many of them would say now, "Krav, I don't remember you ever saying to drive safely."

In my year-end evaluation Brian Donohue wrote: "I commend you for the sensitivity you displayed in the way you advised the students to handle the death of Allyson Rosenblatt. During the week following her death, I saw you many times consoling students for the loss of their classmate. You helped them through their grieving."

On the last day of journalism, in Room 405 where we now had the internet and I had been so encouraged all year by the newsroom-like sounds of students clicking keyboards, I realized Allyson wouldn't fill up that room with her brash, loud personality. I completely broke down and fled before my students arrived. There was a back door which connected to a room with servers in it and I went through there and crossed the hall and hid in an instrument room, where there was a girl cutting my journalism class and getting her instrument to do band lessons. I didn't say anything to her. I returned late to the class. That group had been so special. We remembered Allyson through teary anecdotes about her.

That spring of 1998 had emotional highs, devastating tragedy and even Norman Mailer.

I went with 16 Wantagh students and two other teachers that spring to Adelphi University, which has tremendous programs for high school students, to listen to Mailer speak.

As Vanessa Pozzi and Debra Lozner wrote: "Mailer, now 75, is best known for his novel *The Naked and the Dead*, his Pulitzer-prize winning work *The Executioner's Song* and secondarily known for his numerous children (nine) and his slightly less numerous wives (six, having stabbed but not killed his second wife with a penknife).

"After a 35-minute wait, a hunched man (Mailer) hobbled out from a side entrance, cane in hand, seemingly cranky and impatient."

Their article described how Mailer read from different works and articles and then concluded: "Mailer presented himself as brusque yet brilliant … He is best characterized by his closing quote of the night, "'Lord, prayed St. Augustine, make me pure but not yet.'"

Vanessa wrote in my yearbook: "You've taught me so much in both journalism and creative writing. Thank you."

Allyson's best friend, Lisa Cesternino wrote in that yearbook: "When I was in middle school my brother would always come home and talk about journalism and you. It made me want to take the class. You are the best teacher I have ever had. You have taught me so much about writing. Thank you for always being there … You have made such an impact on my life, and I love you for it."

Allyson never got to write in my yearbook.

Another of my newspaper editors and a friend of Allyson's, Stephanie Lamb, wrote: "Thank you for being there this past week (for us). And even if you don't think so, Allyson did love you just like the rest of us."

CHAPTER 13

More Sadness for Wantagh and then for the Nation

The last full school year of the millennium would bring recognition to Wantagh High School. The high school was named a Blue Ribbon School of Excellence, by the U.S. Department of Education. That made it the fourth out of five of the district's schools to win the Blue Ribbon award and not long afterwards the fifth school won, too.

The community and the district staff felt great pride, but of course tragedy lurked. One April day of that year would forever change education in the United States.

Three months after losing David, in August of 1999 a Wantagh sophomore, who was not my student nor my athlete, Scott DeVerna, died in August from an undiagnosed heart condition—though he was a three-sport athlete.

I didn't know Scott well, but again Wantagh grieved for another student. Did other communities go through repeated heartbreak?

Josh Kanowitz was best friends with Scott. Returning to school in September of 1999, he struggled. He spent a lot of time in Frank Muzio's guidance office, talking about the loss of his best friend.

"Thank God I had Mr. Muzio there for me," said Kanowitz, who took my journalism and creative writing classes and excelled in both. Today he teaches special education in New York City and is a married father of three. "He helped me so much."

The lacrosse team, coached by a Wantagh elementary school physical education teacher, John Cuiffo, created a tradition by awarding Scott's number 22 each season, by team vote, to a senior varsity lacrosse player. The entire lacrosse team continues to vote each year for the teammate they believe deserves the honor of wearing Scott DeVerna's 22.

Cuiffo's lacrosse teams were always in the mix for a Nassau County title, even though the other Nassau teams were among the best in the United States, like Garden City and Manhasset.

Two years after Scott's passing, in what would have been his senior year in 2001, the Wantagh boys' lacrosse team won a state title. To do so Wantagh had to capture a county title over undefeated Garden City, which had handed Wantagh its only defeat during the season. Going into that game Garden City, defending state champs, had been the No. 1-ranked boys' lacrosse team in the nation.

The star of that Wantagh championship team was junior Pat Walsh, a record-setting scorer, who would go on to become a three-time All-American lacrosse player at Notre Dame University.

Many Wantagh players from that team and from future teams would play in college, where they would wear the number 22 on their helmets or uniforms. A few who wore 22 for their college teams were: Jake Gambitsky, an All-Ivy League goalie at Harvard University; Brandon Mangan, a top 10-career points leader and goal scorer at Yale University; Ryan Walsh, an All-American honorable mention at Colgate University; Dylan Beckwith, an All-American honorable mention at Fairfield University.

Cuiffo in 2020 wrote: "More than 50 boys have worn the number 22 in colleges all over the country to honor Scott's memory. There are no words to explain just how much this meant to Maria (Scott's mom) and her family, as well as Scott's friends and teammates. The love and support that every single boy has given to their family over the past 21 years has been immeasurable."

In November of 2020 Scott's mom Maria passed away at age 62.

* * *

My journalism class settled into the Room 405 computer lab and no teachers fought me for a period in that room. That would come in the next millennium. We also had a bank of computers in a room in between Brian Donohue's office and the office of the Social Studies Supervisor, Jeannette Stern. My editors and I would log hours after school there, now that I wasn't coaching. Jeannette, in her 29th year as a teacher and administrator at Wantagh, would endear herself to me for her help and kindness. That would change, however, when she became the principal of the middle school.

My regular English classes had some great students but they weren't honors classes. I enjoyed teaching many bright kids in my electives. That journalism group was talented. They would go on to win 11 awards at the Syracuse contest, including four Golds. No other group of mine would win four Golds in a year. And it's not like four Golds in that contest was a great accomplishment. Other schools achieved it easily. I measured my kids' success against my writers from pervious years. In addition, that staff included two future Emmy-award winners for their work in television—which no other group came close to achieving.

My students laid out the newspaper on Quark Express, a desktop publishing program. That was the first of ten years where my students published five issues per year instead of four. That first year we generated 68 pages, more than the 48 pages from my first year, and at significantly less cost. We just paid for printing on newsprint in black and white. We had four years of 100 pages per year in that run, plus for three years I advised for two issues per year of the middle school newspaper.

While I no longer coached wrestling, countless hours went into teaching writing and journalism, and helping the kids edit and lay out print issues.

Now, there were high school newspaper staffs on Long Island that generated more pages per year than we did. Meanwhile, the average high school newspaper advisor on Long Island lasted a couple of years, due to the massive workload and potential problems with kids writing articles that landed the advisor in the principal's office.

Despite the stress at each deadline—I had to chase down kids and pop into their classes (they called it stalking) to demand they finish their articles that day—I enjoyed helping to put out a newspaper and seeing my students' writing skills improve.

Some even became top professional journalists—like one young lady from that 1998-99 group. Erin Colton, the most determined and hardest-working student I ever taught, did an amazing job with her reporting. She took journalism because her older sister Megan had. She wrote outstanding sports articles as a sports editor in her junior year. She won four Syracuse awards for her junior and senior years, and then attended Syracuse University. She didn't initially get into the Newhouse School of Communications, which was and still is uber competitive. But she got straight A's her first year and that got her into Newhouse.

Many years later, in a *Warrior* profile of her by Grace Tague, Colton said that taking journalism in high school sparked her interest. She said my class was her "first exposure to the world of journalism through writing articles, checking facts, spelling, grammar and taught her how to do everything." But at Newhouse she learned how to become an Emmy-winning broadcast journalist for Long Island's News 12, which serves nearly three million people in Nassau and Suffolk counties, bigger than many of the nation's urban markets.

When I see her on television I can't believe I taught her. A statuesque and attractive blonde-haired woman, she has become an accomplished broadcaster and reporter.

In the *Warrior* article Erin described how in a typical day at News 12, "she wakes up at 2:30 a.m. and is out the door at 3:15 am. She is live on the air by 5 a.m."

In addition to that busy broadcasting career, Colton has been a girls' basketball coach at Wantagh for a decade as of 2020. She works with long-time Wantagh basketball coach Stan Bujacich, who was her basketball coach. With games at night that makes for a super long day, something only Erin could pull off. Colton said it felt weird to coach at Wantagh when she first started but the team became her second family, according to Tague's article.

Colton's parents were both teachers at Seaford High School when David Dubin went there. David then taught Erin, and also had an important influence on her. Erin Colton helped make that group special, along with two seniors: Jason Leff and his fellow co-editor-in-chief, Dave Bauer. Like Leff, Bauer's writing showed a terrific, self-deprecating sense of humor. He would go on to win an Emmy.

Years later, in a *Warrior* profile on Bauer, my journalist Laura Mallon wrote: "Dave Bauer described himself as a 'pretty nerdy guy' while in high school. In his senior farewell he wrote, 'I've been accepted almost as much as any pathetically non-athletic, Ani Defranco-listening, Weezer-loving Honor Student could be accepted in a public high school.'"

A film major at the University of Buffalo, Bauer landed in my hometown of Philadelphia where he collected his Emmy while editing for a TV show called *Philadelphia: The Great Experiment*.

Bauer won Gold at Syracuse for a portfolio of his columns, which included the aforementioned Senior Farewell, a *Warrior* final issue tradition. Bauer described being called a loser, his senior year, by freshmen. "Throughout my career as a Wantagh student, I've thoroughly enjoyed all the alienation and the rejection ... All those Friday nights at home made me one of the best Nintendo players on my block. I know 374 ways to beat you in NHL 95, so don't mess with me."

I visited Bauer in Philly once. He lives across the Schuylkill River from where I grew up.

The first article Jason Leff ever wrote was a hilarious one about sports' mascots. I thought maybe he plagiarized it, as it was so clever. But Leff's genius quickly revealed itself. He won ten career awards at the Syracuse contest, twice as many as any other student journalist of mine ever won. He wrote with humor but, like any great journalist, he was a talented reporter.

Leff recalls those days at the *Warrior* and how exciting it was to get the class into a computer lab "because before that we only used computers to play Oregon Trail." He also recalled the *Warrior* staff getting to shoot photos with a "shoebox-sized digital camera."

Leff graduated from Cornell and got his law degree from the University of North Carolina at Chapel Hill. Today he's an assistant chief counsel at the National Labor Relations Board. He lives in Arlington, Virginia, very close to the parking garage where Bob Woodward and Carl Bernstein met with their secret source, Deep Throat (later revealed to be the FBI's Mark Felt). Their articles and book helped bring down the Nixon presidency and send many of his advisors, attorneys and others involved in the Watergate scandal to prison. The garage features a historical marker.

Leff is relieved that he didn't pursue a journalism career, due to what he calls its violent downsizing.

"Plus I couldn't be interested in blogging, tweeting, influencing, tik-toking, whatever," he said. But Leff still writes.

"Writing is my job," he said. "Just not writing that anyone would want to read. I write legal opinions. I have a special expertise in exciting issues like independent-contractor status and joint-employer liability. My brain is no longer wired in a way that would permit writing in a way that is remotely informative, entertaining, or readable."

And that's a shame, as a Leff email today was as interesting as anything I'd read recently. Back in his *Warrior* days, he wrote a terrific article about Dr. Besculides retiring as superintendent in 1999. And while I wasn't a fan of Dr. Besculides, he did hire me, only due to the persuasive powers of David Dubin.

Leff wrote that Besculides had been Wantagh's superintendent for 14 years, "an especially long time period for a Long Island super-intendent to remain in one district ... the average superintendent stays in the same district for less than three years."

That was prophetic. In the next decade Wantagh would somehow feature five superintendents in a single calendar year.

Replacing Dr. Besculides was Dr. Carl Bonuso. In a district run by Dr. Bonuso, and a high school run by Dr. O'Connor, many teachers thrived. They created a terrific teaching environment as both were upbeat, positive and personable. While my first principal, Frank Mickens, in a few words created a template for how to treat students, Terry O'Connor motivated all of us to reach our potential.

Six years later, in the spring of 2005, Dr. Terry O'Connor was named New York State Principal of the Year by the National Association of Secondary School Principals (NASSP).

Another of my talented journalists, also an eventual Syracuse graduate, Angela Cave, wrote in a front-page *Warrior* article first quoting Dr. Bonuso: "Dr. O'Connor is an exceptional principal. His leadership skills and style have motivated students and staff and this recognition in many ways is reflective of the entire school commu-nity's commendable and collaborative success.

"English Department Supervisor Mr. Donohue calls Dr. O'Connor's leadership style 'inclusive' [because] he sees the bigger picture and raises everybody up."

"'He cares about us as whole people, not just teachers,' said English teacher Julie Magnuson. "'He recognizes our smallest accomplishments with a note, a smile or a pat on the back. Everyone's positive attitude comes from knowing that they work in a positive environment. We are inspired to take risks in education because we know we are supported.'"

These quotes, from Angela's article, show how good leadership in our schools creates a better learning environment for our students, and makes for successful schools. Poor leadership, like I experienced in New York City, makes it harder for schools to be successful. That probably seems obvious, but an administrator might have a great resume and interview well and then turn out to be a poor leader. Or it turns out they're just interested in using a job as a steppingstone to a higher paying administrative job. It's incredible how quickly those faux leaders can muck up a good school district.

In October of 1999 Erin Colton wrote a front-page article about Dr. Bonuso titled: "Leading Wantagh into the Next Millennium." Looking back, it's interesting that two of my students, who would both eventually graduate from Syracuse's Newhouse School of Communications, wrote great articles about Wantagh's leadership.

Erin's article showed how Dr. Bonuso hoped to add more AP courses and have sit downs with small groups of parents and students. He embraced technology and brought video conferencing into the districts, which evolved two decades later into Zoom and Google Meet—helping to save education during a pandemic.

Erin wrote: "Dr. Bonuso has a great relationship with many teachers in Wantagh. All of the teachers are excited about his new position and they are ready to support him in any way they can."

Another strong aspect of her article: "The best quality about Dr. Bonuso is that he enjoys coming to work every day. He loves his job and he loves the Wantagh Schools. He appears as his happy self, all the time showing ... that he does his job but has fun along the way ... Teachers and students are amazed at his love for these schools."

There are superintendents that students and teachers never see. Dr. Bonuso was visible in Wantagh's five schools, always smiling, laughing and leading.

* * *

While Wantagh High School cruised along thanks to the superb leadership of Dr. Bonuso and Dr. O'Connor, in the spring of 1999 two high school students in Colorado planned a massacre.

I have taught sociopathic children, only a few fortunately, and their behavior terrified me, especially after April 20, 1999.

The FBI concluded that Eric Harris was a psychopath and Dylan Klebold was depressed and suicidal. Clearly, both boys enjoyed their killing spree and they had planned to kill significantly more of Columbine's students and staff than their eventual toll of one teacher (William David Sanders), 12 students and themselves.

How many students have uttered the words, "I want to blow up the school." Craziness said in anger. But 99.9 percent of those who've said that never thought beyond the utterance.

Harris and Klebold tried to do it.

The pair planted propane bombs in the cafeteria that they hoped would kill hundreds of students and teachers during a busy lunch period. They made several attempts to detonate them, shooting at them and throwing Molotov cocktails at them. They planted car bombs and carried pipe bombs with them. Fortunately, the cafeteria bombs and car bombs didn't detonate.

Many books have been written on the Colorado school massacre. One of the best is *Columbine* by Dave Cullen (not the same Dave Cullen I taught with at Tilden.)

"Cullen, a Denver journalist, makes the reader care about getting it right," wrote Jennifer Senior in a 2009 *New York Times* book review article. "I expected a story about misfits exacting vengeance, because that was my memory of the media consensus— *Columbine, right, wasn't there something going on there between goths and jocks?* In fact, Harris and Klebold were killing completely at random that day."

In the days and weeks after Columbine I walked the halls of Wantagh High School in a fearful state. Previously, as I passed kids in the hallway I focused on smiling, saying hello and rummaging through my ever-fading memory for their names—especially of students I'd taught in previous years.

Post Columbine I scanned faces and wondered if any of the children were about to pull a gun or were planning a massacre. It was irrational, anxiety-ridden thinking. I tried to visualize exactly what I would do if a kid appeared with a rifle. Could I muster the courage to be a hero? I hoped, if that nightmare scenario occurred, I would protect the children—as so many courageous teachers have done in the mind-boggling number of more recent U.S. school shootings.

After a few weeks my anxiety dissipated, only to return with the next big school shooting. It was so ironic that during my years at city schools, where I knew that kids had weapons, I was never nervous. But after these horrific and tragic school shootings, I feared for students' safety (and my own) in a very safe school.

Columbine ushered in the era of locked doors and video cameras in schools. It's insane to think that pre-Columbine anybody could have walked into Wantagh High School through any one of several unlocked doors in low-trafficked parts of the school. Post-Columbine, instead of affable senior-citizen hall monitors, security guards walk Wantagh's halls and guard doors, most of them retired New York City police officers—unarmed.

It also spawned drills, where we practiced in case an intruder was inside the building or outside the building—all good safety measures.

There were school shootings before Columbine. But that was the turning point—spawning many copy-cat shootings. The only previous one I'd recalled was the 1966 University of Texas tower shooting, where an engineering student had killed 17 people and wounded 31 others in 96 minutes.

There were other shootings I don't remember: at the University of Iowa in 1991, where three professors, two students and the shooter were shot and killed; at California State University Fullerton in 1976 where a custodian killed seven, but not himself, with a rifle he bought at a Kmart.

Among the more-recent tragedies there was the Virginia Tech shooting in 2007, where 27 students, five professors and the shooter died and 17 were injured. It was the third-deadliest shooting by a single gunman in U.S. history.

At Stoneman Douglas High School in Parkland, Florida in 2018, a former student killed 14 students and three staff members: Scott Beigel, a teacher, died helping students hide; Chris Hixon, the athletic director, died trying to help students escape; and Aaron Feis, an assistant football coach, died shielding two students.

President Trump reacted to the Parkland shooting by initially saying, "... no child, teacher or anyone else should ever feel unsafe in an American school." Then he Tweeted: "Highly trained, gun adept, teachers/coaches would solve the problem instantly, before police arrive."

However, there was an armed, uniformed Broward Sheriff's office deputy at the school, just outside the building with the shooter, who radioed that shots were being fired but failed to enter the building and confront the shooter. He was later arrested for criminally failing to protect students during the shooting.

How do we stop this madness?

Clearly, we have too many weapons in this country. Now I'm pro Second Amendment. I feel that we Americans should have the right to own weapons. But I'm amazed that more than 2.4 million AR-15 rifles are being produced and sold annually by American companies. From 1994-2004 there was a federal assault weapons ban. Since that ban expired, AR-15-style rifle production has increased dramatically. Though gun proponents say that more shootings occur with hand-guns than those deadly rifles.

In yet another horrific school shooting, an autistic and anxiety-ridden 20-year-old took his mother's guns, used one to kill her, and then drove her car to Sandy Hook Elementary School in Newtown, Connecticut where he killed 20 six- and seven-year-old students, six staff members and himself with his mother's Bushmaster XM15-E2S rifle and a Glock handgun.

Here was the deadly combination of mental illness, a mental disability and easy access to military-style weapons. In this case, there is no question that the rifle created a more effective killer.

President Obama responded with a televised speech to the nation and said: "We're going to have to come together and take meaningful action to prevent more tragedies like this."

He then said of the six murdered staff members of Sandy Hook Elementary School: "Dawn Hochsprung, Mary Sherlach, Vicki Soto, Lauren Rousseau, Rachel D'Avino, and Anne Marie Murphy expected a day like any other—doing what was right for their kids; spent a chilly morning readying classrooms and welcoming young students—they had no idea that evil was about to strike. And when it did, they could have taken shelter by themselves. They could have focused on their own safety, but they didn't. They gave their lives to protect the precious children in their care."

British friends of mine are astounded at the easy access to weapons, like military rifles, that we have in this country. I have a good friend who is a retired English police officer who says that few of the police in England carry guns.

Since 2009 the United States has had 288 school shootings and the United Kingdom has had zero, according to CNN, which also reported that Canada, France, Germany, Japan and Italy combined have had five.

Even Republicans like former Ohio governor John Kasich say we should have restrictions on sales of AR-15-style rifles, which seem to be the preferred weapon of school shooters. For a final perspective on the topic of military rifles and school shootings I yield the floor to Republican Congressman Brian Mast from Florida, who wrote a 2018 *New York Times* op-ed titled "I'm a Republican. I Appreciate Assault Weapons. And I Support a Ban." Mast wrote that he spent 12 years in the Army and lost both of his legs to a roadside bomb in Afghanistan.

"Most nights in Afghanistan, I wielded an M4 carbine and a .40-caliber pistol," Mast wrote. "My rifle was very similar to the AR-15-style semiautomatic weapon used to kill students, teachers and a coach I knew at Marjory Stoneman Douglas High School in Parkland, Florida, where I once lived.

"I have fired tens of thousands of rounds through that rifle, many in combat. We used it because it was the most lethal—the best for killing our enemies. And I know that my community, our schools and public gathering places are not made safer by any person having access to the best killing tool the Army could put in my hands. I cannot support the primary weapon I used to defend our people being used to kill children I swore to defend."

CHAPTER 14

One Fall Day

I t was a Tuesday, the second week of school. I ran out to get a newspaper during second period, my prep period. The weather was perfect: a still blue cloudless sky, zero humidity and temperature in the 70s.

There was a television in the card store where I grabbed a newspaper. Everybody in the store stared at the TV, and the image of a plane crashing into the World Trade Center. It looked like it was a small plane in that first grainy video and that's what people said before the second plane hit.

The World Trade Center was about 30 miles due west from Wantagh. Some of our students' parents and relatives worked there; others were police and firemen. The tragedy that unfolded that September morning would impact my teaching and our community for years. Though I was incredibly fortunate not to have lost any relatives or close friends in the horrific attack. And I had family and friends working in Manhattan but none in the World Trade Center.

In the high school, during my third period class, we talked about what was going on in Manhattan. We were all traumatized.

As one of my students, Chelsea Jablon, later wrote in the November issue of *The Warrior*: "When I walked into class (the teacher) said, 'Three hijacked airplanes crashed into the World Trade Center and the Pentagon ... Just moments earlier, classmates were concerned with how bored they were during a math lesson ... (Now) students thought of family members and friends in New York ... dads worked in the buildings, moms had businesses across the street, aunts, uncles and cousins had meetings in the city."

It was my first year of teaching eighth grade journalism and advising the middle school newspaper, *Smoke Signals*. I feared that teaching middle school kids would be difficult but after only a few days I knew I had an amazing class.

When I realized that those children were upset, but they didn't know the specifics of what was going on, I began to tell them that we had been attacked, with planes intentionally flown into the World Trade Center towers.

Immediately, a girl burst out in tears, crying, "My dad works there."

"In the World Trade Center?" I said.

"I don't know," she said, bawling.

"Where does he work?" I said.

"I don't know," she said.

"He works in the city?" I said.

"Yes," she cried.

Just then Christine Hult, a middle school English teacher, came into my room and whispered in my ear, "We aren't going to tell the middle school kids exactly what happened so don't talk about the World Trade Center."

"Too late," I said.

The next school day first-year Wantagh Middle School Principal Dr. Jeannette Stern called me to her office. I hadn't been in a principal's office for about eight years for any missteps.

"You were not supposed to tell the middle schoolers what was going on," Jeannette said.

"I'm sorry. In the high school we were talking about it. I came down here and the kids were upset so I told them. It was kind of a crazy day, you know."

She stared me down. Jeannette, a heavyset stern woman, had a bulldog-like face. In complete anger she hissed, "The next time this happens, you'd better not say anything."

Had she really said that? I mean, Jeanneatte had been great when she helped my kids with the *Warrior* only a couple of years before. Now, as both of us began working in the middle school (I only had the journalism class there with the rest of my classes still in the high school), we were off to a very bad start. And while I would put in three years of teaching middle school journalism and advising the middle school newspaper, eventually Jeannette would run me out of her school. She would also eventually run my journalism class out of computer lab 405, which was technically in the middle school but shared by both buildings, which were attached on the second floor but not the first floor.

Fortunately, she was wrong. For as long as we both worked in Wantagh there was no second event in any way remotely similar to 9/11.

Running a school changed her. She tried to micromanage every teacher and every situation. She had been a better social studies supervisor than a principal.

Meanwhile, that year my amazing group of journalism students created three *Smoke Signals* issues, as opposed to the usual two. And that spring in a *Newsday* journalism contest we won Best Middle School newspaper in Nassau County, with a good 20-30 schools entered—including some very strong ones. Rachel Guerrara was one of my best writers. She took journalism in high school for three years and became an editor-in-chief her junior and senior years.

Eighth-grader Scott Duwe was a student who stayed with journalism from middle through high school, but perhaps the best article he ever wrote was his 9/11 piece in the December 20 *Smoke Signals*. He went on to win three Syracuse and Adelphi awards his senior year of high school.

Scott wrote about his uncle—NYPD officer Richard Vitale, a 1979 Wantagh graduate—who ran in and out of the smoking and damaged North Tower rescuing people with NYPD transit officer Ramon Swarez.

"And then as [Officer Vitale] stood at the foot of the North Tower, a thunderous, continuous roar ripped through the eardrums of all people within a half-mile radius," wrote Duwe. "Officer Vitale looked up to see an airplane fly into the South Tower ... He ducked under an EMS truck, barely escaping falling debris.

"Dead bodies spread around all over, the ground a dark mixture of blood and gray soot ... he ran back into the tower to help ... After saving more people he stood outside of the North Tower and there was a deafening roar ... he looked up to see South Tower collapsing

... Panicking, he ducked under a pillar ... and that was all he could remember. The next thing he knew he was awake in the hospital."

The heroism and tragedy of 9/11 were chronicled in great detail at the time but not by many eighth graders. And Scott somehow had a photo of Officer Vitale and Officer Swarez, rescuing a woman, that we ran with the article.

Tragically, Ramon Swarez perished that day.

Swarez was one of 23 police officers to die in the 9/11 attack along with the 343 firefighters and many other rescuers. One of the many firefighters who plunged into the rescue operation was Joseph Downey, a FDNY captain who was the brother of the Division wrestling coach we'd battled against. Joseph Downey had also been a fellow finalist in my college conference wrestling tournament my senior year, for a great Hofstra team. But unlike me he won and then wrestled at Nationals in Oklahoma.

Joseph Downey raced into ruins of the south tower of the World Trade Center on 9/11. Deputy Chief Raymond M. Downey, Joseph's and Ray's father, had also been in the rubble of the World Trade Center that day. He'd been with Mayor Giuliani and Giuliani went one way to safety and Chief Downey rushed further in to save lives.

"He had been trying to help a man who had injured a leg and could not move," said a *New York Times* article from Nov. 22, 2001. "...two fire lieutenants had reported hearing Chief Downey tell firefighters at the north end of the hotel site to flee, saying that the north tower was about to collapse."

While Chief Downey ordered his men to retreat to safety, he ignored the danger and was killed. He was 63.

As of 2019, an estimated two hundred first responders have died from breathing in carcinogens, swirling in the dusty, toxic debris of the collapsed towers that day and in the days that followed. Perhaps half a million people who lived and worked in the World Trade Center area are still at risk of contracting many types of cancer due to their exposure to the disintegrated towers.

A few days after the attacks, as everyone in the New York metropolitan area, and the nation, struggled to understand what had happened, we also attempted to return to some form of normal life—though it would take months to feel normal again. And for many in New York City and its suburbs, life would never be normal again.

That fall I coached Rebecca Mae's youth soccer team and my son's ice hockey team in a competitive (ages six-nine) house league at Superior Ice Rink in Kings Park—as I no longer coached wrestling. My coaching had completely regressed, from head collegiate coach to high school varsity coach to my kids' coach—the opposite of the path most coaches took.

We had a draft each year to pick hockey teams with the other coaches. The draft was supposed to be on 9/11. We had it a few days later. I tried not to think about the mounting death toll at the World Trade Center and focus on our draft. My neighbor Rob Savitsky coached with me and we hoped to have a good team. The draft was a good distraction from the chaos and tragedy.

We started to pick our players when one of the other coaches mentioned that he had worked in the World Trade Center.

"Were you there the other day?" I said.

He nodded. Maybe I shouldn't have asked. But I continued and said, "What happened?" The draft stopped and everyone listened to the following paraphrased account:

"I was working way up in the South Tower, the second tower to be hit. I had been working there eight years before when the World Trade Center was bombed. I always believed, if anything ever happened again I would immediately get out of the building by the stairs. I practiced doing that. So, the minute we felt the building shake from the explosion of the first plane hitting the North Tower, I told everyone in my office we had to get out and to follow me. Most of the workers in my office were young and they hadn't been there eight years before and they were hesitant to leave. But I quickly managed to get everyone, the entire office, to listen to me and head for the stairs. As we left, people in other offices stayed and I shouted at them to follow us but many didn't. We raced down the stairs."

All of us hung on his every word. I felt guilt that this fellow hockey coach had been running down the stairs of the South Tower earlier that week while I had been safe in my school.

He continued his story so calmly it was amazing he didn't get emotional.

"I knew which staircase to take and we quickly got down the stairs to the elevator exchange where we had to exit the stairwell. I wanted to get to the next stairwell but we were blocked by a big Port Authority cop in the lobby there. He said, "This building is secure, go back to your offices." I pleaded with him to let us evacuate the building but he insisted that we couldn't. As I argued with him there was a massive explosion and the entire building shook as the second plane hit our building, above where we were. The Port Authority cop fell over and I screamed for everybody to follow me. We literally ran over him to the next stairwell and raced down that one. It was dark in that stairwell but it was lucky that I had practiced this escape and knew my way. We finally got out of the tower and sprinted away from the buildings. About five minutes after we were out of it the South Tower came down, but every single person in my office was safe. The South Tower collapsed 57 minutes after it was hit while the North tower collapsed one hour and 42 minutes after being struck."

I didn't know what to say. I just looked at him dumbfounded. I tried to think about our hockey draft. We went ahead and picked players. I figured that our team would be terrible as I was completely distracted—unable to think about anything other than his daring escape, and how he'd saved his entire office staff thanks to practicing his escape from the towers for eight years.

We named our team the Orange Crush because we were given orange jerseys. We went 8-7-1 and came in third out of five teams. There was one team that we went 0-4 against, as it was very strong. But we won our playoff semifinal and played that strong team in the championship in February.

We fell behind 1-0 and then tied it thanks to a nice assist by one of Brett's friends Alex Baren. Brett scored but again we fell behind 3-2 after two periods. Brett then scored the tying goal and a short-handed game-winner, for a natural hat trick, to give us a 4-3 win and the championship in that crazy season. And Brett hadn't been near the goal scorer of our best player that year, our next-door neighbor and my assistant coach Rob's son, Ryan.

In a letter to the team's parents, I pointed out that on the last shift of the championship game we didn't put all of our best players out to protect a one-goal lead, while the other team had its best five on the ice. Of all my coaching, coaching my son in ice hockey may have been the most fun and rewarding. I loved skating with the boys at practice and showing them how to use their skates to stop passes and kick the puck to their stick and how to sauce a pass. I enjoyed making the lines and showing the boys and girls how to shut down good scorers. While I also enjoyed coaching wrestling, standing behind the bench in an ice hockey game, even though it was just youngsters in a rec league, was exhilarating as the speed of hockey created an unmatched intenseness.

And while I would never forget how that season began, in the terrifying days following the 9/11 attack, I would dream that one day I could coach my son in high school ice hockey. He played the next year, and once again our team pulled an upset. We won the Superior house league (10-12) title, over a team we had failed to beat in five tries during the season, on a double-overtime goal by Michael Pizza. The final score, 4-3 again.

Dreaming of hockey glory for Brett, like many silly sports parents, I took him to training sessions at the Rinx twin rinks with the best ice hockey teacher on Long Island at that time, Aleksey Nikoforov, a Lithuanian who had played on the Soviet junior national team. Aleksey helped several Long Island boys reach the NHL like: Matt Gilroy, Mike Komisarek, Chris Higgins and Rob Scuderi. He coached many Russian and Lithuanian NHLers; he ran a great clinic for kids.

I would coach Brett one more year in the Superior league. Though that team failed to gain a threepeat for Brett and me. Following that season in the winter of 2004 I took him to a theater to see *Miracle*, the true story of how the U.S. Olympic hockey team stunned the Soviets and then the Finns, to take one of only two U.S. gold medals in men's ice hockey history, in the 1980 Winter Olympics in Lake Placid.

In the incredible U.S. win over the Soviets the score was 4-3. It was our lucky score. But, unlike every other kid who played ice hockey, Brett didn't love the movie. After we saw it he broke my heart and said he didn't want to play ice hockey any more. He was disturbed by the scene where U.S. coach Herb Brooks makes the players skate until they puked after a poor performance in an exhibition tie with Norway.

Ironically, I started coaching hockey at Superior Ice Rink because the rink owner, Richie McGuigan, had asked me to do so alongside a coach named Ernie DiChiara. Ernie screamed a lot, especially at his son Frankie in the six-nine age group. Ernie was a massive former powerlifter who couldn't skate. Richie had known I was a teacher and a coach and he hoped I would be a calming influence on Ernie, who would bench Frankie every game after the first period and scream, "Stop playing like a girl Frankie." But Frankie was a good player. I thought Ernie's tirades were abusive and ridiculous. These were little kids in a rec league. I never screamed at kids at any level I coached.

I always wondered what happened to Frankie. And then while watching college hockey years later on TV I saw that Frankie had become one of the best players for Yale University. He grew into a six-foot-two-inch, 225-pound goal scorer. He went to Yale the year after it won the NCAA Division I title and he started for four years. Perhaps Ernie had it right and I was abusively soft on my kids.

I didn't try to convince Brett to keep playing ice hockey and I would never coach him in high school ice hockey. Brett played soccer, basketball and tennis in school and was on a Suffolk County championship tennis team at Commack High School his senior year which he enjoyed.

After about seven years of no ice hockey he told me he wanted to play again. We went out to a store, very appropriately called Play it Again Sports, which sold good used sports equipment. He grew to six feet three inches, so we had to get all new equipment.

I asked him if he wanted to play in my Monday night ice hockey game and he said he did. I was nervous. In my game the guys didn't like weak players, especially my teammates the Sweeney brothers from Boston. What if Brett were bad? He hadn't played in years. And while there was no checking in my game it could get a little chippy—especially from Mike Sweeney and my good friend Marc Cohen who threw his bulk around.

But Brett's game was solid, like he'd never stopped playing. I played horribly that night. After the game, one of the guys said, "Pete, we really like Brett's game. You suck. So, maybe just let Brett play from now on and not you."

I was thrilled. Not about my fellow Monday Night hockey players' reaction to my play, but that they wanted Brett in our game. Though both of my daughters, especially Dana, loved hockey and were annoyed that I never worked with them on their skating. We'd play some pond ice hockey and a lot of driveway-street and roller hockey. And I was very involved with Dana and Rebecca Mae in sports and other activities. Perhaps most important, Jennifer was thrilled that she never had to sit in a cold rink and watch another ice hockey game, a sport she detests.

CHAPTER 15

Turn of the Millennium Writers

As we crossed into the new millennium I taught several outstanding young journalists, like Megan Gill.

Two other young ladies also in the top-10 writers among the approximately 1,000 journalism students that I taught throughout my career were Courtney Allison and Megan Barry—who took my class and wrote for the school newspaper for all four years of high school.

Megan Gill only took journalism as a senior. She was a witty, tall, blonde-haired teen who, when she wasn't writing hilarious page 2 columns, drove me somewhat crazy. She arrived in Wantagh as a freshman after a Staten Island childhood.

Gill became our star columnist, reminding me a little of my friend Gil, another great columnist.

"The boys in this school are immature and attractively challenged," she wrote in her first column. That did something that no other student columnist had by eliciting a strong reaction from the boys in the school, especially the seniors. They wanted to kill her—not literally.

In the second issue, in December of 1999, she wrote her most infamous piece, "Housewife? I Think Not."

It began: "When asked about my future I can spit out every detail down to what I will be wearing.

"(But) all of my dreams came to a sudden halt on my monthly trip to the psychic on Third Avenue (Manhattan). Among other things I was told I would have four kids and a happy marriage ... This is my own personal hell ... I can't imagine cooking, carpooling and a home with a mortgage.

"The idea of waking up to the same person for the rest of your life ... is absurd ... Now I realize that I am offending every housewife in America but I don't really care. Maybe I'm saving lives.

"I can assure you I was not put here to be someone's wife ... God, all you have to do is look at parents ... There is some scary stuff going on. It seems that once you have a kid your brain melts."

That one didn't anger boys but attracted the attention of the Assistant Superintendent Lydia Begley, who was enjoying the *Warrior* and writing letters to us. She had a chat with Gill. Lydia, now retired and living in Florida, recalls the discussion.

"I wanted her to see perhaps a slightly different perspective," she told Gill from her perspective as a married, working suburban mom. "I loved her spunk and her strong opinions and hoped that she could see that you didn't necessarily have to be a "housewife" or a professional woman with children, but that you could actually have both and that, in itself, was the sweet spot."

Gill recalls it slightly differently and thought she was admonished a bit.

In "Love: Blah Blah Blah" Gill led: "I hate to be the one to say it but to all of you darling little lovebirds who think you are gonna be married in five years, you are soo wrong. I hate walking by people who mutter 'I love you' to each other every hot minute ... It's the most annoying thing to hear couples who have been together for ten minutes shouting, 'I love you.' Shut up!

"Fraggie, my friend, says, 'I definitely think it's possible to be in love with a person after you spend a lot of time with them.' Frankly, Frag I think you are on crack."

She closed with: "I think that when you are 18 you have never experienced anything else and don't know the difference between love and like. So reevaluate your relationships and grow the hell up."

After that one every girl with a boyfriend wanted to kill her. I'd never seen students react so strongly to the school newspaper. They would grab it and turn right to page 2 and read Gill, as opposed to leaf through it in 20 seconds, look at a few headlines and throw it on the floor. Megan loved the notoriety. No student journalist of mine ever achieved a reaction like that again. Of course, in a few years, students would become too distracted by their phones to read anything not assigned for school—and many of them wouldn't read that either.

She closed out her columnist career with, "I would like to thank each and every one of you who so graciously read my articles this year.

"I exaggerated to cause a little harmless controversy that impressively went mainstream. Mrs. Lydia Begley, the assistant to the superintendent, wrote me an angry letter about my anti-suburban life article. Some editor from *Newsday* makes comments to Mr. Kravitz about me. The English department had a meeting about censoring me. And of course students made plenty of comments about the stupidity of my points.

"I succeeded in finding a niche for myself this year in journalism. I have enjoyed my 15 minutes of fame. I hope I have entertained and offended you. Thank you to my loyal readers and the rest of you don't really matter anyway."

Since she only wrote columns, I entered her best three in one portfolio category, Columnist. However, that failed to gain her an award at the state-wide Syracuse contest. Those judges preferred columnists who were essentially reporters. What Gill had achieved as a writer couldn't impact the judges. Again, it was similar to what Gil Spencer achieved as the voice of the *Delaware County Daily Times* over his long career there.

The rest of my students won 12 awards that year at Syracuse, with Courtney Allison winning three, including one for News Story, for a piece she co-wrote with Megan Barry.

Megan Gill went off to Emerson College as a journalism major but transferred to Hofstra where she earned her degree in English literature.

Ironically, she then married a terrific guy, had three boys and today is a suburban housewife—so she is now living her teenage nightmare—the ultimate irony. But that Third Avenue psychic was nearly correct. She just gave Megan one additional child, but who knows maybe she'll have one more.

Megan "nee Gill" Carusona now lives near my old neighborhood in suburban Philadelphia's Main Line, where she is raising her three handsome boys. I met up with her in Ardmore, Pennsylvania, at a Starbucks, in the fall of 2020, where she told me that she had been in a cancer battle for the past year. After a mammogram revealed breast cancer, she underwent a double mastectomy. The cancer and its treatment motivated her to write, but her latest column won't elicit anger or laughter. She published the well-written piece "Breast Cancer? No Thank You" in scarymommy.com in December 2020.

"I was diagnosed with breast cancer a little over a year ago," she writes in a more poised voice than her teenage one. "I was 37 and mom to an eight, five, and one-year-old. I never felt a lump or had a knowing suspicion that something was not right."

It's a powerful piece. Fortunately, it has a happy ending. After a painful year, Megan is cancer free and enjoying parenthood. Somehow, she's also avoided the fate that her teenage self wrote about—brain melt after your first kid.

* * *

The other two young ladies from that period who were outstanding editors and writers were more mellow students than Megan Gill. My journalism program was peaking. My students were winning awards and churning out great pieces in that pre-smart phone world. My English Chairperson Brian Donohue wrote me glowing year-end evaluations like this one: "You like your work. Your enthusiasm for it carries across to your students. They like to talk about you .... they tell me about how you challenge them to meet the needs of the audience and about how they are trying to develop a writer's voice. I like their enthusiasm when they are talking about your enthusiasm.

"And you are good at paperwork."

While of course the last line was ironic commentary on how I was nearly not hired a decade before, it said a lot about how far I'd grown as a teacher. But I still had more to learn and I focused on improving my teaching each year.

I also entered my students' work in another journalism contest, a new one, at an Adelphi University conference. Strict rules permitted each school to enter a maximum of six categories, one article per category. The student writer was supposed to be at the conference, so that eliminated graduated seniors from the competition, whereas you could enter their work in the Syracuse contest.

In those years I could take about eight students to the full day at Adelphi, a short bus ride from Wantagh in Garden City. All of my editors wanted to go. Kids loved missing school for field trips. Though, field trips were a lot of paperwork.

Plus, figuring out which articles to submit proved time consuming.

Our first year at Adelphi was 2001. I had gotten Courtney to write an article about the bowling team. She had no interest in writing sports, yet I even got her to go to a bowling match. Courtney was the rare, very obedient teenager who did what was asked of her.

For some sports articles, my students interviewed the coach and kids on the team—but did not see the team in action. Though I'd always attempt to get them to spectate, I had never asked a student to watch bowling. I'd gone to many of Wantagh's sporting events but not bowling. Courtney's article on the bowling team was well written with a solid lead. I entered it in the Adelphi competition for Best Sports Story.

I never told the kids whose articles were entered. I wanted them to be surprised. Held in a large room, the awards ceremony capped the day with about 200 students from over 30 high school newspaper staffs among the very best in Nassau and Suffolk Counties and often a couple of strong New York City newspaper staffs. It was difficult to win awards.

The announcement of the winners always drew loud cheers from the winning students and their classmates. As a category was announced my kids would all whisper to me, "Are we in this one?" I wouldn't give the name of the student entered but told them if we were in a category.

Presenting awards that first year was the *New York Times* sports columnist Ira Berkow, who had also spoken earlier in the day. Berkow shared in a Pulitzer that year as a contributing staff member to a *Times* series, *How Race Is Lived in America*.

After the honorable mention and third place-winners in the sports category got their awards and shook Berkow's hand, they called the second place-winner.

"Courtney Allison of 'Wantauck' High School (they usually mispronounced the name of our school)," the Adelphi moderator said.

Courtney was embarrassed, especially when Berkow joked about her winning an award for a bowling article. I laughed. Years later kids alleged I cried when they won these awards.

"Courtney, go and get your award," I said. Our kids cheered for her. She went up there. On a big screen was the headline of her article: Bowling Team Ready to Pin Opponents."

The headline on the screen further embarrassed Courtney. The contest ended with the three most prestigious categories; also the hardest to win: Best Editor (which was changed to Most Outstanding Reporter years later), Best News Article and Best Newspaper.

Courtney's name was called and again she went up to the stage and shook Ira Berkow's hand as she won third place for Best Editor. She wasn't embarrassed about winning that one.

Each year I entered a submission in the Best Editor/Most Outstanding Reporter and Best News Article. It would take a decade for one of my journalists to win our first Best News Story award. And it would be another eight years before we'd get another award in Best Editor/Most Outstanding Reporter.

Courtney's two awards were a great achievement. She would win a total of four awards in the Syracuse contest. Courtney was also a great addition to my creative writing class. In a Brian Donohue observation of that class, he described how I had the students read a newspaper article along with a Gabriel Garcia Marquez short story called "Sleeping Beauty and the Airplane."

"Courtney commented on the way the narrator viewed the sleeping beauty in the story," Brian wrote in his observation description. "She also tied the story to a piece of journalism about the rights of women in modern Afghanistan. She found it disturbing that a woman would be stoned to death in a sports stadium for adultery with thousands watching. The discussion was intense."

While Megan Barry didn't win as many awards as Courtney, they often worked together on articles and were great editors and leaders in the journalism program. In Megan's junior year, I helped her publish an article in a *Newsday* insert called *Voices and Visions*, where high school students looked ahead to the coming millennium.

Megan, like Courtney, did whatever I asked of her. They both had great personalities and were hard workers—dream students. They were healthy, happy kids. It's so easy to teach students like them. And several of my other students were excellent, too. These students made teaching fun—something I never thought I'd experience after my Brooklyn and sweat hog torture. But I also had challenging students.

As we were about to head to our faculty holiday party, I showed David Dubin a terrific profile of him in the December 2000 *Warrior*. The article was written by Kristen Dybus and I was very proud of it. David started reading it and his face fell. In utter shock he said, "Why does it say, in Dubin's 'cock' classroom?"

"What?" I said in shock. But it quickly became apparent one of the kids had sabotaged that article and possibly the entire issue. I showed the newspaper to the principal. "You can't distribute this newspaper," said Dr. O'Connor. "You are going to have to reprint it—if you can go through it and find all the bad words."

I couldn't believe it. Courtney, Megan and our other editor-in-chief Vanessa Antoinette, another great writer and student, combed through the entire 16-page issue hunting for "cocks" and other inappropriate words. We did find one more in David's article and another random "cock" elsewhere.

David's initial reaction was: "How can I show this to my mother? She will not enjoy finding a cock in there."

Who would do such a thing? There were 28 kids in the Journalism II class. I left the Quark program open on several computers during class so any editor could work on pages and any kid could have gone to a computer and quickly sabotaged the pages right before we took it to be printed. There were only seven boys in the class. The dean, Ron Lebel, was great at finding student culprits. Ron and I suspected it had been one of the boys.

In no time, Ron had his man, George Ray, who did very little writing in the class. While I was happy that Ron planned to punish George severely, that felt hypocritical because I had sabotaged Ron's

Ed Garcia punishment five years before. Now, I wanted to see George drawn and quartered—figuratively of course.

And Ron did that. He made George pay for the reprint, and he was bounced out of the class with a failing grade. George had to work months as a busboy cobbling up the money. As the years went by, after Lebel, other deans were not as effective at catching perpetrators and punishing them.

The crazy thing is that all these years later David Dubin is friends with the boy who hid "cocks" in the article, "Seaford Grad Sounds Good at Wantagh," which led with how David did the school announcements on the P.A. system every morning.

"We go out to lunch every once in a while," David now says. "He's really charming."

Courtney and Megan continue to be charming, too. Megan has been married a decade and has two beautiful blond children and lives just outside of Reading, Pennsylvania. Courtney is a senior editor in the communications office at New York Presbyterian Hospital, where she puts her excellent writing skills to use.

Recently I chatted with Courtney on Facebook Messenger. She said, "[This discussion] is making me miss my mom, because if she were alive I would tell her, 'I'm talking to Mr. Kravitz!'"

Courtney's mom was a beloved fellow Wantagh School District teacher. She taught at Wantagh Elementary School for 20 years before dying in 2017 from pneumonia, which she developed after being diagnosed with a pre-leukemia condition and breast cancer.

"She's that shining light, the most amazing teacher that you remember for the rest of your life," said her Principal Randee Bonagura in her Newsday obituary. She was only 63 and close to retirement.

"She was an amazing listener," said a colleague of hers, Mrs. Hobbes, in a *Warrior* obituary on her by Annie Goode. "She was always the first to welcome a new teacher to the building. She was a loving, supportive wife and mother. She was so incredibly proud of all that her four children had accomplished when talking about them."

CHAPTER 16

Relationships Off the Rails

Wantagh hired several new staff members. Some of them stuck and a few didn't, like a math teacher named Heather Kennedy, who would have benefitted from a Frank Mickens lecture on her first day in 2005.

My children flourished, Dana was entering her sophomore year at Commack High School and Brett was in his bar mitzvah year. While Dana and Brett were excellent in academics, Rebecca Mae struggled with behavioral issues in school. She was in a difficult phase. We had also moved five miles east to a larger home, a roomy five-bedroom farm ranch, six years before.

Life was great. So, as I was wont to do in blissful moments, I stumbled into a bizarre mid-life crisis. I was in my mid 40s, the perfect time to concoct a creative disruption to my family. Jennifer was convinced that my mental health problems had resurfaced, after a 25-year remission.

My problems had started two years previously with the death of my childhood best friend, Milton Frank, in his early 40s, from cancer.

At the outset of this narrative I described how Milton was there for me when I was hospitalized and quarantined with the virus that lacerated my epidermis into open sores.

As childhood friends, Milton and I played basketball and street hockey in his driveway where Milton would develop his one hoops skill, taking a charge. As the 13th man on the high school basketball team, Milton could take a charge like nobody else. Milton made his younger brother Stephen play goalie in hockey and we shot orange street hockey balls at him, with Milton blasting away at an ill-clad Stephen, whom he'd nicknamed Pudge. Milton was tall and lean and Stephen was a shorter, chubbier prepubescent. Another reason I was at his house often was because he had great snacks and an infinite supply of Frank's soda in a much-more well-stocked fridge than mine.

I wanted to go to Milton's funeral in late August of 2003 in Philly. But there was a lot going on with Jennifer's family and our kids. She had six first cousins nearby, including one who lived across the street, plus her parents and brother both lived a couple of miles away. We were more like an Italian family than a Jewish one.

I should have traveled to Milton's funeral. Jennifer and I argued about it. She said that since I had not kept up with Milton I shouldn't go to his funeral. He had left a message on our answering machine, which ended up as the last time I heard his voice.

My busy Long Island life had separated me from all of my Philadelphia childhood and work friends, like Gil Spencer. I hadn't started texting at that time and it would be years before I'd join Facebook.

I was passive; Jennifer was controlling. I needed to pay my respects to Milton and see his family. But I didn't. I allowed her to dictate my missing Milton's funeral. That created resentment, which festered over time.

Then in the spring of 2005 my father died just short of his 83rd birthday. Jennifer was supportive. We went to my dad's funeral in Philadelphia and then raced right back to Long Island a day later—but that was my decision. I only missed one day of teaching after burying my father. Many colleagues, like David Dubin, expressed surprise that I didn't take more time to be with my family and grieve. I thought I was fine. Jennifer assumed my rush back to work was because I didn't have a good relationship with my dad.

Actually, I loved him and he loved me. We didn't show that love like her family did—with hugs and kisses. Kravitz men don't kiss each other. And I had told her many stories about my youth where my dad had hit me as punishment sometimes because he'd had too many scotches. One time he threw me into a tree. Then I grew older and bigger and he stopped hitting me. I didn't begrudge him. I survived and was fine.

To Jennifer, it reeked of abuse. Her parents had never struck her. Though many parents in those days smacked their children around. My brothers and I were not alone.

My dad, Dave Kravitz, exuded toughness. As I've previously said, he was a World War II U.S. Marine. He then became an IRS agent. He'd grown up poor in the Depression but he got a college degree and eventually became a stock broker and did well. He sent his three sons to college and paid for it. My brothers and I graduated from college with small stock portfolios sans a penny of debt.

His temper, however, could erupt over nothing. My brother Enoch said that when he was seven, he walked to a friend's house and upon returning home played in the sandbox. My dad didn't know what happened to him and was terrified he'd been kidnapped. (Dad was also really paranoid.) Enoch said that he saw dad, 220 pounds with huge arms, running towards him. He didn't know why. Then dad beat him, angered that he never said he'd gone to a friend's house. Dad was happy that Enoch was safe but failed to recognize that he should have been safe from his own father, too.

Dad even once grappled on the sidelines at Enoch's soccer game with another father. He was no soccer mom. Milton's father, Herb Frank, broke up that fight.

But my dad and mom were married for 47 years until he died. Their long marriage somehow survived one awful episode. In the early 1960s my dad loaned his nest egg, that he'd been saving for years, to my mom's father, Bill Flaxenburg, to help his business, United Packaging Company.

Several of my father's friends had warned him not to get involved with his father-in-law. "He's known for the Jewish Lightning," they said. That term, used by plenty of Jewish people, referred to burning down a failing business to collect insurance.

Not only had my dad loaned that money but he went into the business, too. Then his father-in-law said that dad wasn't doing a good job and fired him and never paid back the money, which had saved his company. United Packaging flourished; dad's in-laws grew wealthy. Dad had two young children and a wife but no job and no nest egg. My mom said he wouldn't get out of bed for weeks.

"I would grab his foot and try to pull him out of bed but he was too big and strong," my mom told me years later.

Dad landed in a mental hospital. He was treated with electro-shock therapy. Eventually he recovered, started over and, as I've said, became a financial success. More importantly he kept his family together. And when his father-in-law was dying of colon cancer, dad showed forgiveness and kindness to his mother-in-law.

Does that incident with my grandfather explain my dad's some-times violent parenting? Perhaps. Still, Dave Kravitz ensured that his sons had a healthy relationship. The Marine motto is "semper fi" and my dad was always faithful—to his family. Though, yeah, we dealt with that temper.

In retrospect, I should have seen a therapist and talked about his death. I built up this resentment towards Jennifer for little innocuous comments she made about my dad—or about our relationship. Had I turned my grieving into anger at her?

For example, the last time we saw my dad alive, he was semi-conscious and Jennifer said, "You never know how long he could last like that. It could be months."

He died the next day. Jennifer had said nothing wrong but in my emotional state I misinterpreted her reaction as callous. It upset me that she didn't show more emotion and empathy regarding my dad's death.

My anger irrationally increased and I decided I was unhappy with her and our marriage and I didn't want to be in it anymore. This was much worse than our softball fight over a Bathit at bat a decade previously. I slept on the sofa for a few days after that fight. Now, we talked about splitting up. Our poor children didn't know what had smacked our happy family. Dana and Brett handled this sadness with strength. Ten-year-old Rebecca Mae was completely distraught, crying hysterically, demanding we stay together.

While Raf was the only colleague I talked to about my troubles, a few others sensed something was wrong. Tom Ruane, a social studies teacher who had two children, said to me, "I don't know how I could wake up and not see my children every day."

Julie Magnuson kept asking me if anything was wrong and I kept telling her everything was fine.

During that time, in the winter of 2006, I'd walk through the halls of Wantagh and study the faces of my students who I knew had either one parent or whose parents were divorced. Any hint of sadness in their faces made me fear that my children revealed sadness in their schools, launching me into emotional turmoil. I don't know how I got through those days, how I taught. I struggled to focus on my classes. I had to somehow save our marriage, even though Jennifer at this point was furious at me and believed the marriage was broken.

* * *

While I struggled, this young math teacher Heather Kennedy began a very short teaching career in 2005. Engaged, Heather was a plain-looking young woman. She had a little extra weight. She wore glasses and had medium-length straight brown hair.

In the November 2005 issue of the *Warrior*, in the centerspread with the other teachers hired that year, Heather looks good smiling in her photo—much better than her mug shot two-and-a-half years later. But who looks good in a mug shot?

In the interview article with her by my reporter Rachel Iadanza, Kennedy is asked why she chose to come to Wantagh. "I knew the staff and students and the school had a great reputation," she said.

She had observed Wantagh math classes previously.

Asked what she liked about Wantagh students she added, "The teachers take the students under their wing and they are very helpful. The students are curious, enthusiastic and they react when they understand what I am teaching."

Regarding teachers getting close to students or "taking them under their wing," a little more than two years later in March of 2008, as I drove to work one morning, my cell phone rang and it was Chris Rafferty, my roommate.

"Hey just giving you a heads up," he said. "There are news trucks everywhere in front of the school."

"What? What's going on? I said.

"Heather Kennedy was arrested for having sex with a student," Raf said.

"What?"

I felt sick. One million thoughts pinged through my mind. Could it be true? But she was engaged.

I drove down Beltagh Avenue, the dead-end street that included Wantagh Middle School and High School, and I could not believe what I saw: several news trucks with satellite dishes poking high in the air, police cars, reporters with microphones in kids' faces. It was a surreal scene, like something from a movie. I'd never experienced a media crush. As I slowed down to drive around the back of the high school and park my minivan, a reporter knocked on my car window and screamed, "Could I ask you a question?" I drove on. I envisioned every single Wantagh parent and grandparent thinking that all of the teachers in the high school were perverts. I held out the hope that there was some mistake.

But as I got to school and talked to colleagues I knew it was no mistake. Newspaper leads in the city and Long Island reported that Kennedy, 25, had had sex with her male student, 16, in a car in a school parking lot. Kennedy was charged with rape and endangering the welfare of a child. She was released on a $35,000 bond. A Wantagh spokesperson said that Kennedy was "reassigned out of the classroom to her home pending the outcome of the investigation." She was placed on paid leave.

A revolting feeling overwhelmed me. Across the New York Metropolitan area, TV and print news blasted the name Heather Kennedy, a Wantagh teacher. Though nobody knew the name of the boy, except some Wantagh students, staff and community members.

Nobody had seen this coming. Heather appeared professional. She was around the kids a lot, like many younger teachers, including me my first year. But who would take things beyond that?

She had annoyed me a few times, though, when I had insisted my student sports writers get information from her about her track team, which she did end up coaching. They were unable to get it. I hunted her down and said, "Heather, can you please just email me names of your best athletes, captains, the team's record? It will take you two minutes."

She said she would. She didn't. I had to go to her classroom again. But that wasn't unusual. There were coaches who just didn't promote their teams. And like a lot of young teachers she seemed overwhelmed.

As for her victim, I had taught him two years before in a terrible freshman English class. It was close to the sweat hogs. My son Brett, about 13 at the time, once came to school and sat in on that class and afterwards said to me, "Dad, you need to be tougher with your students. Kids would never treat a teacher like that in my school [Commack]."

But Kennedy's victim was very quiet. He never disrupted that class, though he was friends with the rowdy band of boys who did. He was a small, skinny, pimply boy, even as a junior. You see TV shows and read about other reports of female teachers having sex with their male students and it seems like the boy is always handsome. This boy wasn't. I just kept wondering why Heather got involved with him and felt tremendous anger at her for doing so.

I eventually taught the boys' younger brother and his sister. They were nice kids, not as quiet as he was, better students and more involved with school activities and sports. His younger brother was a terrific ice hockey player and played for the school club, the Baymen. I'd occasionally go and watch the Baymen's games to support the players and I once sat next to his mom at one of his games. She was very nice, and attractive. This was five years later. It appeared that the family had recovered from the trauma. I didn't ask her anything about her older son as we mostly talked about her younger son and his ice hockey ambitions.

The story was: perhaps the first time Kennedy had sex with the boy, he picked her up in his car at her grandmother's house. He was nearly 17.

"The pair then stopped at a darkened high school parking lot, talked some more and then had sex, said Detective Lt. Richard Zito," in a *Daily News* article titled "Teacher accused of sex with student," from March 28, 2008.

"Things unraveled as the boy's father grew worried when the teen blew curfew—and didn't answer his cell phone because his battery died," continued the Daily News article. "The teen finally called his father from the teacher's phone. 'The son made up a story about where he was,' Zito said, but the father didn't believe him and later got him to confess. Zito said the father had reservations at first about whether to prosecute and waited a week."

At the time I understood that the boy's father, a police officer, first went to Wantagh's superintendent and told him what had happened and said to him, "What should we do?"

Dr. Bonuso allegedly said, "You are going to report this to the police."

The night that this went down, several of my younger teacher friends were out at a bar with Kennedy. Sometimes I would join them but many of them were single or didn't have kids. I wasn't out that night with them in Massapequa. Several of the guys said Kennedy was drunk and flirtatious. She came on aggressively to a couple of them but they rebuffed her advances.

As for the boy, he seemed okay when I saw him. I said hello in the halls. The impact on him was unclear. Kennedy got out on bail, and while awaiting sentencing in July of 2008 she was arrested a second time for having sex with the boy five times.

That landed her in prison for nearly eight months. As soon as she was released from prison in March of 2009, she was arrested a third time for writing the boy letters while in prison, a violation of an order of protection against her that she wasn't supposed to contact the boy.

After the third arrest Kennedy had to register as a Level Three sex offender, surrender her teaching license, and not have any contact with the boy for four years.

In the midst of Heather's prison time and several arrests, among the reporting on her was this: "This defendant disgraced not only her school, but her community and the entire teaching profession," said Nassau County Assistant District Attorney Jaime Johnson in a somewhat sensationalized *Daily News* article, "Long Island teacher Heather Kennedy wrote letters to teen lover from jail, say authorities."

That quote nails it. I felt disgraced by her conduct. I felt like Heather had let everyone down. We teachers are there to nurture the children but also to protect them, while teaching them how to learn and encouraging them to be mature, good citizens. I still felt compassion for a young woman who made the worst decision any teacher could make. She ruined her life.

I felt compassion for her victim, too. Knowing his friends well, I'm sure there were high-fives with him early on. However, I'm nonetheless convinced that the long-term impact on that boy, almost any boy who ends up in this situation, was not good.

"Predatory teachers often possess a willingness to abuse their authority—as well as psychological flaws," said Australian forensic psychologist Tim Watson-Munro, in a *Daily Mail* July 2020 article. "They're immature, they enjoy the power... [but the victim who survives] being sexually abused by a teacher, whatever the gender, [feels] betrayed, humiliated and exploited."

* * *

Two years before Heather Kennedy's life imploded, in early 2006, while I hid my marital strife from nearly every one of my friends and especially my colleagues, I tried to repair the damage I had done to our marriage. To give Jennifer more space I stayed with Jennifer's cousins, a few miles away.

I woke up at 4:30 a.m., drove home and made the kids' lunches (as that had been my job) in the morning before school. I returned at night to help them with homework. Trying to end our marriage now seemed like the most asinine thing I had ever concocted. I loved Jennifer. I struggled to function as I thought about the pain I had caused her, the kids, her parents, my mom—who was upset with my actions and let me know it in a rare assertive moment for her.

Jennifer said for us to have a chance I had to see a psychiatrist and get "a drug" to help me. Talking to the psychiatrist helped. I hadn't had any serious therapy since my mental hospital outpatient days and there was a lot to talk about. The anti-anxiety pill seemed superfluous, but I took it for a couple of months. It didn't help.

Among the many things I discussed in therapy was how I had allowed Jennifer to talk me out of missing Milton's funeral. It had occurred nearly three years before but still weighed on me. I recognized that I had to be more assertive in my marriage, assuming we could repair it. If something were that important to me I couldn't just give in to avoid conflict.

Jennifer could have walked away and nearly did. I was also extremely lucky that her cousins let me stay in their home. I had no family in New York nor other friends I could have stayed with. Our marriage could easily have ended but it survived and became stronger.

The students of Wantagh, who looked upset about parental strife, also helped save our marriage—even though none of them ever knew about our troubles. I couldn't allow my children to grow up in a broken home and wear sad faces in their schools, so I did everything I could to strengthen our relationship. While I my told my students many anecdotes about my family, I never said one word about this drama.

At that point Jennifer and I had been together for 24 years and married for 19. I worked on my issues. (Though it would take several more years before I learned to put the toilet seat down.)

Successful relationships have deep foundations in trust. I had never worn a wedding ring after our Brooklyn landlord Don Clarke's crackhead maintenance man stole mine. And even after this nearly marital-ending time, I continued to not wear a wedding ring because I'm jewelry phobic—perhaps that's another mental illness issue. Jennifer had always shown great trust in me.

It took months to regain that trust from her. And while a marriage is like teaching a difficult class in that you never know when the next disruption will arise, we are together today in 2021. We just celebrated our 34th wedding anniversary.

CHAPTER 17

Life Imitates Art

I taught the first chapter of a novel called *Summer Crossing* by Steve Tesich, who is better known for his screenplays *The World According to Garp* and *Breaking Away*. He won the Academy Award for Best Original Screenplay for the latter.

Summer Crossing opens with the 167-pound state wrestling final between the fictitious Presley Bivens, going for a threepeat as Indiana state champ against the novel's narrator Daniel Price. Price leads 8-4 in the third period.

"Everybody wanted me to win," Price says. "[The ref] wanted me to win. Even [Bivens's] hometown people wanted me to win. Everyone wanted the legend to fall."

Bivens has only one move, an incredible neck bridge. You can't try to pin him or he will arch up on his neck, bridge you over and pin you.

"... that neck of his, a massive, frightening neck; dinosaurs had necks like that," Price observed.

This bout will be the career finale for Price's Coach French and he's never had a state champ. All Price has to do is not try to pin Bivens in the final minute and he'll win. Then Bivens suckers Price into putting him on his back.

"Don't do it!" Coach French screamed.

I won't spoil what happens. Read the book. It's a great novel. Only the first chapter has wrestling in it. I gave my book to Frank Muzio. I'm not sure if Frank read it, but it ended up on his office bookshelf at school. I rescued it from his office and now it lives on my bookshelf.

In Frank Muzio's 16th and final year of coaching wrestling at Wantagh, in his final bout, a ninth grader named Paul Liguori wrestled in the 96-pound New York State Final at the Nassau Coliseum in 2006. A few weeks before, Paul had won Wantagh's first county title in 19 years. Like Coach French, Coach Muzio had never coached a state champ. He'd never even had a wrestler reach states prior to Liguori.

In a front-page *Warrior* article, my reporter Jackie Iaquinta wrote, "In front of nearly 10,000 fans, Liguori beat Casey LaNave of Chenango Falls High School by a score of 9-5 ... (to become Wantagh's first state champ in 37 years.)"

The year before Liguori had reached the county final as an eighth grader. Also reaching that final that year for Wantagh was Al Iaquinta, Jackie Iaquinta's brother. Liguori and Iaquinta both took second.

And while Liguori would win four county titles, a second state title, and then place third at states his junior and senior years and graduate from Harvard, "Ragin" Al Iaquinta would achieve much more fame as a top UFC fighter. He lost a five-round decision to UFC Champ Khabib Nurmagomedov at the Barclays Center in Brooklyn in 2018. But he went the distance with Nurmagomedov, unlike many of his opponents who lost by submission.

Frank Muzio's hard work and development of a youth program built the foundation for wrestling success at Wantagh. When he stepped down, his assistant Jim Murphy took over as head coach. An NYPD officer, Murph moved with his family to Wantagh. I taught all three of his kids.

Now, there is a bit of controversy attached to the incredible run of wrestling success for Wantagh after Frank Muzio. One opposing coach, Plainedge's Rob Shaver, accused Wantagh's coaches of recruiting kids—much more of a problem in basketball than wrestling. For years Shaver forfeited to wrestlers he thought had moved to Wantagh from other towns for wrestling. I worked the scoreboard at many of these dual meets and tried to talk to Shaver, as I had coached against him, but he wouldn't talk to me. He's a big grumpy guy. Or maybe going up against Wantagh made him grumpy. Some of the kids he forfeited to had gone to elementary school in Wantagh. So, I'm not sure if moving as young kids counted in Shaver's mind as recruitment. His concept had some merit but was not particularly well defined.

Shaver's coaching instructions to his wrestlers, in these meets, impressed me as tactically brilliant. Shaver is a terrific coach. But the Wantagh kids were better because they wrestled year-round. Their coaches took them to tournaments, wrestling clinics and training. I could never coach wrestling at Wantagh again because I was unwilling to dedicate my life to the sport like the Wantagh coaches did. Shaver did some of that with his kids but not to the degree of Wantagh's many coaches. And I believe that that intensive, year-round effort made the Wantagh teams great, not kids moving to Wantagh. A grappler could move there in the hope of improving, but not do so.

In addition to coaching wrestling, Shaver successfully coached football at Plainedge. But not without some controversy of his own. He was suspended for one game in 2019, as the head coach of Plainedge's football team, for violating a Nassau County sportsmanship rule designed to prevent teams from running up the score.

I knew the Barbato family had moved to Wantagh from Garden City. After the move Joe Barbato became a two-time state place-winner for Wantagh and that helped him get into Harvard. So maybe moving to Wantagh paid off for that family, as Joe got a Harvard education.

Another wrestler, Jose Rodriquez, came to Wantagh in 2012. He reached the state final that year. The next year his father moved with him to Ohio, where he wrestled for Massillon-Perry High School and won two Ohio state titles. He wrestled for Tom Ryan at Ohio State and made Division I nationals his red-shirt freshman year. I taught Jose in English his one year at Wantagh. He was a good kid and did his work. But he got in trouble at Ohio State and was charged with assault, with another Ohio State wrestler, for a bar fight.

Jose then transferred to Notre Dame College in Ohio, where he won a Division II 141-pound National Championship in 2019.

Jim Murphy coached Wantagh through 2011, where he helped Liguori, Steven Bonanno and Johnny Greisheimer win state titles. National Wrestling Hall of Fame coach Paul Gillespie took over and he, along with several assistant coaches, led Wantagh to even greater wrestling glory. Gillespie had coached Long Beach in the 1990s. Our wrestlers rarely beat his.

In the Muzio-Murphy-Gillespie run there were seven wrestlers who won ten state titles, nine additional state finalists and 17 additional state place-winners, through 2020. The team won an incredible nine Nassau County team titles and four times had the most team points at the New York State tournament.

Irwin Loew had three boys wrestle. Matt was a two-time state runner-up and Jonathan, who now wrestles at Cornell, was a state champ. The only Loew I taught was the youngest, Jenna, and she was on a volleyball state championship team.

When Frank and I had coached, our lofty goal was for a kid to place in the top six in Nassau County. Murphy and Gillespie raised that bar for Wantagh's elite grapplers—anything shy of the state final was practically a disappointment.

I used to wrestle with the kids, during Frank's time, in the room and then in the halls. I would go after the guys I had weight on. Then I picked on the wrong kid. Joe Kavanagh was the best Wantagh wrestler I ever saw, among these many greats. I had him in English and journalism. He was not the best student I ever saw.

For some reason, demented old age, I thought I could go upper body with Joe. He was one of the best in the nation at throws and he was my weight. I was 50 years old. I locked up with him and he instantly threw me six feet into a wall. He laughed. I did too as I was uninjured. That ended my hallway wrestling.

Joe was another one who Rob Shaver forfeited to. Though Joe would have pinned any of Shaver's guys anyway. In the state final his senior year he pinned the Suffolk County champ at 189.

After a meet at Plainedge, Joe's mom, a stunning-looking woman, got into a physical confrontation with a Plainedge wrestler. I watched her try to wrestle in that fight. Her boys didn't get their wrestling skill from her. And you remember my rule from the city, never break up a fight with a girl—especially not an attractive mom. I dared not untangle Mrs. Kavanagh and the Plainedge kid. Security guards broke it up.

Joe tried to wrestle at Hofstra. He lasted maybe a week. He would have been a top five NCAA place winner on talent. Though he didn't have the work ethic and hated listening to coaches.

Of all these great Wantagh wrestlers, the only one who placed in DI Nationals was Steven Bonanno, who is now an FBI agent. He took eighth for Hofstra.

Johnny Greisheimer had a great college career, qualifying for three NCAA Division I tournaments. He just missed placing in Philadelphia in 2011. I was there watching him, encouraging him. That was his best NCAA tournament.

Johnny had been a dedicated and disciplined student. He sat in front in my freshman English class. He didn't make weight for the post season that year. Utterly distraught, he believed his wrestling career was over. For weeks I calmed him by saying he had a lot of years left.

I also always told him to do his work and that at college he'd be a student-athlete, not just an athlete—as I told all of my students. Johnny listened. He went to Edinboro University in Western Pennsylvania and every holiday he'd stop by the school and show me his GPA, which he was very proud of.

While he never made All-American, he had some great wins. In the 2016 NCAA Championships at Madison Square Garden I sat with Johnny and his dad, in his excellent Edinboro seats. We watched Isaiah "Imar" Martinez of the University of Illinois, who at that point had won two Big 10 titles and an NCAA title as a redshirt freshman.

"Think anyone will ever beat Martinez again?" I said to Johnny.

"I beat him," Johnny said.

"What? Where? No way. You are full of shit." I had thought Imar had only lost once at that point.

"At the Midlands two years ago," Johnny said of the Northwestern University December open tournament.

So in Johnny's redshirt senior year he defeated a guy who would go on to compile a 116-3 college record, win four Big 10 titles and reach four NCAA finals, winning two of them. He even battled five-time world and Olympic champ Jordan Burroughs, in a very close best of three, in the final at the 2019 U.S. World Team trials.

Today Johnny is a state trooper in the Florida Highway Patrol. I've gotten together with him in Florida. He'd love to wrestle me and get me back for a few of my hallway beat downs on him but now he's 200 pounds of solid muscle and I'm not stupid.

More education advice: Don't hallway wrestle state champion wrestlers, especially after they've graduated and bulked up.

CHAPTER 18

Turnover at the Top

The back end of the decade of the aughts brought great change to Wantagh's leadership.

At our first faculty meeting Terry O'Connor announced that the year would be his last, in September 2007. He'd been a Wantagh administrator for 19 years. The faculty loved him. The kids loved him. We wondered who would follow him as principal.

"It has always been Dr. O'Connor's goal to take what was a good school and turn it into a great one," said David Dubin in a *Warrior* article. "He managed to fill the school with people who want to be here."

In the last *Warrior* article on him Dr. O'Connor said, "Wantagh is personable. Wantagh is a place where we all know and love each other ... that's the special part of Wantagh ... Here, we grow up together, we know each other, and it's a good atmosphere."

Dr. O'Connor said this a few months after Heather Kennedy created the perception that our happy high school had hidden flaws. Additionally, the Great Recession of 2008 caused Long Island home-owners to decry any raise in taxes. Wantagh residents responded by voting down our budget in June for the first time in two decades. A contingency budget re-vote also failed and the Wantagh School Board had to cut $1.5 million from its initial proposal of a $64.7 million budget.

The Wantagh community created a plan to fundraise the money to save school sports and extracurricular activities, which were first on the chopping block. The name of their group was S.O.S.—Save Our Students. It was the summer of car washes and fundraisers.

"Despite the mishaps that have gone on over the past couple of months, Dr. O'Connor believes Wantagh is going to be just fine," wrote my assistant editor Tara McLoughlin.

Before retiring Dr. O'Connor smoothed the transition to the next principal, who would be Carolyn Breivogel—the first female principal of Wantagh High School in its 54 years.

Our new high school administrative leadership team of Principal Carolyn Breivogel and Assistant Principal Jim Brown were prepared by Dr. O'Connor. But with the budget going down and parents scrambling to fundraise, they were faced with huge challenges.

While many teachers missed Terry O'Connor, Carolyn and Jim had both been guidance counselors. That gave them psychological insight into navigating the tricky relationships among parents, teachers and students.

Carolyn had also served as assistant principal for Terry O'Connor for the previous seven years, and prior to that she had been a Wantagh guidance counselor. Jim Brown had been the director of guidance in the high school for seven years. The duo had worked together. Their leadership displayed an initial calmness. Panic would have been the easy alternative.

Carolyn's attractive smile and easy-going demeanor hid her determined inner strength. Jim was handsome and dapper but also driven and determined. They sent out positive vibes. Nonetheless many teachers were concerned.

Leadership change wasn't confined to Wantagh that year. In November 2008 Barack Obama became the 44th president of the United States. Wantagh was a very conservative community, with about 75 percent of the kids and parents not excited about President Obama. Wantagh was and still is working class and White—with a small upper-middle class.

My student editors chose not to put Obama's historic win on our front page. They went with a Homecoming article. Obama was bumped into a side front-page tease-box. Though that was less a political move and more the girls in charge preferring Homecoming. Plus, the election was right at our deadline. And I always tried to have the kids decide the front page, unless they couldn't and then I'd pick the article.

Many teachers were happy with Obama being bumped. One thinks of suburban New York teachers as being liberal. But about

40 percent of the faculty was conservative, like my good friend and social studies teacher Mike Tallarine. Mike was one of many young teachers who I had become friends with in and out of school. We played in a monthly teachers' poker game, golfed together and frequently ate lunch together in the faculty room.

Mike, who loved the *New York Post* and hated the *New York Times*, had grown up in nearby Farmingdale, where he played football and lacrosse. His father had been an NYPD officer and then in his retirement a Wantagh H.S. security guard; his wife had been in my first journalism class. He applauded my students bumping Obama off page 1 to page 7. Mike also loved to scroll through the *Warrior* and ridicule our headlines while suggesting much more witty headlines—like his beloved *Post*.

"I'm sorry that I'm not teaching tabloid journalism to your high standards," I said in response to his critiques of each issue.

"I'm surprised you took Obama off the front page since you are the editor," he said.

"I'm not the *editor* of the *student* newspaper," I said. "I'm the advisor." I knew Mike teased me but his constant poking succeeded in irritating me—his goal perhaps.

My associate editor Chris Eisenhardt quoted Obama's opening speech as president: "If there is anyone out there who still doubts that America is a place where all things are possible; who still wonders if the dream of our founders is alive in our time; who still questions the power of our democracy, tonight is your answer ... In a country where the black race was enslaved only 145 years ago, a black man was now soon to be the leader of the free world."

While Obama dominated newspaper headlines and articles across the country and around the world, Wantagh residents focused on fundraising to save sports and extracurriculars.

"Local officials called the recent efforts of a Wantagh parents' group in raising $650,000 to restore sports and extracurricular activities cut for budget reasons a great victory for the community," began a February 2009 *New York Times* article by Linda Saslow.

That article, "From Educators, Caution on Parent Fund-Raisers and Foundations" focused on how school districts couldn't depend on being saved by community-run fundraisers and featured a photo of Wantagh wrestlers. We all hoped that the incredible communal effort to save sports and extracurricular activities was a once-in-a-generation moment.

My journalism program and the print newspaper were safe from budget cuts but were attacked by an unforeseen administrative maneuver. The middle school principal, Dr. Jeannette Stern, who had run me out of teaching middle school journalism because she didn't like how I taught it while advising the middle school newspaper, now went after my classroom.

The computer lab that I had helped develop a decade before and had been home to my journalism classes was technically in the middle school. Though it was located in the middle of the high school and the middle school.

Unlike just a few years before, many teachers now vied for computer lab time for their classes. I always got two periods scheduled for the Room 405 computer lab for my journalism classes. But Jeannette, realizing that Carolyn was new, decided to challenge her, in a turf war, for the second semester of that 2008-09 year. She tried to punt my class out of that room so she could put a middle school art class in there. There was no other available room, however, with computers to put my class in. The key to the popularity of my elective class, and its learning environment, was its newsroom-like relaxed feel with some instruction but mostly the clicking keys of students writing.

Jeannette would never have challenged Terry O'Connor. But she figured that she could just blitz Carolyn. Another factor was that Jeannette didn't like me. It had only been four years since she'd run me out of her middle school, which she controlled with an iron fist.

Carolyn fought for me and our high school students. But Jeannette won and my journalism class was homeless. My kids were distraught. First they had to deal with the budget voted down and now we had no classroom.

Jeannette's double punch of ending my middle school journalism class and then throwing us out of Room 405 hurt my program, and in some ways it never fully recovered from that in terms of numbers.

I had never had to recruit kids for it. Now, I had to battle other elective teachers for students.

We migrated to different available rooms. Then Carolyn Breivogel had a musty storage room converted into a very small classroom with computers. It got us through the year. That room would eventually become an office for the popular Social Studies Chairperson Dr. Christopher Widmann. I would spend a lot of time there, especially arguing and laughing with Mike Tallarine. Mike could be very humorous.

Carolyn would then create a high school computer lab for my journalism classes, only to see my numbers decline. A young art teacher swiped that lab for his graphic arts classes. Keith Hunter, another Seaford grad, drew big elective numbers. My journalism class headed back upstairs to Room 405 after Jeannette Stern retired. In my latter years I often taught in four different rooms. I didn't mind that though, as I walked and burned calories. But my journalism class remained in Room 405.

One of my very talented writers, Jill Bongiorni, who Julie Magnuson called her "star pupil" succumbed to senioritis in the spring of 2009—aided partly by Dr. Stern's booting our class out of the computer lab.

I had hoped that Jill would step up as a leader and do more writing her senior year. She still wrote some great front-page articles. But the Journalism II class had shrunk to 22 students, my fewest students in over a decade. And there were long stretches where Jill lost all motivation.

"This year I've gotten written up and suspended for the first times in my life and my name gets called down to 104 (the dean's office) more times than all my other years combined," Jill wrote in her senior farewell.

Another member of that group, whose academic demise had begun her freshman year, was Ashely Exner. Ashley was a lively cheerleader. In the rare moments where Ashley felt inspiration she wrote well. But she and her best friend Kristina Codi, another cheerleader, worked more on cheer routines in class than articles.

"If you know me you might think that I never listened to anything any of my teachers said to me over the past four years,"

Ashley wrote in her farewell. "In particular, Krav has said many things to me. 'Ash are you going to finish an article? Ash you have so much potential, why don't you use it?'

"And to be honest, I really didn't listen to anything he ever said to me.

"But one day Krav said something that I really did listen to. On a trip to Adelphi this year for a journalism conference, on the bus, when asked what he liked about being a teacher, he said, 'I like being around kids, because kids are always looking to the future. All kids feel like there is something out there waiting for them, some kind of hope.'"

Among that group there was one young lady who always had it together and kept it together through our nomadic class journey that year. Jackie Dresch, freckled, adorable and uber-determined, was devastated by the impact on her senior year from the budget being voted down. In the first issue she wrote an editorial demanding that in 2009 community members vote for next year's budget as well as every student over the age of 18.

She continued pounding out one great article after another. Jackie had been upset that her great work junior year didn't win anything. As a senior her determination finally paid off at the Adelphi contest. She won Gold for Most Outstanding Reporter and Bronze for Best Feature Article. Chris Eisenhardt won Gold for Best Sports Story. It was a rare double Gold at Adelphi for my kids. Ashley and Kristina had their finest moment in journalism, leading cheers as Jackie and Chris were called up to the stage. I might have shed a tear of pride that day.

Jackie also won two Syracuse awards, including a Gold. Then she attended Syracuse and graduated from the Newhouse School of Communications. From there she would work for ABC News and come back and talk to my journalism classes about that job in Room 405, the room her senior class was exiled from, using the smartboard to show some ABC News clips that she had worked on. Next she landed a job at HBO. And now she's on the strategic communications team at The College Board. She is one of many of my former students I'm so incredibly proud of.

As for Jeannette Stern, after a 40-year Wantagh career as a teacher, president of the teachers' union and social studies department chairwoman, she retired as middle school principal in 2010. Jeannette didn't get to enjoy retirement for long as she died in October 2015, the same year that Joel Dick died.

Wantagh United Teachers President Tom Vereline, a middle school teacher, said (in an obituary), "once you got used to Stern's oversized personality, you came to learn that she had a big heart. She loved her staff," he said. "She loved her students, she loved her colleagues, she loved being an educator and she loved Wantagh.'"

While I had my battles with Jeannette, I had hoped that she could enjoy a long retirement. I bore no grudge against her nor the many other administrators who didn't like me or agree with my teaching techniques. I didn't teach and work my butt off for administrators. I did that for my students. So, if an administrator didn't like how I did something, as long as my students benefited, I didn't really care. Though I don't recommend that strategy for young teachers.

I do believe there is nothing worse than seeing a teacher retire and then not get to enjoy it. Jeannette died from cancer at age 67.

And while it would seem that Jeannette would have been the last administrator to give me a hard time, she wasn't. There was one final surprising battle waiting for me in my long war with administrators.

CHAPTER 19

More Administrative Turnover

Wantagh's Superintendent Dr. Carl Bonuso announced his retirement, as did the assistant principal who supervised the dean's office and the music department, Ron Lebel, in the spring of 2009. The administrative stability I'd experienced had been remarkable.

Dr. Bonuso put in 26 years at Wantagh, 39 years in public education, as assistant principal, principal, assistant superintendent and a decade as superintendent.

Outside of Dr. Bonuso's paperwork comment about me, my every single interaction with that always-smiling, pleasant and humorous man was a delight. And Ron Lebel had done a great job with the dean's office. If a kid did something wrong, Ron handled it. His screams penetrated the walls. He'd been a music teacher at Midwood High School in Brooklyn for 15 years, so he could project his voice. He arrived in Wantagh as a dean in 1989.

Additionally, three years prior English Chairperson Brian Donohue had retired after 35 years. Brian worked as an engineer on submarines and he began teaching English and math at Wantagh before switching over to just English. He became the department chairperson in 1990, a year before I arrived. While I got off to a bumpy start and Brian didn't know what to make of me, we came to appreciate and respect each other. I succeeded with my students because of all these amazing administrators for my first nearly two decades.

Taking over for Brian was Rebecca Chowske, a tall intellectual with a narrow face and glasses. Rebecca had many excellent ideas. She founded a company, SNOsites.com, that created websites. At her urging I put the *Warrior* on the school website, where you can read it today (https://thewarrior.wantaghschools.org). Also, during an observation of my Journalism I class, she showed me a streamlined method for posting my assignments. She had great software and tech skills.

Rebecca, who had us call her Becky, had a lot of other excellent ideas for improving instruction. One was for regular senior teachers to teach mini courses on subjects that interested us, which we finally implemented in 2011-12. Teaching non-honors seniors was a huge challenge, as I had learned with the sweat hogs. They didn't just check out in the spring, they checked out in October. The idea behind Becky's mini-courses was that they could evolve into semester senior classes—I would teach sports literature and nonfiction, David Dubin would do a broadcasting class, David Garey would teach horror. That quickly came to fruition. And Becky reminded me each January to recruit for journalism, which was necessary to keep the classes running. I appreciated that.

Becky's first couple of years went well. She had taught English in another district for 16 years before coming to Wantagh to be a supervisor. Though she had a little Joel Dick in her: she cobbled reading and library, plus additional duties, into her English department supervisor position—a resume build-up that hinted at her desire to move up the administrative hierarchy. She liked official sounding titles and hers became Director of English Language Arts.

One negative was Becky's own teaching. She taught a couple of honors classes, initially. While she knew her subject, her students didn't like her lack of pizazz. Her teaching also cried out for humor. She appreciated the wit of David Dubin, however. In fact, she loved David Dubin. David's teaching still shone with his students and colleagues, too.

Another English teacher who Becky admired was Violet Turner. Violet's students relished her quirkiness and storytelling. She had taken over creative writing and also advised the school literary magazine. I had gotten her to enter the literary magazine in the Syracuse contest and her kids did phenomenally well, racking up many more awards than my newspaper kids did each year. I was thrilled for Violet and her kids, as many of them wrote for the literary magazine and the newspaper.

Violet's group won 26 awards at Syracuse in 2007-08, while my kids had a down year, winning only five awards.

"Mrs. Turner is clearly a dominant state-wide force in literary magazine advising," I was quoted in a *Warrior* November 2007 article. "The hours she puts into that magazine are enabling countless Wantagh students to be recognized in a state-wide contest ... We have some great writing programs here. We are producing great writers."

Violet took over the high school literary magazine, *Escapades*, in 2003 and the Syracuse awards piled up. She also entered a national contest at Columbia University and taught a workshop on contest day at Columbia. She suggested that I enter the newspaper in the Columbia contest and take some kids into the city for it. But the Syracuse and Adelphi contests were enough. There were other Long Island school journalism contests, too, but I didn't have the energy for any more.

Our English department exceled under Becky as it had under Brian Donohue; we had many talented teachers like our drama teacher, Heather Romano, who had taken over that role from David. Two years after debuting at Wantagh, Heather completed the intense application process and was awarded a Fulbright Scholarship in Japan in 2004.

She spent three weeks there "visiting schools, experiencing Japanese culture, staying with families and attending seminars," wrote one of my all-time best journalists Angela Cave, and her co-author Nicole Lauterbach.

"The fascination that the Japanese schoolchildren have with the teachers is also a result of their homogeneous society: being a 5-feet-9-inches tall and blonde, Ms. Romano stood out in a striking way," Angela and Nicole wrote.

Three years later Heather used her boundless energy to win a radio station contest that benefited sick hospital patients. Thanks to Heather's efforts, the entire cast of the Broadway musical *Rent* sang a number of songs from their hit show on the Wantagh stage. My editor-in-chief, Katie Ciasullo, closed her front-page piece on the show with, "Even teachers were elated afterwards. 'I would give up everything to have a voice like that!' said band teacher Mrs. Dragovich."

But leave it to Becky to hire an English teacher who had a voice good enough for Broadway. That 2007-08 school year she hired a rock star. A very straight rock star, too, as opposed to a grungy tattooed one. Lean, tall and handsome with short hair, John Hampson was the lead singer of the Long Island band Nine Days, which had topped the Billboard charts with the No. 1 song, "The Story of a Girl," which he'd written about his wife Theresa, who taught Italian at Wantagh High School.

"Instead of having hour-long concerts or gigs, [he's] now performing in 40-minute periods," wrote Jill Bongioorni and Jackie Dresch in John Hampson's *Warrior*-debut article. "Like being on stage you still have an audience who you are trying to reach out to, but ... the audience has notebooks and binders. And, as Mr. Hampson points out, in the classroom, "Nobody claps when you're done."

The day before vacations I dropped by John's room as he played his guitar and sang for his students. The kids clapped for him and demanded an encore—and late passes to their next classes.

However, by 2017, John said (in an LIHerald.com article) that his students no longer cared about his music career: "I'm their English teacher and I'm making them read *Catcher in the Rye* or something."

I cared. And I frequently questioned John, who recounted many stories about his concert days. Nine Days played at the 2001 NHL all-star game and I'd asked him questions about the hockey players' reactions to his band. But John had no interest in ice hockey. He did like baseball and rooted for the Mets and the Red Sox, an unusual combination for a Long Island guy.

Unfortunately, the Internet helped make it hard for John to make a living from his music. Epic Records dropped him and the band, and the gigs dried up, though he continued to write incredible songs and (with Nine Days) compiled two solid albums: *Snapshot* and *Something out of Nothing*. Unfortunately, neither of those two albums nor the two previous ones after his hit, *The Maddening Crowd*, had an impact. To support his family, with young twin boys, he took on a real job.

In Becky's early years the 12 members of Wantagh's English department were mostly happy with her, except during the year-end 11th-grade New York State English Language Regents test.

While Becky did well with the day-to-day dealings, she became extremely stressed setting up that exam. She wanted us there 20 minutes early. If you got there ten minutes early you were late. Hence, I frequently incurred her wrath, as I meandered into the gym to proctor for that test. I didn't teach 11th graders, like Julie Magnuson—who arrived 30 minutes early and made sure her students were ready, which included a couple of pieces of candy on their desks.

Also, as David read the initial listening passage to the 250-or-so students in the gym, Becky insisted on his comfort. She once ripped my water bottle out of my hands and handed it to David to make sure his throat wasn't dry. I'm not sure she was aware she had done that. She zoned into a bizarre mental state during that test and the days leading up to it.

"She broke out in hives," said another excellent English teacher, Tracy Nieves. Her face turned red and blotchy, thanks to June Regents exam stress. In Becky's defense, it had become an overwhelming task to set up that test. While most of the approximately 250 juniors took the exam in the gym, many others were scattered in different special education rooms around the school. Years before we had lost a test, Leah Neverka's, and Leah's name was bandied about every year at Regents time. Becky was determined that that would never happen under her watch.

Now, not every member of the department went to her defense. Michael Loicano took on an English-teaching leave replacement position in the fall of 2007. His new teacher article was written by Brittany Fitzpatrick, a solid writer for me. (Brittany's younger sister Kiera would arrive a few years later and become one of my best writers ever.)

Loicano, who earned his undergraduate degree from NYU, was extremely witty and smart. In his *Warrior* profile he lobbied for a permanent job at Wantagh.

"Although his reign upon (his) English classroom will be short lived he hopes to attain a permanent teaching position here at Wantagh High School," wrote Brittany, who I called Brit Fitz.

"There are endless treats to having Mr. Loicano stay solid here, like film projections and extensive lesson plans chock full of informative goodies," Brittany wrote. "It would be a mistake to let a gem like this go."

Loicano's position did become a full-time tenured spot for the next year. He had to apply for it. In the end it came down to Loicano, who we called Lois, or a former Wantagh journalism student of mine, Christina Tepedino. Loicano viewed himself as a shoo-in for the job. After all, Tepedino had never taught. And her University of Scranton undergrad education didn't compare to his elite NYU one.

Chris Rafferty and I had interviewed Christina initially and strongly recommended to Becky that she move forward for the position among the many applicants. In the end Christina got the job. Loicano was enraged. He blamed Becky and Christina's mom. He played in our teacher's poker games, though not a very good poker player, and he would spend half the game badmouthing Becky.

"Becky only chose Tepedino because her mom had pull in Wantagh," he said. None of us knew where this crazed conspiracy theory originated. I defended Becky, and also I knew Christina's mother had nothing to do with who got the full-time and tenure-track position. Several of us told Loicano that what hurt him was how he hung around with veteran teachers and acted like one of us in that he didn't volunteer to take on any clubs or extra activities.

So, you young teachers, do as much as you can when asked to become the tenth grade class advisor or run the Key Club. Nobody wants to advise the Key Club but you need to take it on with enthusiasm.

Christina is now Christina Bewick. She teaches English at Wantagh Middle School.

Loicano ended up getting a full-time, English-teaching job in another Long Island district, married a Wantagh girl, had a kid and now lives in Wantagh. We played poker in his basement and right away he would attack Becky.

"Mike, enough, please just check, raise or fold," we said, repeatedly.

* * *

A science teacher named Odysseas Svolos replaced Ron Lebel as dean. We called him Ody. And if we thought Ron Lebel could scream, Ody's voice competed with a jet engine. He also had the strength of Hercules. He never lifted weights; he was about 240 pounds of muscle.

Ody was, and still is, a friend. He tutored all three of my kids in science and was a very good teacher, though Ody teased his students with graphic language. We all figured one day the dean would remove him from the classroom, not that *becoming* the dean would remove him from the classroom. He'd also been a very good head girls' soccer coach and assistant girls' lacrosse coach for our outstanding lacrosse team.

Before he became dean (he only did that job for a year), Ody would enter the faculty room, as I ate lunch, and pinch me in the side with his powerful paws. I told him not to do that while I chewed food.

He didn't listen. One day he pinched me hard and I snapped. I usually remained composed, and while Ody had about 30 pounds on me I went after him. I squared off in a wrestling stance. He remained seated in a chair. I cuffed him in the head a few times but realized that it would be difficult to get him out of that chair so I could crunch him with a good wrestling move—like my body-lock. I tried to rip him out of the chair. While I had begun this wrestling match angry both of us started to laugh and gasp for breath. Other teachers watched in horror, especially the females, thinking this was a serious fight. But it was just two big guys wrestling in the teacher's lounge.

Finally Ody shot out of the chair and took me down with a nice single leg. He won the wrestling match. Though I had made my point. I never again endured his potent pinch when he entered the faculty room.

* * *

Regarding the top position in the district, Wantagh hired long-time Assistant Superintendent Dr. Lydia Begley. She became Wantagh's first female superintendent.

"Less than 22 percent of all school superintendents were women," my editor-in-chief Marissa Boyle wrote in her featured piece on Dr. Begley.

Dr. Begley, like Dr. Bonuso, smiled easily. She was slim, attractive, and fit with blonde hair and a kind smile. And like many other leaders in our district then she saw how critical technology would be to Wantagh's future.

"She [Dr. Begley] believes that the faculty's job is to teach the students communication skills [and] the use of technology," wrote Marissa. "Whether it is new computers or smartboards, Dr. Begley believes that the innovative environment will change the structure of learning."

Administrators like Dr. Begley kept our school district at the forefront of public-school education. In a short time, we had a smartboard in every classroom. I became addicted to my smartboard and would never use chalk or whiteboard markers again. We had very good numbers of students graduating and going on to college. And so many of them have become productive members of our society.

* * *

We had a female superintendent, female principal and Becky, who kept changing her title and was now the Department Chair of English Language Arts. Some other male teachers complained that every new hire seemed to be female.

As the years went by Becky struggled to handle the stress of the position she had created. Though it looked great on her resume, she snapped easily at ten teachers in the department. But never at David or Violet. They were her favorites. Playing favorites didn't seem to be the best leadership approach.

Becky looked down on me; she viewed me as non-intellectual and sports-obsessed. She failed to recognize the depth of my reading. While much of her reading then focused on education, especially towards gaining her Doctor of Education (Ed.D.) degree, I devoured nonfiction—travelogues, anthropology, history, biography, counterculture like Miller and Kerouac, science, adventure like Beryl Markham—and fiction.

More significantly, regarding leadership, sports teach you how to be a leader. Who in our society leads better than a great coach? Take the greatest National Hockey League coach of all time Scotty Bowman, who led his teams to nine Stanley Cup championships.

"Bowman has a complete and undistractible team focus," wrote Montreal Canadians great Ken Dryden—a Cornell grad, a lawyer and a former Canadian Parliament member—in his book *The Game*. "He has one loyalty—to the team; not to individual players."

Becky's department was her team and her ability to lead us often faltered. She did pull off a spectacular achievement, however, when she procured tickets for a number of sophomores, me, her and three other teachers to see Elie Wiesel speak in the spring of 2010 at Adelphi University. Brian Donohue had taken us to see Norman Mailer and now Becky had gained access to another legendary literary figure.

I was the first in the department to teach Wiesel's short and terrifying Holocaust memoir *Night* several years before. That year it was taught in tenth grade.

Wiesel, then 81, spoke for an hour to an audience of 1,000, many of us students and educators.

"To combat repression, racism and anti-Semitism, victims must speak out and schools must teach morals, said Wiesel," wrote *Newsday's* Dave Marcus in "On LI, Wiesel urges next generation to battle hatred."

In the *Warrior* Kelley Garland paraphrased Wiesel: "If schools began to incorporate morality in lessons, perhaps ... racism and hatred will begin to diminish."

Unfortunately that hasn't happened.

Despite Wiesel preaching against hatred, and his hopes that world politicians would cease using scapegoats and hate to gain and remain in power, as the decade of the teens went on more world leaders were propelled by divisive politics, embracing the Nazi's propaganda tactic of the "big lie" to divide nations throughout the world.

Wiesel also talked about literature. Though I have to disagree with something he said about *Romeo and Juliet*. He said it was a play about hatred. Having taught that play well over 20 times I would say it was about hatred and love at the same time.

Who am I to contradict the late Nobel laureate, author of 57 books and a survivor of the Holocaust? But in *Romeo and Juliet*, Romeo says to Benvolio:

> "Here's much to do with hate, but more with love
> Why then, O brawling love! Loving hate
> O anything, of nothing first create!
> O heavy lightness! Serious vanity!
> Misshapen chaos of well-seeming forms
> Feather of lead, bright smoke, cold fire, sick health!"

Shakespeare juxtaposes love and hate, and many other things, throughout the play. But I don't think his theme is focused on solely hate—if anything it's about the ying-yang nature of all things.

Getting students and teachers to see Wiesel speak was Becky at her finest. Unfortunately, stressed out, exhausted Becky appeared more frequently.

Once I left my homeroom 20 seconds before the bell rang and from down the hallway she screamed at me not to leave my homeroom early. Though I had to race all over the high school and to distant Room 405.

She became the first administrator in 24 years to admonish me for wearing jeans.

"Only wear jeans on Fridays," she said sternly. And I'll give her that one as my colleague Rich Colavita often said, "Kravitz is intense about everything except his attire." Luckily for me, Jennifer was sound asleep when I left the house, as a few times I went to school in an inside-out short-sleeve fancy shirt.

In another example of stressed Becky, several teachers and students had gathered in David Garey's room in June of 2010 to watch a World Cup soccer game on his Smartboard. Classes were over and we were working on grades, proctoring, organizing our rooms, putting away books and watching a little soccer. David Garey loved soccer, especially watching the U.S. men's national team. And I had watched practically every U.S. game in the World Cup for two decades.

The U.S. battled Algeria, in its home continent of Africa, though over 4,000 miles away from its home country, in South Africa. The game was tied 0-0 after regulation. If it ended in a draw the U.S. would miss advancing out of the group stage and into the knockout round of 16.

We were all quiet and bummed, as it wasn't looking good for the U.S. team, which had been favored to beat Algeria. With minutes left in stoppage time, U.S. goalie Tim Howard tossed a pass to America's star player Landon Donovan, who sprinted down the field. We all rose in anticipation of a scoring chance. Donovan passed to striker Jozy Altidore, who passed to Clint Dempsey. Dempsey, a great finisher, shot and we opened our mouths ready to scream but his shot was blocked. Yet Dempsey quickly tucked the rebound in the net and the U.S. had an incredible 1-0 victory. The USMNT had won its group for the first time in 80 years and we screamed louder than Odysseas Svolos.

Becky had been walking down the hall and heard the screaming. She burst into the room in the midst of our victory celebration of high fives.

"What is going on here?" she screamed. "You are watching soccer? You are supposed to be grading. Pete, why are you doing this?"

Why had she singled me out? We'd finished the English Regents. She should have been relaxed. And there were other teachers there.

The students fled in mid celebration. She ruined our incredible soccer moment. I didn't care that she'd screamed at me. I hadn't done anything wrong. Besides, what could she do to me?

CHAPTER 20

Becky "The Bulldog" Chowske

Becky patiently waited two years to clarify how I needed to collaborate with her about education.

In my two decades at Wantagh, I never had a bad observation or year-end evaluation—outside of that near-disastrous-first year.

Education was in its usual state of flux. Two years into Obama's first term he wanted to ensure that students succeeded in public schools, especially in poor communities. There were billions of federal dollars that states could get if they followed Washington's recommendations, especially in how teachers were evaluated.

"The initial Race to the Top grants provided $4.3 billion to states if they agreed to adopt certain policies, such as using test scores to measure teachers' effectiveness and – in what was seen as an implicit endorsement of the Common Core State Standards – adopting high standards," wrote Elizabeth A. Harris in a *New York Times* 2014 article, "Cuomo Fights Rating System in Which Few Teachers Are Bad."

Becky immersed herself in these Common Core standards and the potential changes coming in education. I did not. I kept teaching my English and journalism students literature, nonfiction and writing. My methods were effective. My students did well. The Common Core was just the latest educational jargon for the same things we'd always done. My journalism students' success had proved that my writing-teaching methodology was effective—at that point my kids had won over 150 awards in the Syracuse and Adelphi contests. At Adelphi the year before, 2011, Kiera Fitzpatrick won a Silver for Most Outstanding Reporter, and we won another Silver and Bronze. We were about to go on a nice run at that contest.

I also had been teaching what we called an Inclusion (or as I always called it a collaborative) English class for five years with a special education teacher named Lisa Watkins. Lisa had been a special education elementary teacher in Wantagh for many years before coming up to the high school. We had a lot in common. We were both University of Delaware grads, lived a mile apart and her youngest and my Rebecca Mae were in the same grade in Commack schools. They would even both eventually graduate from the same university.

Some educators didn't like teaching Inclusion classes. I loved them. Lisa had about eight-ten special education students main-streamed with a regents class. Lisa, her aide, Ellen Kelly, and I could outnumber a difficult 30-student class. I felt that working with those two made me a better teacher and all of my students benefited.

Lisa, in 2021, still teaches at Wantagh, and she is as good as any teacher in that school—though she plans to retire at the end of the year. Small, thin and indefatigable, she quickly saw how I taught and always prepared great material and fun assessments for our students. Her special education students, along with the rest of the class, bene-fited tremendously from her efforts.

Many ninth-grade parents I'd see, in the school and at sporting events, would tell me they hoped their child would get me as a ninth-grade English teacher. Some years I'd have two ninth grade classes or even three, though usually only one with Lisa.

Becky planned to observe my class with Lisa in January of 2012. She was also going to observe my roommate Chris Rafferty. Raf madly prepared for his observation, as if he were untenured. Raf worried about all of the changes in how we were being evaluated. His teaching and prep were fantastic so I found it curious that he tried to create a perfect lesson for his observation with Becky. Lisa and I prepared, too. Though not with the same diligence as Raf. It was just my observation and not Lisa's, as she'd already had hers.

Becky observed the class. It went well, I assumed. This was her sixth year of observing me. I had never received a bad observation or year-end evaluation from her. Her observation report said that my lesson "didn't meet state standards." Not even Joel Dick had ever said that about one of my lessons, though he'd fired me several times in two years.

I prided myself on being a good teacher, not a teacher below state standards, so Becky's lesson write-up flabbergasted me. I showed it to Lisa and she expressed shock. In fact, a week later, Lisa wrote Becky the following: "How grateful I am for Pete's efforts and attitude toward making our program work. His empathy towards my most-challenged students is incredible. He finds a way to include them in our lessons in a way where they won't feel self-conscious."

Before my post-observation meeting with Becky, I studied her report and read through the standards that she said I didn't meet. I walked into her office, sans a greeting, and said, "This observation was ridiculous."

"The lesson didn't meet state standards," she said.

"You've observed me for years and I've never had a lesson that didn't meet state standards. So all of a sudden I can't teach," I said.

"It's not about your teaching," she said. "It's about observing how much the kids learn. This year doesn't count. But if you are observed to be below state standards next year and following year you can be fired."

I just stared at her.

At that moment I realized that she looked like Big Bird—tall with a beaky nose. Oh my God, a Big Bird ice hockey player had cross checked me in 1974 and now I had been assaulted by a Becky Big Bird. I was glad my kids didn't watch *Sesame Street* anymore.

For the first time in 20 years an administrator had threatened to fire me. I vacillated between viewing this observation report as a bluff or worrying that she would try to fire me. I tried not to obsess about it.

I talked to David. "Well, she just observed me and spent half of the lesson debating with the kids and ruined my lesson," he said. "But of course she called it a great lesson."

David could have the worst lesson and she would call it "highly effective."

I poured through her critique and checked it against the standards. It was definitely the most I'd looked at a lesson report. I usually took a quick glance and piled it on my desk, which was infamous for its stacks of papers.

I kept discussing "the lesson" with Jennifer. "She won't fire you," she said.

"I realize she can't fire me now. And it will take a lot of changes for her to fire me in two years. But my lesson was not below state standards."

"So don't worry about it so much."

I refused to accept her write up. I asked my union rep, Lisa Fugazzi, to talk to Becky with me. I poured through everything Becky had written. And then I spotted something. Wow. I couldn't believe it. Had Becky really screwed up that badly?

I emailed Becky and told her I wanted to have a meeting with her and my union rep. She responded that she'd asked the principal to be at the meeting, too. So, a meeting was set up with Principal Carolyn Breivogel, Assistant Principal Jim Brown, Becky, Lisa and me. Meanwhile, Becky insisted I sign the observation report and I refused until after our meeting.

I could not wait for that meeting.

* * *

I wasn't the only teacher having issues back then. The school's extremely successful head football coach Keith Sachs was removed as coach by the school board, right before his 20th season. The school board's actions did not impact his job as a physical education teacher nor as the school's baseball coach.

At a school board meeting in the auditorium packed with nearly 200 students and residents in June of 2011, several community members and students demanded the board reinstate Sachs, who had won over 100 games, a Long Island title in 2001 and a Nassau County title in 2003.

"Wantagh senior Ryan Sliwak, who played football and baseball for Sachs, gave an emotional speech ... about his coach's impact as a father figure," wrote Andrew Coen in the *Wantagh-Seaford Patch*. "Sliwak lost his father in the terrorist attacks of September 11, 2001 just days before his eighth birthday. 'I feel like I'm losing my dad once again,' said Sliwak."

I was at that meeting; Sliwak spoke profoundly and powerfully. His father, Robert Sliwak, perished in his Cantor Fitzgerald office. He went to Seaford High School, where he was a star athlete.

The decision to not reappoint Sachs had nothing to do with the school's athletic director. It had nothing to do with Superintendent Dr. Lydia Begley, who wrapped up her second year running the district. It was a decision made by the Wantagh School Board, whose members refused to explain why.

As a teacher, I saw the behavior of the School Board members as pure cowardice. They had Dr. Begley speak to the outraged community residents as if she had something to do with dumping Keith Sachs. The board's president was Jean Quinn, a Wantagh graduate, who had been an aide in the high school. I had taught her children. Another powerful board member behind the maneuver was Michael Cucci, who would spend a total of 18 years on the board, many of them as president.

Years later I was told that Quinn and Cucci wanted to punish Sachs for the manner in which his marriage blew up. Sachs lived in Wantagh; his three children went to Wantagh schools. Quinn and Cucci, if that allegation about the marriage were true, decided to stand on some type of moral high ground by removing Sachs.

They hid behind the public face of Dr. Begley and the board's attorney, Christopher Venator, and refused to explain their actions to the community.

As if that weren't bad enough, the board brought in a guy named Tom Casey to replace Sachs. After long successful stints as an assistant football coach at Garden City High School and assistant baseball coach at Division High School, Casey had four short coaching jobs. Casey's sister had coached my son in travel soccer (to a pair of state cup finals) and she was a successful coach and teacher at Great Neck High School South. Their father Tom Casey, Sr., had been a teacher, coach and top NCAA basketball official.

And while Tom Casey, Jr. was a winning coach in his one year at Wantagh, as someone who was supposed to represent the moral high ground, football players described inappropriate comments he made to students. Several parents demanded that he be dismissed as coach and as a result he resigned, a few months after the season ended. Casey was out and Sachs was back in.

Again, behind all of this was Wantagh's School Board led by Jean Quinn and Michael Cucci.

But that was only the beginning of the craziness. Dr. Lydia Begley was offered a position at Nassau BOCES (the Board of Cooperative Educational Services for the county's 56 school districts). After ten years as assistant superintendent and nearly three years as superintendent, Dr. Begley fled Wantagh. We teachers had liked Dr. Begley and thought she had done a good job and were sad to see her go. But many of us suspected that it must have been very difficult for her to work with a difficult school board.

"I thought I would finish my career at Wantagh but that was not the case," she told me years later. "I left because I simply could not continue to give tacit approval to bad decisions that were harmful and unprofessional. I guess I should thank the Wantagh Board because if I hadn't left, I would never have experienced my wonderful years at BOCES."

The school board hired Dr. Richard Marsh as an interim superintendent. He resigned for personal reasons after five months on the job. Dr. Bonuso returned as the next interim superintendent.

Then after spending thousands of dollars to search for the next superintendent they hired an upstate New York superintendent, Philip D'Angelo, Jr., from the Skaneateles School District. The board gave D'Angelo a five-year contract. His run as superintendent lasted about three months and he was gone.

So much for my two decades of stability in Wantagh. This school board was wacky. At first the board issued a statement saying it approved a leave for D'Angelo, again following its recent policy of a lack of transparency for its actions.

"Wantagh school board president Michael Cucci referred questions to the district's public relations firm," according to a *Syracuse Post-Standard* article by Catie O'Toole. "[Then Cucci] asked, 'Can I ask you one thing? How is [the] Skaneateles [school district] now?'"

That article further quoted Skaneateles School Board President Evan Dreyfuss as saying, "This is surprising to me. I had no inclination ... [and] hope he's okay personally and professionally. People here liked him. He was a standup guy ... In my six years on the board there was no misconduct, no reason to reprimand, nothing of that nature."

Some of the mystery was clarified at the September School Board meeting, where a board resolution revealed that D'Angelo was "suspended with pay pending an investigation." A Wantagh elementary school principal, Maureen Goldberg, was named "acting superintendent."

We now had our fifth superintendent in one year. That must have been some kind of record. The Board paid Maureen and continued to pay Phil D'Angelo his salary. D'Angelo then landed a job running the Millbrook Central School District as superintendent in West Chester County, New York. He worked there for six years and retired in 2019.

It was never revealed what he had allegedly done. Cucci did say at the December 2012 school board meeting that a district investigation on D'Angelo had been completed but he wouldn't elaborate.

I even asked one of Cucci's daughters, who had been my student, if she ever knew what happened and she said, "My dad won't tell me." And I've heard allegations from Wantagh teachers about D'Angelo's conduct at Skaneateles but I failed to verify anything.

Maureen Goldberg proved to be an excellent superintendent. She ran the district for five years and returned stability to Wantagh's schools.

And after his 18-year run, Michael Cucci was voted off the school board in 2017. Though not before his leadership helped put the district in poor financial condition, according to current district officials. Cucci's budgets essentially borrowed from the future. As a result, for the 2021-22 school year Wantagh asked the community to support a property-tax increase of 3.82 percent. As it pierced the two-percent tax cap, Wantagh needed 60 percent of residents to approve the district's proposed budget in the annual vote. It only got 51 percent, though a re-vote passed.

* * *

The date of my principal's office meeting, for which I was pumped up, was January 27th, a Friday in 2012.

Instead of hitting Becky with her *faux pas* that I had uncovered, I decided to bring up a procedural point to see how she would react. I said that she hadn't informed me at our pre-observation meeting how much observations were changing and that this one would be treated differently from every other one of the past five years, indeed the past 21 years. Past practice was a big education concept. With our principal Carolyn sitting there, I said, "In our first meeting this year Carolyn showed us these seven standards and said we were all good teachers and no administrators would use them to hurt us. I think you should just amend this report to show my lesson met state standards."

Becky went off on me. No wonder Jim Brown had called her "Becky the Bulldog." She said the lesson did not meet the standards. She appeared angry. I was calm.

Then Carolyn asked me how I would rate my lesson.

"It wasn't my best," I said. "But it was well above state standards. And it met every single standard."

Becky glared at me. The big bird bulldog wanted a fight. I hit her with the bomb.

"Okay, Becky, let's talk about those standards you said I didn't meet," I said. "There are three of them. First is Standard 3, which says to 'create a challenging learning experience.' Next is Standard 5, which is 'assessment for student learning' and finally there is Standard 6, which is 'collaboration.'

"All over this report you write that I don't collaborate. Your recommendation is that I need to discuss my lesson and unit objectives with colleagues. And while you call this an Inclusion class, I taught it with a collaborative teacher, who I have collaborated with for five years. So, how could this lesson fail to meet the Standard 6 for collaboration?"

I dug my eyes into her. Her whole face collapsed. She suddenly appeared exhausted. She tried to say something but stuttered. What could she say? She realized how badly she'd screwed up.

Carolyn's body language showed her recognition that Becky had this lesson going down before it started.

I interrupted Becky's attempt at speech and said, "Standard 6 should have been a strength not a weakness. I mean, come on, didn't you see Lisa in the classroom with me as we taught the class together? If that's not collaboration what is?"

She had no choice but to agree with me. While I made compelling arguments for the other two standards which I felt my lesson clearly met, she gained a second wind and fought me on those two and wouldn't give in, even though I outdebated her.

I had been more prepared. I knew my standards. She had forced me to pay attention to them. I had the standards with me in a format that Carolyn called "the placemat" and Becky asked to see my placemat several times.

Lisa, my union rep, at this point said, "How many standards need to be met for this lesson to meet state standards?"

Becky had no idea. Not even Carolyn had any answer to that.

"Next year we will use a rubric, not this form," Carolyn said.

An hour into the meeting, I again said that Becky should just rewrite her report to say my lesson met state standards. Her face turned red and blotchy, she took off her glasses and wiped her eyes.

"I only got three hours of sleep last night," she said.

I didn't feel bad for her. I kept hammering away. I pointed out that Lisa Watkins had 13 of the 22 students in her group and that one of those students, a boy with Aspergers, began the reading (*Great Expectations*) by doing a brilliant English accent. Once again, I demanded that what she saw as a weakness was a strength. Challenging a child with Aspergers to read dialogue with an English accent clearly met Standard 3, "creating a challenging learning experience." Becky made a weak argument for why it didn't, which made no sense.

Finally, after 75 minutes Becky gave in. She recognized that she had her ass kicked in front of the principal and assistant principal, who she had asked to be there.

"What if I rip up this observation?" Becky said.

"No!" I said. "My lesson met state standards and I want you to rewrite it to show that."

"I vote for the rip up," Carolyn said.

I felt Carolyn had been supportive and wanted some type of compromise so I agreed to the rip up, even though it meant that Becky was going to observe me again.

Becky ripped up the observation report. Then she admonished me, with what little energy she could summon, and said I had to see her regularly to discuss the problems of this class so she could help the children. I nodded but had no intention of doing that. Lisa and I would collaborate and teach our students without her help.

At the end of the day I emailed Carolyn: "I appreciate your mediation and your outstanding show of leadership. I was very upset. I feel better now. This has been a long and upsetting two weeks for me, since that observation, but I've learned a lot from it."

"I am glad you feel better," Carolyn wrote. "You are a teacher with many gifts! We are lucky to have you. Thank you for putting your heart into what you do."

Clearly, the reason Becky overlooked collaboration is because she wanted me to collaborate more with her, to pop by her office and discuss my classes. At that point she had little fires everywhere and was a year and a half away from her Ed. D in Education Leadership and School Reform. But the problem was that no number of graduate classes could help her understand how to lead. She looked down on me because of my sports background. She saw me as a jock, a dumb wrestler, not a "fellow intellectual." But if she had coached as much as I had, she would have had a better understanding of what good leadership was. The redo observation went much better and that was the last time she ever observed me.

Becky's climb up the administrative ladder had begun. She had been given an administrative elementary position, which was viewed as a step toward her becoming principal of Wantagh Elementary School when its principal retired in July of 2013.

But that first year didn't go well. Within months the elementary teachers revolted against her leadership. Several of them signed a letter to Superintendent Maureen Goldberg demanding that Becky not become their next principal.

After one more year as an elementary supervisor in Wantagh, Becky, now Dr. Chowske, left the district. She headed to Eastern

Long Island to the Shoreham-Wading River School District, most famously known as the Long Island community whose completed nuclear power plant was never fully operational. Strong opposition to the plant led to it being decommissioned in 1994. Today the Shoreham Energy Center site features two 100-foot wind turbines. Shoreham-Wading River is also famous among the New York wrestling community for producing four-time state champ Jesse Jantzen, who was Harvard's first NCAA wrestling champion in 66 years in 2004. No Long Island wrestler has won a Division I title since Jantzen—going into the 2022 national tournament.

Shoreham-Wading River officials created a position as humanities director for Becky. She did that for two years. But the commute from Western Nassau County was too much so she took a position at Manhasset High School, in Nassau County, where she is today in 2021, as its district coordinator of English language arts and reading.

I have been very critical of Dr. Rebecca Chowske for how she treated me in her last two years at Wantagh High School. She did a good job in her first four years, where she supported my journalism program; she had good ideas. David Dubin, who retired from Wantagh in 2016, was hired to teach AP English classes as a leave replacement in Manhasset for a semester by Dr. Chowske.

"She's much calmer now," David said. "And she praised your teaching, saying that your journalism class was a happy combination of structured and free. That you set the bar for every journalism class she has seen since."

I bear her no ill will. And if she's in her fourth year in a great district like Manhasset, she has figured out the human connection required for educational leadership.

CHAPTER 21

A Journalism Rebound

While Becky's last year, 2012, created two weeks of stress for me, after the collaboration meeting I thrived.

My journalism program rebounded. I had several years with at least one outstanding writer, starting with Kiera Fitzpatrick. While 2009-10 was a low point for Syracuse awards—as we only won three, our fewest in 23 years—my young journalists had great success for the rest of that decade.

Kiera always came up with a well-written front-page story. Her sophomore and junior years featured her byline on six out of eight front-page articles. That continued in her senior year. Her best piece, which won her a Gold at Syracuse and Best News Story at Adelphi, was about the death of journalist Marie Colvin. Kiera came up with the headline: "Uncrowned Queen of Intrepid Journalists."

Kiera's lead: "The siege of Homs in Syria led to the devastating deaths of thousands of Syrians. Western foreign correspondents also fell victim to the perilous warfare. Marie Catherine Colvin, a 56-year-old award-winning American journalist who worked for *The Sunday Times* in London, was killed by a rocket fired by the Syrian military, February 22. Marie Colvin is survived by her mother, Rosemarie, two sisters and her two brothers Michael and Bill residing in New York.

"Bill Colvin, a retired NYPD detective, is currently a security guard at Wantagh High School."

Since Marie's brother Bill Colvin worked in our school, Kiera interviewed him. He gave her insight into his sister Marie Colvin, what motivated her, and exactly what had happened to her in Syria. Bill Colvin still works at Wantagh, where he continues to be a popular and tireless security guard. I always felt safe with Bill around.

We ran a photo of Marie Colvin wearing her black eye patch. "Due to a blast by a Sri Lankan army rocket-propelled grenade,

Colvin lost sight in her left eye," Kiera wrote. "Thereafter, she wore an eye patch. This eye patch became a symbol of not only the dangers of foreign corresponding, and the downfalls of her passion—but also, it became a symbol for Marie Colvin...[she] became recognized for her eye patch and her fearless spirit."

Also killed in the attack was a 28-year-old French photojournalist, Remi Ochlik.

"After Syrian President Bashar al-Assad pledged to kill any journalist who set foot on Syrian soil, her desire to expose the inhumanity made her stay," wrote Kiera. "... the Syrians targeted the makeshift media center where Marie Colvin and Ochlik were located."

Winning any award for News Story didn't happen often for my kids. In 20 years at Adelphi, Kiera's Gold for Best News Story was our only Gold in that category. Indeed, two of our four awards (over those 20 years) for News Story, the most-competitive category in both contests, were by Kiera. She made her readers, her fellow students, understand Marie Colvin and how, despite great danger, she reported to the world what was happening in Syria.

Colvin's life has been immortalized in books and film. *In Extremis, The Life and Death of the War Correspondent Marie Colvin* by Lindsey Hilsum came out in 2018, as did the film *A Private War.*

Kiera's stranglehold on the front page was broken by her protege, Lindsey Cohen, a junior, who wrote about an emotional and powerful Challenge Day program on the only front page that didn't include a Kiera byline over a two-year span.

I was extremely disappointed when Lindsey failed to win an Adelphi award her senior year, 2013. Though one of her best pieces was her last, which came after the Adelphi contest, her Senior Farewell.

I'd inherited the senior farewell concept from previous journalism teachers. I told the kids to write about their experience in the Wantagh School District. They could write about an elementary school teacher, a class, a year, or summarize their entire educational experience. Most students wrote about some aspect of high school.

I shared Lindsey's 2013 Farewell with seniors every May thereafter to show them a senior farewell to model. As a teacher who taught writing and who wrote myself, I always felt that this had been a courageous piece of writing, especially for a 17-year-old.

Lindsey, who was also very visual and today has a career in fashion, came up with the art for her piece. We got the art teacher, Keith Hunter, to put a photo of Lindsey into Edvard Munch's painting "The Scream."

Lindsey's lead: "In preparation for my first day of freshman year, I decided to try out a new persona. A daring one. I would go to a new place to get my eyebrows waxed. I walked in feeling like a certified boss, acting all nonchalant and what not ... After I was made into a bonafide wax-figure, I looked into the mirror ... I bawled and threw a hissy fit ... The whole nail place laughed at my reaction. Half of my left eyebrow was hacked off. My prized possessions were disfigured. And if that didn't foreshadow the rest of my high school experience, I'm not sure what did."

She then wrote a brief summary of each year of high school and gave each a little headline. *Ninth grade: the good, the bad and the UGGly. Eleventh Grade: I'd rather be in an insane asylum*: "I think I was the only one not excited to be an upperclassman. All this meant to me was more responsibility. Things are about to go 'Bad Girls Club' real quick.

"I had two different groups—one that was more my speed and the other that I had been part of for many years. From this large group, three of us stuck together ... Our friendship was all hunky-dory until March. That's when we became immersed in big drama ... but it was more of a silent kind of drama. I was totally caught off guard and confused. 'What was going on?' I constantly asked. No response. It was like they just decided, 'Let's exile Lindsey' as if I were some illegal immigrant. By the time it was over, my friendship with my three best friends was over."

When that final *Warrior* issue came out on June seventh, I had conversations with some upset former friends of Lindsey's and fielded parent calls over the article. Yet I admired her ability to turn the drama into humor and to write about such a painful experience. Few high school kids had to courage to do that.

At the Syracuse contest, in the fall of 2013 after her high school graduation, Lindsey won a Silver for Columnist, as her Farewell was part of a portfolio of her senior-year columns, and she won another for News Story for an article about Superstorm Sandy.

When I look back at my journalism instruction at Wantagh, I have to put Lindsey and Kiera among my top-five, all-time writers. They improved as writers thanks to their talent and because I gave them the freedom to write about what interested them. Their print articles, combined with success in the Syracuse and Adelphi contests, built their confidence. And I simply taught them what I had learned from my teachers and writing mentors, among them some great journalists and newspaper editors.

Kiera and Lindsey's written goodbyes to me conveyed that I still had a strong impact on these children, despite aging—which sapped my energy and intensity. In her Senior Farewell postscript Lindsey wrote a few shoutouts. To me she wrote: "Krav—I know you hate cliches but this lends itself to one, you truly believed in me from the beginning and have really been a mentor. You have listened to every word I have ever said. You've stayed late after school when we had to get an issue out. It was a huge challenge to follow Kiera but you made me feel just as able ... I can't thank you enough."

All successful careers reward you in different ways. In teaching, you appreciate kids expressing their thanks for your effort. And while the job has a great deal of stress at times, seeing these teenagers grow up and blossom into adults is the best reward. One good aspect of social media is that it enables you to see this take place.

Kiera wrote in my 2012 yearbook: "Undoubtedly, you have made the greatest impact on not only my high school career, but my life. Thank you for truly inspiring me. Your class not only drove me to find a passion but to have confidence. I'll truly miss writing for you and your crazy emails. Never change, you are an amazing teacher. Throughout high school you acted as a father figure to me. You always knew what to say and I think you really allowed me to strengthen my relationship with my father ... Thank you for everything. I can't say enough. Thank you for believing in me when I didn't."

While Kiera didn't pursue a writing career, today she's a nurse working with medically fragile children. Some are on ventilators while others suffered severe abuse or are in palliative care; they suffer from cancer and rare genetic disorders.

* * *

The year after Lindsey graduated, it appeared we'd be shut out at the Adelphi contest. In the previous 13 years we had only been shut out once, a decade before. As the awards were called out, we won nothing in the first five out of six categories we'd entered. I thought about what to say to the kids on the bus ride back to school.

We were down to the last category we were entered in, Most Outstanding Reporter—our last hope. We didn't get Honorable Mention, nor Bronze. I figured that Silver was our last chance. No Silver for Wantagh. I sagged in my seat. The kids comforted me.

"And the Gold for Most Outstanding Reporter goes to Dan Parker from Wantauck High School," the moderator said.

"Great job Dan," I screamed. The kids cheered. My most outstanding editor-in-chief Dan Parker had saved us.

The next year, 2015, Bianca Buffamonte, a senior, took journalism for the first time. Her older sister Stephanie had been an editor a few years before. Stephanie, a good editor, got a TV news reporter job in Wisconsin and now is much warmer working for Orlando Fox 35 TV in Florida.

Bianca immediately displayed incredible writing talent. She won four awards at Syracuse in four different categories. That achievement helped that group win 16 awards at Syracuse, the most ever in a single year for one of my staffs.

Bianca also led the way at Adelphi by winning our second straight Gold for Most Outstanding Reporter. Also taking a Gold that year at Adelphi was a freshman, Grace Tague. Grace won for an opinion piece about how her home, which had been flooded 16 months before in Superstorm Sandy, was still not repaired and habitable due to bureaucratic delays by the Town of Hempstead and insurance issues.

The majority of awards in these contests were won by seniors—rarely freshmen. Grace would win two more Syracuse awards and one more at Adelphi. She would take the class three out of the next four years.

As I raced towards age 60, losing all semblance of coolness caused my journalism numbers to tumble. It's amazing that great kids like Grace stayed with the class in order to be part of the school newspaper. Because as we reached the next decade, the 2020s, newspapers struggled financially and cut jobs. A career in print journalism has lost the popularity it had in the 80s and 90s. During this time I Googled Frank Mickens to locate him so I could thank him. Instead I found his 2009 obituary.

"Mr. Mickens created a haven within the walls of the school, at 1700 Fulton Street, and a chance for children to succeed," wrote Dennis Hevesi in a 2009 *New York Times* obituary. "Mr. Mickens's efforts drew national attention and were compared to those of Joe Clark, the baseball-bat-wielding principal in Paterson, N.J., who was the subject of the movie *Lean on Me*."

Mickens retired at age 58 after 18 years as Boys and Girls Principal. He died five years later. A *Daily News* article by Joyce Shelby said that Mickens retired with 309 unused sick days.

"I worked from six a.m. to nine or ten at night, five days a week, plus Saturdays, Sundays and holidays," Mickens said.

I felt terrible that I hadn't looked him up years before so I could have thanked him for his speech from 25 years before, on my first day as a teacher, to tell him how much those *nine* words did for my teaching career and my thousands of students—and my three children.

CHAPTER 22

My Children's Education

Rebecca Mae had struggled to maintain focus in school. But after tenth grade she matured and her behavior improved, as did her grades. She reverted to bad habits her senior year, doing little work in 2013. Rebecca wasn't as strong a student as Dana or Brett, but she still hoped to attend a good college.

Dana had graduated from the University of Michigan with an industrial and operations engineering degree. That helped her land a good Wall Street job. Corporate Wall Street quickly bored her. She fled New York for a job for a more granola corporate setting at Epic, a medical software company just outside of Madison, Wisconsin. She liked the Epic campus, especially the culinary choices there.

Brett was also in Madison in his junior year, working towards his geotechnical engineering degree, at the University of Wisconsin.

Rebecca Mae applied to several colleges and universities and was accepted to nearly every one of them, however, she was waitlisted at Wisconsin. Her junior year she attended a soccer clinic run there by the Wisconsin women's coaching staff. She didn't do well in some of the drills; she didn't know them. She scored in the scrimmage, as she could always put the ball in the net against top competition. She wasn't a DI prospect, though in my delusional-sports-parent mind I believed she could be.

She played for Commack's varsity soccer team and for top travel teams. She was aggressive, strong and fast with a huge left leg. Her Commack team upset No. 1-seeded West Islip in the Suffolk County Class AA quarters, led by an eventual Division I Boston University four-year soccer player, Erin Neville. However, Commack dropped a 1-0 game in the semis.

Rebecca's soccer skills and dedication to training peaked in her junior year. Her interest in sports faded. She dropped basketball after sophomore year and then said she would not play lacrosse her senior year though she had been a varsity player sophomore and junior years.

Meanwhile, we got to work on trying to move her off the wait-list and gain acceptance to Wisconsin. Frank Muzio, my former fellow wrestling coach, was now director of the guidance department at Wantagh and suggested that we reach out to admissions at Wisconsin as they probably only had one person who worked on all Long Island student applications.

He was right. And that admissions person was named Rebecca. Rebecca wrote Rebecca a letter, saying that the last admitted student from her high school to enroll at Wisconsin had been her brother from three years before and that she would enroll at Wisconsin if she were admitted. Her SATs were borderline, though she took them and the ACTs several times. Dana and Brett loved to read but Rebecca didn't, and it showed in her English and reading standardized test scores.

The weeks passed and we didn't hear from Wisconsin. We sent a deposit to Penn State. She would return to my home state and be a Nittany Lion. She was happy with that decision.

Then we heard from Wisconsin. She got in; she wanted to go.

Jennifer didn't think she should. "Rebecca, Wisconsin is really a difficult school," Jennifer said. "And we'll lose our deposit to Penn State."

Rebecca loved the city of Madison and the beautiful campus on an isthmus, though she was unsure of a major. Jennifer confided to me that she feared Rebecca might flunk out. I believed if she worked hard, she could succeed at UW Madison. She competed with her siblings and I knew she wanted to do well like they had. Plus, she wouldn't major in engineering. When she really wanted something she worked hard. I was more upbeat than Jennifer about her prospects. We owed her a chance so she headed Midwest to Madison, and that settled all three of our children in the Wisconsin capitol.

In our visits there from 2010-2017 we enjoyed great meals in terrific restaurants, devoured cheese curds and consumed

Leinenkugels in the summer sun at the Student Union on Lake Mendota, munched out at the giant Sunday farmer's market, watched football games at Camp Randall with its earthquake-like third quarter jump-arounds, explored Frank Lloyd Wright houses and quirky Wisconsin sites like the House on the Rock, and of course played pond ice hockey. Nobody ice fished.

Brett graduated in four years, in 2014. I was incredibly proud that we had another engineer. He'd fared better than Frank Lloyd Wright and Charles Lindbergh, both Wisconsin engineering dropouts.

Brett earned his master's degree in geotechnical engineering from the Colorado School of Mines, and today he is building solar farms and wind turbines all across the United States.

Dana disliked the less-intense version of corporate America and got a two-year degree in graphic design at Madison Area Technical College. She worked as a graphic designer in Madison. She was much happier.

As for Rebecca Mae, she worked incredibly hard and graduated in four years with a higher GPA than her siblings. All of our children had higher college GPAs than either Jennifer or I had. Today Rebecca Mae is successful at selling a real estate social-media platform for a New Zealand-based startup. And ironically her boyfriend went to Boys and Girls High School for a year where his principal was, yup, Frank Mickens. After three years of working for a real estate company as a graphic designer, Dana Rose interviewed for weeks and landed a job as a graphic designer for Square Roots, "an urban indoor farm growing food and training urban farmers." Co-founded by Kimbal Musk, Elon's brother, it currently has two locations: Michigan and Bedford-Stuyvesant. Jennifer and I are incredibly proud of our three children.

My teaching improved my parenting and bolstered our kids' excellent education in Long Island's public schools. I was on the same schedule as them. I had insight into their high school work and was fortunate to know talented colleagues who tutored them in math and science; I helped them in English and social studies. I tutored for the SATs and ACTs and I showed them various techniques beginning with practicing timed tests; I went over tricky grammar questions. Jennifer and I were a very good parenting team with different skill sets. Parenting three children dramatically improved my teaching, too.

CHAPTER 23

Faith—But Not in Shap

The journey through my teaching career would be incomplete without attempting to characterize Kevin Shapiro, a respected (sort of) member of the social studies department.

David Dubin discovered Shapiro, whose mom owned a place in Cherry Gove, Fire Island, where David summered. He later called it a mistake bringing Shapiro to Wantagh for an interview, and additionally professed regret for fighting for my hiring. In my case David did a good thing for the community. As for Shap, well—you judge.

Shapiro's epidermis features a multitude of tattoos. They are not on his forearms nor his neck or face but he vows, as he rolls into his 18th year of teaching at Wantagh here in 2020-21, that when his boss Dr. Christopher Widmann, who he calls Dr. Wid-money, retires he will properly ink his neck.

To say Shap is a character fails to observe the scope of his outrageous personality packed into his small body. While I can only go by his students' claims that he's a good teacher, he is an excellent poker player. He'll bring a couple of 40-ouncers of gnarly beer to the games and get "kermuzzled." The more kermuzzled he gets the better he plays. In an aggressive teachers' poker game, he's tough out. I hate going against him as he three bets and chirps incessantly.

About a decade ago, in a game at my house, he confused my big red double front doors with the toilet and urinated on them.

"Shap you dick, that's not cool," I said.

"Wha-" was his answer, as he finished off Jennifer's favorite bottle of flavored vodka. I had also repeatedly warned him not to pet our crazy dog, Toby. While very cute, Toby harbored an intense dislike of humanity (except for our family and a few female friends), though he was great with other dogs. Shapiro stroked Toby's head despite my repeated warnings for him to stop.

"Yo, this dawg loves me," Shap said. A snapping sound followed as Toby's teeth slashed into Shap's hand. I quickly removed Shap from the sofa, lest he drip blood on it. Usually when Toby bit someone, one of the kids' friends, we rushed to his aid. In Shap's case we laughed.

Meanwhile, he has four kids and a lovely wife; he's a great father.

I was shocked that he had a bar mitzvah. The way he speaks you'd think he grew up in Bed-Stuy during my Boys and Girls High School days. When you ask him where is from, he says, "Roncompton." Which means Ronkonkoma in Central Suffolk County. But he graduated, allegedly, from Ward Melville High School, which is in a pretty nice community.

In our first *Warrior* article on him, the headline read "The Original Wangsta." David Dubin rushed into my room waving the newspaper at me and said, "You can't publish this!"

"Why?" I said.

"You can't have a headline that calls Kevin a wangsta. You are going to have to reprint."

"Nobody will care," I said. I mean, it wasn't like there were cocks in Shapiro's article. Besides in those days, 2003, few people knew that a wangsta was a White gangster. In time one of Kevin's many nicknames among faculty became Wang.

His students' love for him didn't help him get his grades in on time. And grading had become much easier thanks to computerized programs that crunched the numbers. Long gone are the time-consuming days of calculators. If grades are due at midnight, Shap will scramble to punch the final numbers in by 11:59 p.m., driving Dr. Wid-money to drink a 40 of Pabst Blue Ribbon.

In our teachers' monthly poker games, we keep standings—with the title awarded to whosoever compiles the most points after 12 monthly games. Shap refers to himself as "the world's greatest poker player." He was the world's greatest without a title until 2014-15 when he won the last monthly game to edge me out for his only Wantagh Teachers' title. I came back two years later to edge him out for my only crown. Several guys have multiple titles. The best poker player without a Wantagh title is currently Jay Apfelbaum, a math teacher who often starts out with a huge chip stack but whose uber aggressiveness invariably falters.

Kevin Shapiro loves the New York Mets, perhaps more than he loves his children or his pit bulls, which he calls his "bullies." Every year he tries to bet anyone on anything about the Mets. "They gonna win the World Series, huh!" he says. That's cost him—the Mets haven't won since 1986.

One year he bet Rich Colavita $50 that Mets knuckleballer R.A. Dickey would win the Cy Young award as baseball's best pitcher. It was a silly bet. Colavita jumped on it especially when Shapiro refused any odds, which should have been about 500-1 in his favor. What happened? Whaddya think? R.A. Dickey became the first knuckleball pitcher to ever win the Cy Young, in 2012. If Shapiro had made that bet at a Vegas sports book he could have won tens of thousands of dollars.

The poker crowd is always betting. One of the best poker players, Antonio Benito, a Spanish teacher, is quick to bet on anything. When we have a teachers' golf foursome, there's usually a lot of low-stakes action—featuring payouts for birdies and greenies but never sandies, because I'm too good in the sand.

One of our favorite parkland tracts is a public gem called Town of Oyster Bay, only 5,800 yards from the white tees but filled with tight, perilous holes.

Mike Tallarine shanked a shot into the woods on No. 2 there, a decade ago, and instead of blaming his poor swing, he proclaimed, "There are gremlins here." Since then we refer to the course as Gremlins. Our most infamous hole there is No. 6, a downhill par three. Mario Espinosa, a Spanish teacher who we call Espo, declared on the tee that he could reach the green with a seven-iron from 160 yards.

Physics teacher Rich Colavita quickly calculated—in the hard drive that is his brain—that based on Espo's swing speed, a 20-mile-per-hour wind in his face, and the now-increased psychological pressure, a seven-iron would never reach the green.

"Bet $5 that you can't," Rich said.

"I agree," said Espo.

His shot landed 30 yards short. "Double or nothing," said Espo, teeing up another ball.

"Okay," said Rich.

That shot landed 20 yards short. He was getting closer.

"Double or nothing?" said Rich.

Espo's final attempt again sliced well short of the green. And while Espo paid Rich the $10 for the initial double or nothing, he has claimed that he did not verbally confirm that second double or nothing.

Anytime we golf at "Gremlins" Rich insists that Espo owes him another $10. Pretty much anytime we talk golf, Rich insists Espo hand over $10. Whenever we step on the No. 6 tee someone says, "Betcha I can hit the green with a seven-iron."

If Espo is there, he neither laughs nor acknowledges the legitimacy of Rich's demand for $10. Mercifully, Shapiro is never there—though if he threatens to try golf his non-stop chatter would be unacceptably annoying.

Shap's golfing wouldn't be as bad as David Dubin's attempt to golf. David lacks the least bit of athleticism and harbors a deep dislike of all sports. After a few terribly frustrating months he had me sell his clubs, golf bag and crappy golf balls on eBay. I got him about a hundred bucks and didn't even take a cut.

* * *

Coaching a high school golf team is a coveted position and Rich Colavita had always dreamed of doing it. When the Wantagh boys' varsity golf position opened up in 2009, Rich applied for it. Though he had never coached a team at the high school. I told Jennifer that the job was open and she insisted that I put in for it, too. I wasn't sure. At that point Brett and Rebecca Mae were playing a lot of sports and I wanted to watch them. But Jennifer pestered me so I applied for the position. Rich and I became the frontrunners.

The more I thought about it, I realized I might enjoy the very short fall season—which featured warm, dry weather, as opposed to chilly, wet spring golf, when the other half of Long Island's teams played. John Cuiffo, who had stepped down as lacrosse coach to become athletic director, faced a difficult decision in choosing between Rich and me. That gave me an idea.

"Rich, why don't we co-coach," I said. "We can split the salary and that way if one of us has to do something the other one is there to cover."

Rich liked that idea as he didn't care about the full salary, nor did I. Cuiffo loved that he didn't have to choose one of us. A golf partnership was born that has lasted to this day, here in 2021.

In our first year we had a terrific team. We had several very good golfers. We went 9-5 and defeated golf powerhouse Massapequa once, dropping the second match. We would never come close to beating Massapequa again. Kevin Fanning and Andrew Onufrey qualified for the county tournament.

I guess my wife was right, as I have enjoyed coaching golf. There are no fans nor referees. If the kids disagree about a rule, we coaches tell them to work it out unless they can't and we reluctantly step in. We are not allowed to coach the boys in competition. It's less stressful than coaching wrestling.

We practice at the five-course Bethpage municipal golf facility, but never on the famous Black course. During practices Rich and I play nine holes with the kids. Both Rich and I are about 12 handicappers with different skills. A lefty, Rich has a perfect swing; I scramble well with a solid array of chips and flop shots.

Coaches play in the middle of matches, which consist of three foursomes. We need to be near the kids, who will be a couple of miles out on the course, in case something happens. What could happen? An injury from a kid tripping over a root or getting hit by a ball. A golfer nearly stepped on a big fox once; luckily it didn't bite him.

As we readied for year two, our school board cut the golf team—yet another of that whacky board's decisions. It would save them $14,000 for the coach's salary, bussing costs and green fees. Every dollar counts, but in a $70 million budget was that a necessary savings?

Meanwhile, the board said that the parents could fundraise the money to save the team. The parents of our two best senior players,

Andrew Onufrey and Mike Robbins, quickly got to work. They had recent practice from when the district budget had been voted down.

Within a month the golf parents had fundraised the $14,000 and the golf team was reinstated. Wantagh parents love their sports teams. The board never tried to dump us again.

We had 24 boys and girls try out for the team in 2012. We had to cut. Cutting a child from a team is a horrible experience for the child, his or her parents and for the coaches. No coach wants to tell a kid he or she has been cut. Rich and I rated all of the kids at the driving range on hot August days before classes start. Then we took them all out to play nine holes. The kids who scored the best made the team.

Since we did not have a girls golf team, girls could play on the boys' team. Three girls tried out. One girl made the team—a small seventh grader named Faith Francioso. Rich had a lot of faith in Faith. "She is going to be our greatest golfer ever," he said excitedly. I didn't see what he saw but she was good.

One of the girls we had to cut, a senior named Kristen Struzzieri, had looked good on the range but couldn't break 60 for nine holes. We also had to cut an all-state wrestler, Dan McDevitt, who had potential but also shot a high score. I played in his group and can still see him slicing a shot into the woods on No. 4, a short and easy par three, on Bethpage Yellow—the easiest of Bethpage's courses.

We felt awful about cutting both of these seniors. At parent-teacher night Kristen's parents confronted me. They were upset, especially her mom.

"Didn't you tell her that she would probably make the team?" her mom said.

"First of all, Rich said that," I said. "She did great on the range but we had 24 kids try out and we had to base the final cut on what they shot for nine holes. We kept 13 kids, which is a lot." Her dad accepted that and Kristen got over it pretty quickly. But sports cuts linger with parents.

Meanwhile, the five-foot-two-inch seventh grader Faith earned one of the six starting spots on our varsity squad. Rich was right, she was a prodigy.

It was unfortunate that we didn't have a girls' team. Faith was a varsity starter for six years. She qualified for the boys' county tournament from freshman year on. She had learned the game in the First Tee program and played in many outside competitions. She improved every year. By her junior year she was a two handicap. She drove the ball down the middle, around 220 yards.

From freshman year on she played in the No. 1 spot and often beat other teams' best male players, from the same tees as the boys. We switched into a different conference that included South Side, Oceanside and Garden City—very strong teams, all of which practiced and played home matches at country clubs. One year we were going to play at the famous Men's Club (Garden City Country Club)—rated as one of the top courses in the nation. But when the club's members learned we had a girl on the boys' team, we instead played at the Cherry Valley Club— also a nice tract.

Faith's junior season was interrupted by a trip to California, where she played with a senior tour pro in The First Tee Nature Valley Open at Pebble Beach. *Newsday's* golf writer Mark Herrmann wrote about her trip there, the summer before she went, in "LI's Faith Francioso to play in First Tee Open at Pebble Beach."

"So far, she says the most beautiful course she ever has played is Sebonack in Southampton," Herrmann wrote. "She has seen Pebble Beach only on TV. 'TV probably doesn't do it justice,' she said, adding that her parents both will go to California to see her among golf's legends. 'I'm still kind of speechless.'"

In a *Warrior* article my editor-in-chief Grace Anne McKenna quoted me: "Faith is an extraordinary golfer. This season I was astounded how she beat the No. 1 golfer from nearly every team we played. These are boys who hit the ball significantly further than her and are very low handicaps."

Despite our fall season, our individual county championship was in the spring. So, in the spring of 2017, Faith, along with two of our other golfers—a big Spaniard, Raul Fernandez, whose family had left Galicia, Spain some years before, and James Tucker—all qualified to play in the Nassau County tournament.

Faith, who always played from the same tees as the boys, shot an 80 on Bethpage Blue on day one to make the cut, becoming Rich's and my first golfer to do so. Day two, on a very long and difficult Bethpage Red, she shot an 85 and finished just outside the top 20 out of nearly 130 golfers, all of whom except her were boys.

That earned her a two-page spread in *Newsday*. The second graph said that Faith had been only the third girl to ever make the cut at the Nassau County boys' championship.

The first girl to do it, Annie Park of Levittown, not only made the cut but won the tournament in 2012 with a stunning four under par 66 on Bethpage Red on day two. She followed that up by capturing the NCAA Division I Women's Golf individual title by six strokes as a freshman leading USC to the team national championship. Park has been on the LPGA Tour since 2016 and has won a tournament there.

Faith's talent didn't compare to Annie Park's, however, had Faith played on a girls' team she would have contended for multiple girls' county championships. But in the 2017 *Newsday* piece by Sal Cacciatore, she said she was glad she didn't play on a girls' team.

"I really like the competitive environment. I'm not saying it's easier for the girls (teams) but I do think being in an environment where it is all boys has really pushed my game and myself as a person."

During her senior season in a match against Sewanhaka, Faith battled an excellent No. 1, Tim Na, who bombed the golf ball. On the match's fifth hole, No. 13 on Eisenhower Blue, Na aced the 296-yard par four.

On the last hole of the match, as Faith lined up her final putt, I walked over to her and said, "How many strokes are you down by?"

"If I make this putt I win by one," Faith said.

I couldn't believe it. Na had a hole-in-one on a par four and yet Faith had a chance to beat him. But she lipped out that putt and they tied with 38. Fernandez shot a 36 that day. He was having a great season. Our team total was 206, the lowest ever for one of Rich and my teams, as we won that match. In our golf matches you totaled the five lowest scores out of the six players who competed and the team with the lowest total earned three points with each victory worth a point—we won 7.5-1.5.

Rich and I didn't coach Faith in terms of how to play the game. She competed year-round and had professional coaching. We played many practice rounds with her and she beat me every time, though she wasn't even paying attention or keeping score.

The only bit of coaching I ever suggested came in my last practice round with her before the county tournament in her senior year. On the ninth hole at Bethpage Blue, she was annoyed that her second shot landed short of the green. She wanted a birdie on that hole. She had a short pitch shot left.

"If this were Tiger," I said to her, "he wouldn't be thinking about how he should have made a birdie, he would focus on holing this pitch to make a birdie." She hit that pitch an inch from the cup.

In the county tournament that year she shot a four over 76 in round one at Bethpage Blue. That put her in fifth place. The top nine would qualify for the state tournament. I followed her during day two on Bethpage Red in her final holes.

She mounted a back-nine charge paring holes 14-17, including the very difficult uphill, 470-par four 15th, but came up just short of qualifying for states. She finished in the top 20.

Coaching Faith was a pleasure. No other golfer of ours has ever reached day two of the county golf tournament. And we've had some good ones. She wound up being a four-time boys varsity golf team MVP.

Now a junior at Elon University in 2021, Faith is in her third year on the women's golf team, where she cracked the starting lineup in the spring. She's doing well academically. She was a straight-A student in high school. She is a quiet, wonderful young lady, and certainly was the most successful athlete I coached at Wantagh in seven years of wrestling and 12 years of golf.

CHAPTER 24

Can I Retire Now?

It was my 29th year of teaching in New York's public schools and my 26th at Wantagh. By the time that year had ended, if I could have retired I would have. But I needed to get to year 30 to maximize my pension benefits.

My ninth period freshman class took me back to my JHS 142 days. I had a senior sports fiction/nonfiction class that one boy made unteachable. I dealt with a sociopath and struggled with Jimmy Joyce—the best athlete I ever taught but not the best student—in two classes and a study hall.

And while my teacher/student relationship with Jimmy Joyce was complex, I liked him and tried to keep him focused on his studies. Jimmy fooled around, seeking my attention and laughter from his friends, though he was very intelligent.

In January of his senior year his misdeeds left me with no alternative but to call one of his parents. I didn't want to call either, as I knew they were both disciplinarians—but I had him three times per day and needed him to listen to me.

His dad, a massive weightlifter, had been banned from going to Wantagh baseball games for screaming at umpires and coaches. I knew his mom better as I'd taught Jimmy's older sister and had Jimmy in freshman English. Jimmy's mom was also ripped with muscle from intensive weightlifting. She seemed more reasonable, however, so I called her.

As a result, his friends claimed that she'd thrown Jimmy out of the house and he was homeless. He brought an overnight bag to class and pulled out his toothbrush to prove that he had to sleep at different friends' homes. His acting didn't match his athleticism, convincing me it was a ruse to gain sympathy.

Calling his mom led to his improved behavior. His Journalism II class was the smallest I'd ever had with only 11 students in it—nine girls and two boys. I struggled to get Jimmy to write anything.

While students did not have to write articles that made it into print, I tried to create the incentive for them to do so. It increased the learning experience for students to attach their byline to a print article. I campaigned all year for Jimmy to publish his articles in print—with a byline.

He wrote three articles that landed in the last two print issues.

Meanwhile, Jimmy's athleticism astounded all of Long Island. He closed out his junior year by leading Wantagh to a state title in baseball, Keith Sachs' second state title as a baseball coach.

After a great season and postseason run through Long Island opponents, Jimmy, a hard-throwing righty, pitched a one-hitter, leading Wantagh to a 2-1 semifinal win over previously unbeaten Queensbury High School in the state semis. Then in extra innings, with the state championship game tied at 5-5, Jimmy rocked a two-out fastball over the fence to lift Wantagh to a 6-5 state title victory over Williamsville East.

As a fall encore, Jimmy helped Wantagh go 12-0 in football and beat Boomer Esiason's alma mater East Islip 21-14 for the Long Island Class III championship in front of over 5,000 fans. That game concludes the football postseason as New York does not have a state football championship. It was Keith Sachs second L.I. championship as head coach.

Jimmy helped Wantagh break a 7-7 tie with a one-handed, leaping interception to set up a TD giving Wantagh its first lead of the game. And then he helped Wantagh return to the state baseball championship game in the spring of 2017. It was an astounding calendar year of success. I wrote *Sports Illustrated* attempting to get him in *Faces in the Crowd*—an unsuccessful effort.

One thing I wouldn't do for Jimmy was fix him up with my golfer Faith. I never paid attention to who the kids dated. True, I had once over 20 years before suggested to one of my wrestlers, Mike Russo, that he go out with Erin Barry and they did eventually marry and have a beautiful family today—you might recall from earlier. But that began and ended my student matchmaking. Jimmy's movie-star handsomeness got him girlfriends. Faith had had a boyfriend for a short time.

"Krav," Jimmy said to me in the middle of his senior year. "Fix me up with Faith."

"No way," I said.

"Come on Krav, you owe me," Jimmy said.

"What?"

"Remember when I was homeless because of you?"

"You were never homeless," I said. "And if you like her go ask her out yourself."

"She'll listen to you, Krav," he said.

I'm fairly certain that the best athlete I ever taught and the most successful athlete I ever coached at Wantagh never got together.

* * *

My ninth period freshman class only had 17 students. Yet three girls made my attempts to teach it utterly miserable. One of the girls was named Barbarino. That connection to John Travolta's infamous character, Vinnie Barbarino, was bad karma—for sure.

Ms. Barbarino was the physical antipode of Vinnie. She was a pretty, short, brown-eyed girl, who was not as disruptive as her famous fictional TV namesake. And she wasn't loud like disruptive girl No. 2, whose piercing cheerleader voice could crack an eardrum. That girl also once tossed her massive backpack at me as if she were hallway bowling for Kravitz. I somehow dodged her toss, as she was a strong and athletic young lady, with an incredible soccer throw in. Her older brother had been one of my all-time best-behaved students. The third girl who was tough to teach was just somewhat hyper. Her older brother had also been hyper, though her older sister was well behaved.

I had the three girls sit in different corners of the room. I dreaded ninth period, as the trio had post-lunch energy and required way more attention and focus than I, on the back nine of my 50s, could muster.

Nearly all of the other students in that class were reasonably well behaved, outside of a bit of freshman immaturity. One student, Johnny King, was a very good ice hockey player. I called him Johnny Hockey, referring to the New Jersey-born-and-raised phenom on the NHL's Calgary Flames, Johnny Gaudreau. I ended up skating with Johnny Hockey in a few open skates. He was a small freshman who tried to dangle through everybody. As a senior he grew into a bigger and more well-rounded player who did well in junior hockey.

That year in a *Warrior* article on the school ice hockey club, the Baymen, my reporter Bridget Connolly included my skate with the boys.

"Over the holiday break, a number of the Baymen players played open ice hockey at Long Beach Arena with Mr. Kravitz, a long-time Wantagh English teacher who has played recreationally for nearly 30 years," wrote Connolly. "'I was truly impressed with every one of the boys' hockey abilities,' said Kravitz. 'Connor Green skates like Bobby Orr. Kieren Baisley is super-fast with great hockey sense. Zach Candela was an all-around amazing player and Johnny King, while only a freshman, was hanging with the big boys.'"

That quote helped me teach a lesson on hyperbole. And it highlighted an era of great hockey by the Wantagh-Seaford Baymen. I taught all of those boys as freshmen and convinced Baisley, Green and Candela to play on the golf team, with Candela becoming an excellent golfer. In addition, Baisley and Johnny Hockey were sports editors for me on the *Warrior*.

My period-nine trio of hyper girls, meanwhile, was enraged that I'd skated with Johnny Hockey. He was quiet and better behaved than the girls, though he had a few moments of disruption. It seemed as if the trio at times dragged down other kids into their behavioral abyss. The girls were a year-long, non-stop-bouncing-out-of-their-seats disruption. And I will admit that dealing with gimme-gimme attention was not my strength.

That year I also had a student who the other kids insisted was a sociopath. The boy was in my first-semester inclusion senior sports class. Let's call him Leonardo MacDonough—not his real name. With the special education teacher Kathy Butler sitting behind him Leo behaved, so much that I questioned the kids' stories about his violent exploits. He was bright and loved history. Though it was a sports class, historical issues often popped up, whether it was from reading the W.P. Kinsella's novel *Shoeless Joe* and his short story "The Last Pennant Before Armageddon" or watching films like *Cinderella Man* or *Secretariat*.

Kathy Butler and I collaborated beautifully, as Lisa Watkins and I had. Kathy graduated from Wantagh. Her younger sister had been in my first class with Marylou back in 1991. Her dad, Joe Delgais, often subbed in Wantagh back then after a 35-year teaching career at Baldwin High School. He'd also coached several varsity high school football teams and coached Wantagh's seventh grade football team. Kathy's children went to Seaford but she had a niece and nephew at Wantagh. My Wantagh teaching for nearly three decades created a small-town feel. My connection to the Delgais family ran so deep I felt a part of it.

Toughness defined Kathy. No kid fooled around in her presence. She was my perfect compliment. I dreamed about having her power to shut down the most hyper student. Kathy just looked at Leo and he shrank in his seat. But again, that was an exhausting year for me with Jimmy Joyce and the ninth-period-trio of rambunctious girls.

In the spring of 2016 Kathy had been inducted into the Nassau County High School Athletics Hall of Fame, as she had been one of the first windmill-female softball pitchers on Long Island. Among the 31 inductees with her in the class of 2016 were Julius Erving of Roosevelt High School and Al Oerter, four-time Olympic Gold Medalist in the discus, from Sewanhaka High School.

My associate editor Jacqueline Schroder wrote a front-page article on Kathy, for which she won one of three Golds that year in the Syracuse contest where we totaled 13 awards. Kathy also played softball at C.W. Post College (now known as Long Island University Post)—and is also in the New York State Softball Hall of Fame.

Leo was such an excellent student the first semester that I thought the kids were pranking me about his alleged incidents. I'd seen no hint of misbehavior from him. Then came the second semester, when I no longer taught Leo, with Kathy Butler hovering over him. He began to appear in my period seven class. I'd politely say, "Leo, could you please go to your class." Off he went—without any issues. At first I didn't ask him what class he had.

That period seven senior sports class quickly roiled out of my control, due to a couple of boys. The main disruptive one we'll call Ronan Gottschald, another *nom de guerre*. Ronan was smart, sought attention, and spewed racist commentary. I addressed his racism the moment he uttered it. Every child in that class was White. The decade of the teens continued to bring very few African-American students to Wantagh. Also, that class, like most of my sports litera-ture/nonfiction classes, had few girls—13 boys out of 17 students. Except for Ronan they were all good kids, with a couple of minor behavioral issues, which Ronan exacerbated.

By that 2016-17 year I started my sports class with an excerpt from Andre Agassi's autobiography *Open*, followed by a *Sports Illustrated* article "Did This Man Really Cut Michael Jordan" by Thomas Lake. Then came a documentary, *Tiger Woods: The Rise and Fall.*

Now, like a lot of White kids who had racist tendencies, Ronan liked Michael Jordan. I never heard any racist comments as we read about the great cutting myth, how Jordan was put on the JV in tenth grade and not the varsity because the coach Pop Herring needed height. Another sophomore Leroy Smith, who was six feet seven inches tall, made the varsity over the then much-shorter Jordan.

Ronan made no racist remarks as we watched Jordan's angry Basketball Hall of Fame acceptance speech and Tiger Woods' incred-ible chip shot on No. 16 at the Masters that led him to victory over Chris DiMarco. And Ronan did well on the assessment for that Agassi-Jordan-Woods unit, which was always an essay comparing how those three greats were parented. (Agassi's and Woods' fathers were completely over-the-top sports dads, especially compared to Jordan's mellow father.)

After Ronan saw that I didn't scream and send kids to the dean, he became bolder with his attention-seeking behavior. And we were on our third dean after Ron Lebel and Ody's one year. We now had Jennifer Santorello as an assistant principal and dean. Santorello was very good at some aspects of that position. We were still writing cuts and misconducts on paper and she computerized all of that which was much more efficient. But she was no Ron Lebel when it came to dealing with difficult behavior. Santorello always said, "Call the parents." She appeared very focused on climbing the administrative ladder and moved on after three years. That's not criticism. She was intelligent, had technological savvy and was a good hire for a higher-paying district.

Ronan took advantage of my patience and created obnoxious noises with his phone to disrupt his class—making his friends giggle. At first I couldn't figure out who was doing it, though I suspected him. And about the same time Leo stopped sitting in the class and began to hide in the back of the room under a long computer table that I used for the newspaper kids after school. Ronan and others helped hide Leo from me.

It became a game. How long will it take Krav to see that Leo is under the back table?

At first I showed patience, then I became annoyed.

"Leo, what class do you have?" I said, as he sauntered out of my room.

"I don't have a class," he lied.

I looked up his schedule, which I should have done at the start, and saw he had John Hampson's senior elective on song lyrics a little way down the hall. John later said that Leo was really abusing the bathroom pass at that time.

I spoke to John and told him what was going on with Leo. But Leo was very clever and he probably came up with other reasons why he *had* to leave John's class. Now, at this point I should have called his parents. That was my mistake. Call the parents. Don't hesitate out of kindness or patience. But Leo had been so great the first semester, I was sure he would finally listen to me and stop hiding under the desk. I should have seen the behavioral disconnect. And perhaps I didn't realize that his early good behavior had only been due to Kathy Butler.

One morning he hid under the desk in my senior class. As he left the room I angrily warned him to never do it again. Later that same day, with Ronan blocking him, I spotted Leo hiding there. I couldn't believe it and I snapped.

I usually had tremendous patience. In all of my years at Wantagh, with the sweat hogs and many crazy stunts pulled by teenagers, I had only lost my composure a couple of times. But Leo drew the magma of hot emotion up into my brain.

As Leo walked out of the room I left with him, abandoning my class—which I shouldn't have done. I would have walked him to the dean's office but Santorello was on a field trip that day. I walked into John Hampson's class with Leo, shut the door, and exploded.

"What is wrong with you Leo?" I screamed in his face, in front of John and his students. "How many times did I tell you to stay out of my class?"

I was a foot from him screaming at full volume.

"Fuck you, you pussy," he screamed back at me.

"Don't talk to me like that," I screamed.

I wanted him to try to punch me and then I would slam him with a wrestling move.

"Why don't you hit me you fucking pussy!" he screamed.

John Hampson stood there, amazed.

"It was pretty intense," he later said. "I remember him (Leo) seeming stunned that his complete lack of respect had finally caught up with him." Then John called the office and asked for a security guard to be sent immediately.

"Hit me," Leo screamed. "Go ahead you coward." I had enough composure to be surprised at this effort to bait me into throwing the first punch. I was much bigger than him, by about 70 pounds. I watched his hands hoping that he would throw the first punch. I wouldn't use fists. I visualized the body lock I would clap on him but only if he threw the first punch.

A security guard—Bill Colvin, our best one as I've said—came in and hauled Leo away. He knew all about Leo, as he knew every troubled kid, and took him to an empty back gym to let him cool down. Leo was very upset and angry—and possibly unpredictably dangerous at that point. I apologized to John Hampson and didn't look at the students in Leo's class. I walked back across the hall and quickly composed myself.

I entered my class. All of my students sat there.

"What happened?" they asked me. I wasn't sure if they'd heard the screaming. Because the doors had been shut, it appeared they hadn't. I was happy that I hadn't lost it in front of my class. And I was really glad no kid in John Hampson's class had videoed me. I'd seen many phone videos of teachers losing it and it's not a pretty moment for us educators.

I called Leo's mom. I was nervous, ready to apologize for screaming at him. Instead, she apologized to me, saying he shouldn't have repeatedly interrupted my class. I was surprised, but most Wantagh parents supported the teacher. And Leo had had many previous incidents, as the kids had said. It wasn't like this was isolated. He never hid in my period seven class again.

I also emailed Ronan's mom. I became certain that he was making phone noises. That helped shut that down.

Then I deviated from my syllabus by declaring war on the racism of Ronan and a few others by showing films like *42*, *Invictus* and documentaries about African-American athletes. I had the kids write a paper comparing and contrasting Nelson Mandela to newly elected President Trump. Trump quickly became very popular in Wantagh even though his attempt to build a massive catering hall and restaurant on state land in Wantagh at Jones Beach would have cheated our community (and other local municipalities) out of about $1 million in tax revenue five years before.

I carefully avoided sharing my opinion about Trump, or any politician, with my students, though I did echo how the film *Invictus* showed that Mandela had saved his nation as president. I added my opinion that in rescuing South Africa, Mandela saved several other countries in the southern part of the African continent. While the White-minority government had imprisoned Mandella for 27 years, upon his release, instead of seeking vengeance, he sought reconciliation. Instead of dividing his nation, he brought Whites and Blacks together. My students appreciated Morgan Freeman's brilliant

Mandella in *Invictus* and I emphasized that Mandella was one of the greatest political leaders in world history.

Jennifer and I had traveled to South Africa six years before, I described to the kids that incredible land, and how it was doing better than it had in the Apartheid era, but there were still too many shantytowns (townships) lacking running water and proper sanitation.

By the end of that semester, Ronan's views had been impacted. My barrage of films, articles and anecdotes had forced him to think more than just react. He was a smart kid. I'd erred in not contacting his mother right away regarding his behavior. But his, and other students' racism had lessened. I hadn't obliterated it, but I had opened minds with a major assist from my smartboard, streaming the brilliant acting of Morgan Freeman and the late Chadwick Boseman—as Jackie Robinson.

* * *

Jimmy Joyce's year in my journalism class had been a challenge. He did the minimum amount of writing. For the third print issue I finally persuaded him to publish a short viewpoint in print, without a byline. The piece was titled "Can Baseball Team Do It Again?"

His lead, "Does Wantagh baseball have what it takes to repeat as New York Class A State Champions?" He pointed out that in the 62 years of the school's existence only once had teams had won back-to-back state titles, and they were the 1992 and 1993 boys' soccer teams coached by Tom O'Leary.

As I noted, Jimmy helped lead the team to a second straight state championship game. One of my former sports editors, Owen O'Brien, wrote the June 10, 2017 *Newsday* article on that game:

"BINGHAMTON, N.Y.—Jimmy Joyce took a moment to reflect.

"After Wantagh finished one win shy of its second straight baseball state championship, Joyce leaned over the railing at the top step of the dugout, gazing at the field for the final time in a Wantagh uniform.

"'It's probably one of the best things I'm ever going to go through,' said Joyce, who will play at Hofstra next season. 'I'm grateful for my coaches and my teammates. Every once in a while, I try to stop and take a look around and take it all in just because I know I'll never have it again.'

"The Warriors lost to Vestal, 2-0, Saturday in the Class A state championship ..."

While Jimmy didn't lead Wantagh to back-to-back state titles, his teams won back-to-back Long Island championships. (And the next year Keith Sachs' boys would win a third Long Island title but lose in a close state semifinal.)

I did manage to get him to write two bylined articles. In the last *Warrior* issue his piece was titled "Bald is Better" and it focused on teachers who shaved their heads. I was one of three teachers in the photo above the article, along with social studies teachers Mike Tallarine and Sean Naughton.

Jimmy listed several teachers who shaved their heads and observed about me: "Mr. Kravitz has shown students photos of his younger days when he had long luscious golden locks. He says that in about his late 30s students would allege he had a comb over so he just started shaving his head."

In a later paragraph Jimmy added: "Some students have suggested that Mr. Kravitz looks like Bruce Willis. He likes hearing that as who doesn't want to be confused with a movie star?"

While Jimmy sometimes displayed immaturity in the classroom, he always led on the athletic fields. He has matured into a terrific young man. He was poised for a breakout season in 2020, when he was named Division I Hofstra's Student-Athlete of the week, after pitching an early-season, complete game, 2-1, two-hitter win over Nevada.

After that great start the season was sliced to only 14 games due to COVID-19. In an interview with axcesssports.net Vinny Messana asked Jimmy: "How would you characterize the brief (2020) season?"

Jimmy: "We were going to be special; we were finally figuring it out and it's a shame everything got cut short."

He then asked him about his high school coach, Keith Sachs, and how his teams had 26-straight playoff (appearances) and two state titles.

Jimmy: "He cares about you like [a] son...He loves all his athletes and he's been doing it so long. He's so smart he knows the moves before [they] happen. Especially with his sidekick [assistant coach] Mike Ninivaggi, they are unstoppable."

Jimmy's 2021 Hofstra team wasn't as good as the previous year. He had the lowest E.R.A. and the lowest WHIP among starters, in addition to the most strikeouts on the team, 89 in 73 innings pitched. He made the Colonial Athletic Association Academic Honor Roll. He's become a true student athlete at an outstanding academic university—long since overcoming his youthful silly exploits to gain attention.

While always in awe of Jimmy's athletic prowess, I never stopped pushing him to learn, write and recognize that academics were also very important to his future. And he has shown a recognition of that in college.

A final Jimmy Joyce note: he became the 14th Hofstra baseball player in 56 years to be drafted by a Major League baseball team. The Seattle Mariners took him in the 16th round in 2021.

CHAPTER 25

Some Good Writing

While teaching journalism was a challenge, at times frustrating, seeing a student work on an article, revise and then publish a terrific piece that teachers praised and that won awards created wonderful gratification.

I regret not devising a better method to teach interviewing skills. I had been a good interviewer during my reporting days. I experimented with kids interviewing friends and relatives, but I never developed those lessons like I did some other aspects of my instruction. Many kids struggled to pull off good interviews.

Students mostly wrote viewpoints. I emphasized objective reporting. They constantly injected their opinion—often in a concluding paragraph—and I'd have them edit it out and we'd make the piece objective. Of course, some of their opinion pieces were excellent and many of the awards my students won were for news columns, sports columns and entertainment columns.

While the numbers in my journalism program dwindled as I aged, I reached out to more students not in the classes and had them contribute to the print newspaper. I continued to enter articles in the Syracuse contest and take the kids to Adelphi for that contest. Additional field trips helped to attract a few more students to my classes, so we also attended a Hofstra University Journalism Press Day seminar, with no contest.

We took to the tradition of publishing an article about that press day trip. In the 2018 trip my outstanding editor Jenna Miller led with: "Hofstra University holds a High School Press Day dedicated to educating high school journalists on current trends in journalism and how to work on their skills in the field. Students from Mr. Kravitz' Journalism I and II classes were among over 200 students to attend this year's Press Day."

As the Hofstra journalism seminars didn't excite the kids, I detoured to the bio lab where they enjoyed a lecture by Hofstra's outstanding biology professor, and one of the goalies in my ice hockey games, Professor Michael Dores. Professor Dores' brilliant lectures became a staple of these trips, though they had nothing to do with journalism. The kids would say to me on the bus, "Are we going to the biology lecture?"

"Professor Michael Dores gave us a sense of what it's like to hear a college lecture," wrote Ava Kornbluth in 2019. "His cellular biology [lecture] was very interesting. He also showed us brain cells he was growing under a microscope."

His lectures fascinated me. And he's an equally outstanding goalie. Born and raised in Colorado, Professor Dores graduated from the University of Oregon and then earned his doctorate at Northwestern University.

As I creep past 60 years of age, I play in two ice hockey games a week with him, though I rarely score on him—he's a very young and flexible 30-something. The goalie I usually defend is Jim Carey—neither the former Washington Capitals goalie nor the brilliant comedic actor. This Jim Carey is a successful business owner. Both Michael and Jim are outstanding butterfly goalies—though there are still a few antediluvian stand-up goalies playing in these games, too.

Excuse yet another ice hockey digression. Jennifer says I'm obsessed with the sport. Michael Tallarine thinks I want to live in Canada. Yes, I enjoy playing and watching ice hockey. I also enjoyed teaching and creating a publication with so many amazing student journalists. I've characterized many of them, and there are many more I didn't discuss. Here are just a few from my last years of teaching journalism at Wantagh—along with one young lady who was not a student of mine but whose story must be shared.

The Brittanys

In my final decade of teaching, several groups stood out for their outstanding writing, like the 2013-14 crew. One young lady was a small senior named Brittany Giannandrea. She worked very hard for several weeks on the following article, which began: "On that

Wednesday September morning I woke up at 5:30 a.m., checked my phone and saw two text messages, one from my best friend and one from my boyfriend at the time. 'Hey girl what's up?' wrote my best friend, Brittany.

"'Nothing much just getting ready for school,' I said.

"I got ready for school. We sent multiple text messages back and forth until about 6:15-ish. She said she was ready to cross Sunrise Highway so I told her to be careful and text me when she crossed the street.

"She never answered me so I texted her asking what she was doing because school was starting. It was before homeroom and I looked at my phone again. Her dad, Danny, had called me and I had missed it. I thought nothing of it and just carried on with my morning thinking it was a mistake or that he was trying to find his daughter.

"He called me again during second period. I couldn't answer. He called again at the end of third period.

"'Hello?' I said.

"'Hi sweetheart are you in school?'

"'Yeah,'" I said. "'What's up?'"

"'Nothing. I was wondering if you were with your father. Can I call him? Is he working?

"'You can call him,' I said.

"'Okay sweetheart I love you.'

"'I love you too, bye,' I said and hung up the phone.

"I was walking in the hall and looked at the most horrible text that I have ever seen that said that my best friend, Brittany Vega, had been hit by a car and was dead."

* * *

Brittany Vega hadn't been my student. And she'd only been at Wantagh High School a couple of weeks when she was killed crossing the street walking to school, September 22, 2010.

I remembered her because she sat in Chris Rafferty's homeroom in our shared classroom, Room 129. I was often in that homeroom getting materials from my desk. She was a small, quiet freshman, who sat a couple of seats away from my desk. It was yet another mind-bending tragic loss of one of our children.

Brittany Giannandrea's powerful piece about her friend won a Gold for Columnist at the Syracuse contest. In the decade of the teens my students won 73 awards in the Syracuse contest but only 11 were Gold.

Sandi Lee Vega, Brittany's mom, wrote a *Newsday* article about the day her daughter died while trying to cross Sunrise Highway, not an actual highway but a very busy road, where motorists drove at highway speed. Brittany was killed crossing at a light.

"Brittany, 14, had gotten up early and instead of taking the bus, decided to walk to school, apparently to meet a teacher before class," Sandi Lee wrote in the September 2012 *Newsday* piece. "Although she was forbidden to do so, she crossed the busy six-lane Sunrise Highway and was hit by a car. The driver, who remained at the scene, was not charged. A bank surveillance video showed Brittany used the cross-walk, but was wearing a hood, blocking her peripheral vision."

In addition, Sandi Lee suggested the following for parents in that column: "I also urge all parents to teach their children—even very young ones—how to cross the street. It's not enough just to look both ways. Teach them to keep looking around, and not to let hoods block their vision. Teach them about traffic lights and signs, crosswalks, and to push the signal button to get more time to cross. Always cross only at corners—and never text or talk on a phone while doing so."

She characterized her daughter: "Brittany was our first-born, a freshman who was optimistic about attending Wantagh High School. She was a Girl Scout, loved music and was the kind of person who befriended shy, ostracized kids. Others came to her for advice. At home, she was helping her two-year-old brother recover from burns he suffered when he fell into embers of a dying campfire weeks earlier."

Brittany Giannandrea and her best friend Brittany Vega shared a first name and looked alike. One of the final lines of Brittany Giannandrea's article was: "I don't remember much of freshman year. I failed most of my classes ..."

Brittany Vega's death was the last I experienced of a student while in school. But throughout that decade of the teens I went to funerals for students who had graduated—most of them due to drug overdoses.

Megan

The last student I taught who had lost a parent in the 9/11 terrorist attacks was a junior in the 2017-18 year.

Megan Fehling, a tall and quiet young lady, was a good student. She took my Journalism I class and wrote an article titled, "When Will Athletic Opportunities Be Equal for Men and Women?"

Her lead: "Usually boarding school has a negative connotation. That's why when I tell friends I chose boarding school at 13, they appear shocked."

The article explains that Megan picked Wyoming Seminary, a prep school in Wilkes-Barre, Pennsylvania that had a girls' ice hockey team. She enjoyed playing ice hockey there, however, Wyoming Seminary dropped its girls' ice hockey team, while keeping the boys' ice hockey team. Megan left that prep school, as a result, and returned to Wantagh. She graduated from Wantagh in 2019. Her prep school experience viewpoint won a Bronze for Sports Columnist in the Syracuse contest.

Megan's dad, Lee S. Fehling, had been in Engine Company 235 in Brooklyn when he lost his life in the towers. He was only 28 years old. Megan's older sister Kaitlin had been my student, too. Lee Fehling never met his younger daughter as Danielle Fehling gave birth to Megan about five weeks after 9/11.

Kaitlin graduated from Hofstra and Megan is in college in Boston in 2021. She appears to like it there and said she was doing really well, despite college life in a COVID-19 world. Sadly she's not playing ice hockey in Boston but said she still enjoys watching it.

Keira Young

Late after school one day in 2018 I saw a female teacher with a female student, who exited the teacher's car. As I had erred in permitting Marylou into my car in my first year at Wantagh I spoke to that teacher and told her to rethink driving a student anywhere.

"Do you know who that girl was?" she said.

"No."

"That's Keira Young."

I didn't know Keira, then a freshman. But like all of Wantagh I came to know Keira, along with her story.

In her senior year she wrote the following post on Instagram: "On August 22, 2012, I was nine years old in the car with my dad, sister and brother. We were all crying and as I caught my breath I asked my family, 'Who is going to be there for me at my cheer competitions?' My dad and siblings promised me that they would never miss one competition after that. About an hour before this conversation we lost our beautiful mom to breast cancer. Our world was shattered in front of our eyes. My mom was my biggest inspiration, supporter and the reason I started cheerleading."

Six years after losing her mom, Keira's dad Keith Young, a retired FDNY firefighter, lost a battle to a rare cancer, synovial sarcoma, in March of 2018. He developed the disease as a result of his exposure to carcinogens while cleaning up at the World Trade Center site after the 9/11 terrorist attacks. So once again, here was the impact of 9/11 on Wantagh, and our students.

Keira still had her older sister Kaley and her older brother Christian, both Wantagh grads. While Keira never took my classes I chatted with her frequently. Any time I saw her in the halls I'd ask how she was, how she was doing with her classes and her cheerleading. A few teachers, especially another English teacher and her cheer coach Alex Grange, and members of the community gave her adult guidance.

On October 21, 2018, the nation met Keira and her two siblings on the TV show *Shark Tank*. Their father had been a terrific chef. He'd won food competitions and cooked for his fellow firefighters at his firehouse, Ladder 156 in Brooklyn.

From here the story was told well by one of Keira's best friends and one of my editors, Grace Kane, in a November 2018 *Warrior* front page article.

"The Young children started preparing and getting ready for the show," Grace wrote. "The three of them practiced their pitch and gathered all of the info they needed to make a great presentation. They researched the sharks and watched a series of old *Shark Tank* episodes to see what they would be up against."

They pitched an invention by their dad called The Cup Board Pro, a bamboo cutting board, and the sharks ate it up.

"The sharks [offered the Youngs] an unbelievable deal," Grace wrote. "All five sharks (Daymond John, Mark Cuban, Lori Greiner, Kevin O'Leary and guest Matt Higgins) agreed to contribute $20,000 each for 20 percent of the company. The money the sharks earn from their profits will go to the fundraiser of the Young's choice for other firemen who were affected by 9/11-related illnesses. According to Kaley, there are over 2,000 firemen who are currently ill.

"Within 24 hours of the episode airing, the Youngs received orders for an incredible 34,000 boards, which is over $1 million in gross sales.

"The Wantagh Board of Education offered the school grounds ... for the event. They set up a blow-up screen to watch *Shark Tank* as it aired ... The outpouring of support was overwhelming. They also raised money for a family friend who was currently fighting breast cancer. One of the sharks, Greiner, called and donated $5,000 to the cause.

"'The hardest part was keeping our outcome from four months before a secret from friends and family,'" says Keira.

It was a great front page that included a photo of Keira's beautiful smile, taken by Grace. I was surprised that neither the piece nor the photo won awards for Grace, who was a terrific writer and editor for me. But what mattered was how much the Youngs gained from *Shark Tank*. Their story left the sharks in tears.

Keira is now headed to a college with a lovely campus, in a warm southern city, for the fall of 2021. She is a sweet and adorable young lady. She was a terrific cheerleader in high school, part of multiple county champion cheer teams at Wantagh. She always seemed happy and never complained when I talked to her. She had a lot of friends. Though no number of friends and adult support can make up for the loss of her parents, who sounded like they were an amazing couple who had met in high school.

On the third anniversary of her dad's passing she posted the following on Instagram: "I have had an indescribable pressure pounding on my chest all week. I miss you so much it literally hurts. I hate to believe it has been three years without you. I miss your voice, your smile, your laugh, your inappropriate jokes, your heavenly meals, hearing you say, 'I love you.' I would do anything in this world to spend one more second by your side. I love you forever and ever and ever my best friend."

Nyatasha

Nyatasha Jackowicz is a unique young lady with a unique name that is easy to misspell. She didn't take journalism until senior year. I hadn't recruited her. I knew of her because she was one of two girls on the wrestling team, the other being her younger sister Katrynna.

She worked hard and wrote well so I made her one of three editors-in-chief, along with another talented writer Matthew Schroh and Jaiden Molyneux—a witty, charming young lady but not the hardest worker. How could a Francophile like me not make her editor-in-chief with that French surname? After all, Jaiden's Norman ancestors helped conquer England in 1066.

Jaiden wrote a few light pieces like her "No Shave November" article about several teachers who didn't shave for the month of November as part of a fundraiser to help Wantagh students with financial needs. Jaiden also photographed 18 teachers and administrators for the piece. She wrote well, her wit shining through, but she shirked her editorial responsibilities.

On the other hand, Nyatasha diligently completed her editorial jobs and took on the duties of others. She wrote several excellent articles, including one about her wrestling experience. She created her headline, as a good editor-in-chief should: "Grappling Beyond Gender Barriers."

The piece appeared in our February 2016 issue, just in time to enter it in the Adelphi contest. And it won a Gold there for Best Sports Story. That was one of our best years at that contest. Sara Sneddon took a Silver in the always-difficult News Story category and Matthew Schroh won Silver for Most Outstanding Reporter.

Nyatasha's lead: "For a girl, walking into a wrestling room full of teenage boys stresses the nerves. First there is the stale odor of sweat. That alone would put off most non-wrestlers. Then there are the looks. Yet imagine walking into that same wrestling room as a girl who is about to join that team.

"Despite being female, a phrase that I find somewhat frustrating, I have won matches. Not only have I won but I've pinned male opponents. Thanks to my background in judo, a martial art, I am no stranger to close contact sports and from my training under our team's coaches I'm prepared to take on any challenge."

No way I hallway wrestled Nyatasha. At that point she might have tossed me into the lockers. However, I wasn't a proponent of girls wrestling boys. And this comes from a coach whose best-ever golfer on a boys' team was a girl. While wrestling was great for Nyatasha, building her confidence, I believe girls should wrestle girls. Of course, there were very few girls to wrestle. So she had to wrestle guys.

In her article there is a photo of Nyatasha having her arm raised after a JV bout vs. a boy. Nyatasha stares into the camera—victorious, defiant. The boy looks dejected. And there have been some girls who have reached boys' state tournaments. I'm glad we now have women's wrestling in the Olympics and about 30 colleges with women's wrestling teams. I applaud that.

But to me it's a no-win situation for a boy. It's painful enough to lose in wrestling to a superior opponent, but for a boy to lose to a girl is emasculating. Winning by the boy means little because it's expected.

Nonetheless, Nyatasha had a great senior year of high school and was a brilliant writer, editor, copy editor and tireless worker. I wished she'd taken journalism previously. She also won two awards at the Syracuse contest, one of them also for her wrestling article.

She graduated from Bryant University in 2020. She played on the women's rugby team. I feel so fortunate to have been her teacher. I believe she will achieve something special.

So many wrestlers become uber successful, as long as they don't end up in Congress ranting and raving like one particular two-time

NCAA wrestling champ from the University of Wisconsin-Madison. I won't name that congressman—as the last thing I want to do is get political.

Okay, I can't help myself. What is it with Wisconsin? That state and its universities produced Senator Joseph McCarthy, Alberto Fujimori—the Peruvian president who earned his Masters at the University of Wisconsin-Milwaukee and saved Peru from terrorists only to be impeached for corruption and human rights abuses and then imprisoned—and controversial Wisconsin former Governor Scott Walker, though he's a Marquette dropout who is 36 credits short of his undergraduate degree.

Grace Anne

Grace Anne McKenna's father, James McKenna, a former Marine, suffers from severe anxiety linked to PTSD—a result of trauma from rocket and missile attacks in the first Gulf War. Grace Anne's mother Christine was left to work, pay the bills and raise their four children, including twin boys, Grace Anne and her sister.

I never saw a more incredible job of parenting than that of Christine McKenna. Her youngest, Mary, was a remarkable swimmer who was the star of Wantagh's team as an eighth grader, breaking long-time school records in several events. Grace Anne took journalism for four years and was one of my best editors and writers and hardest workers. She was also a terrific swimmer for my roomie Raf's swim and dive teams.

I didn't realize how damaged their father was from PTSD until I read the following cutline under a photo of Grace Anne's dad in a 2017 *Newsday* article by Martin C. Evans: "Former Marine Lance Cpl. James McKenna, 48, of Bethpage, suffers from post-traumatic stress disorder that his doctors have linked to rocket attacks he experienced near the Kuwait border during the 1991 Gulf War. The effects—including sleeplessness, depression, mood swings, alcoholism—became so severe that in 2007 he moved out of the Wantagh home he shared with his wife, Christine, and four children."

That article chronicled how James McKenna "was rejected for benefits from the Veterans Benefits Administration when he applied

... that rejection came as financial pressures related to his inability to work pushed his family toward foreclosure and threatened his wife and four children with homelessness."

Despite the desperate situation in her homelife, Grace Anne wrote terrific articles, came after school, edited and did layout. She never appeared to have a bad day or showed the least bit of distress. She worked hard and asked for nothing. So many students with less to grapple with needed support and deadline extensions while dropping journalism to the bottom of their to-do lists. Grace Anne agreed to write any article, whatever the topic, from sports to news. These well-written pieces came in before the deadline. I felt bad asking her for yet another article. I didn't want her to stress her. While I knew her father was ill, I didn't realize how severely, and the desperate financial position the family was in.

How did that child work so hard with a perpetual smile? I wrote her a couple of recommendations and after I read a scholarship one to Jennifer she cried—a rare emotional reaction for my wife.

That one concluded: "I never encountered a student who was more deserving of a scholarship than Grace Anne McKenna based on her effort, ability and need. The university that she attends will be lucky and I truly believe that she is the kind of human being who this nation desperately needs as we move forward into uncertain times."

Grace Anne was my only student to win awards at the Syracuse contest four years in a row; she was an editor-in-chief for three years. She won a Silver in that most difficult category of News Story her senior year and also saved us once at the Adelphi contest as our only winner.

The summer before her senior year she attended an academic journalism program in Washington, D.C. and contacted her Republican congressman, Peter King. She managed to get an interview with him. She came to school that year with the article already written, which ran with a photo of Grace Anne and Congressman King, who was a powerful Republican force in Washington. He served in Congress for 14 consecutive terms from 1993-2021.

Her junior year she wrote two articles about teachers that landed on the front page. The first she co-wrote with her friend Grace Tague about a middle school shop teacher Vic Heepe, who was in his 50th year of teaching in 2017-18. What better tribute to Wantagh than a teacher who spends half a century educating its students? Though he wouldn't tell the Graces if he would retire at the end of that year, he did. He also made them take about 100 photos of him. Vic was 70 years old but looked 20 years younger and had the vanity of a 20-something. After we'd settled on a great photo of him, he handed me a photo he wanted me to use. Instead I used Grace Tague's shot.

Grace Anne's other front-page piece was about the retirement of Jennifer deLyra. Grace's concluding paragraph was a quote by Principal Breivogel: "I met Jenn when we were both young mothers 29 years ago. Since that time Jenn has remained a popular teacher, and senior member of the social studies department. She epitomizes the woman who can do it all."

And when Superintendent Maureen Goldberg retired in 2017, Grace Anne wrote an award-winning article about how then-Assistant Superintendent John McNamara took over the top position in the district. It was a stable transfer at the district's top position, unlike the tumult into which Goldberg had stepped five years previously.

Grace Anne quoted Maureen Goldberg: "I've learned what a wonderful community Wantagh is ... I've been here for 40 years. I've learned also to share with people what a wonderful career being in education is. You find yourself giving to the students and the community. For most people, including myself, it makes you feel good."

A senior year front-page article by Grace Anne described how a former Wantagh diver, Andrew Capobianco, won an NCAA DI title for the University of Indiana in the three-meter dive. "As a seventh grader in 2011, Andrew broke a 22-year-old Nassau County high school diving record," Grace wrote.

Grace quoted Raf: "I referred to Andrew as the 'ice man.' He never froze under pressure and just had this unbreakable determination and concentration."

Capobianco won again as an eighth grader, breaking his own record. During Capobianco's two years at Wantagh, Raf gave a part of his coaching salary to dive coach George Taylor, so that Taylor could coach Capobianco. Raf, a great swimming technician, made sure his talented young diver had expert dive coaching.

Capobianco then moved to North Carolina for high school and trained at Duke University. In 2021 Capobianco continued his grace in midair by winning an Olympic silver medal in Tokyo.

Grace Anne also continues to be uber successful. During her 2020-21 sophomore year at Boston College, she sent me articles she wrote there for *The Gavel*, which calls itself the progressive student voice of Boston College.

And Grace Anne's father has improved. He has a full-time vet dog, who helps with his panic attacks. While he's lived in VA care facilities for the past decade, the family hopes he will one day live on his own. He finally received full VA benefits and is 100 percent service-connected disabled due to PTSD. James McKenna is able to phone and text his family. And they all got together and enjoyed a New Year's Eve dinner to begin 2021.

Despite the tragic, incapacitating injuries her father received in warfare, Grace Anne is yet another of my Wantagh students to thrive as she continues her education. A successful career awaits her. Grace Anne recently wrote me: "In the letter that I gave you before graduation, I included a quote by Henry Adams. It said, "a teacher affects eternity; he can never tell where his influence stops." I can assure you that the influence you have had on my education and maturity is still so strong." If you teach, you recognize that one Grace Anne McKenna in one class, one year, in your teaching career makes you incredibly fortunate.

Jill

I'd reached my 27th year of teaching journalism and advising the Wantagh school newspaper. Who advised a high school newspaper for so long? Yeah, I got a stipend of a few thousand dollars, which was an incentive. But burnout had set in—finally. As much as I enjoyed teaching journalism, I didn't enjoy recruiting for it, nor hunting kids down at each print deadline to wrap up an article, take a photo or do layout. And that spring a virus smacked us. No, not that virus. That would come the next year. Three major viral episodes interrupted

my life: the one that lacerated my skin in 1980, this 2019 virus—
which I will explain presently—and then COVID.

I recruited vigorously in December and January. I spoke to
English classes, including eighth grade classes in the middle school.
I especially tried to get kids who I had in freshman English who
were good writers and well behaved. The perfect example of that
was Jillian (Jill) Laino. She had been a great English student in my
ninth grade class. It wasn't easy to convince her to take journalism
her senior year. She nearly bailed on me, but I somehow convinced
her to be one of my 14 Journalism II students. I had another 18 in a
raucous Journalism I class the first semester.

In addition to doing a nice job as a newspaper writer and editor,
Jill was the star libero of our volleyball team. What is a libero?

It's a back-row defensive specialist who doesn't rotate out of the back
line. Unlike the rest of the players on a girls' volleyball team the libero
is often short and wears a different jersey from the rest of the team. Jill
was a short, fit, always-smiling brunette. Her easy-going personality
combined with a silly side made her a joy to teach and create a newspaper with. My female students had many different personalities. But
if I recruited a strong female writer, I went for a pleasant one, like Jill.

Jill was a tri-captain of the Wantagh girls' volleyball team, which
often battled for a Nassau County title. In a sports viewpoint in our
second issue that year Jill wrote about her volleyball team's season.
That article won one of our two awards at Adelphi in March of
2019, for Best Sports Story. Add to that: Jill was named MVP of that
November 2018 state volleyball tournament.

* * *

Jill's senior year was off to a perfect start. Always cheerful, she
floated carefreely through the rest of the year—despite the aforementioned virus, a ransomware virus attack on our school district
on May 1, 2019—which knocked out our email, smartboards and
servers. It turned the last two months of school into a living hell
for teachers, like me, who had become dependent on technology.
Luckily our attendance and Google classroom still worked, as they
were not hosted on Wantagh District servers. District administrators

refused to pay a bitcoin ransom, hired a company to help restore the network and servers, and set about reconfiguring our computer network to protect against future attacks.

Most teachers struggled to teach—as we reverted to chalk. Though there were a few teachers who were minimally disrupted, like Julie Magnuson, who'd begun teaching with me 28 years before. Julie still looked young, seemingly not aging though she turned 50 that May. She hadn't embraced technology. I was shocked that she rarely used her smartboard. If my smartboard went down I couldn't teach. Julie fared better in the ransomware-virus attack than most teachers.

The virus attack also made it impossible to put out a fourth print issue of the *Warrior*. It was the first time we failed to get out a print issue in my nearly three decades of advising the *Warrior*. But my student journalists continued writing and posting articles on our website, like this one by my outstanding co-editor-in-chief Jenna Miller: "The attack began, it is believed, when a staff member opened an email containing a harmful attachment that triggered the virus to infect their computer; it spread throughout the district computers and servers and eventually made its way to every computer in the district.

" ... as of May 9, the Wi-Fi in the high school had been restored. Starting May 13, some Chromebooks began to work again. The desktop computers which run on shared drives had to be re-imaged before they could work again. Students and staff returned from a long Memorial Day weekend and (some) computers were back along with Smartboards, which had been down for 27 days."

Jenna further described how teachers, including myself, worked around the virus attack. We brought in our home laptops and we tapped into our phones' hotspots for Wi-Fi. Art teacher Mr. Hunter's graphic design class went back to cutting up magazines in a return to traditional art. I found an old DVD player in my attic and hooked it up to my Smartboard.

I thought things could never get worse. Then another virus arrived one year later that virtually stopped the earth from rotating on its axis—as far as humanity was concerned.

* * *

Jill became yet another of my terrific student journalists to enroll at Syracuse University—though she was an Education major. Her freshman year, in the fall of 2019, I had her stop by the ESSPA conference at Newhouse School of Communication to the awards ceremony. I thought she could pick up the Syracuse awards we'd won, including hopefully one for her. But there was something off at the conference and awards ceremony that year. The ESSPA advisor, Sherri Taylor, a Syracuse University graphics design professor, seemed less organized and on top of the high school journalism contest that she had run so brilliantly for over 20 years.

I had emailed Sherri and told her Jill would stop by. But she said she hadn't had time to look at my email. She didn't have our awards ready for Jill. Jill said things were disorganized. She saw one plaque there for us: a Gold, which turned out to be for Sports News from an article by Nicole Hooker. But Sherri wouldn't give Jill the plaque. And Jill's great volleyball columns didn't win.

My group ended up winning only seven awards that year, including a Gold for Jenna Miller, our lowest total in seven years.

It turned out that Sherri was battling an illness. She ended up dying a year later, October 19, 2020, from that illness, not from COVID.

"During her 30 years at the Newhouse School, Taylor built a reputation as a funny, tough and kind teacher who was passionate about design and dedicated to her students, always holding them to a high standard," wrote Wendy Loughlin in a newhouse.syr.edu obituary.

I was shocked by Sherri's death and that she had been so ill—even in the deadly year of 2020. She was one of those people who it seemed would always be there. She had done a terrific job with the Empire State Scholastic Press Association state-wide journalism contest, with its extensive winners list and judges' comments that I utilized as a teaching tool for my students.

Though I'd only met her on my two trips to the seminar/contest in the late 1990s, we constantly emailed and spoke. In one of my last emails to her in early 2020, I told her I contemplated retirement and she said, "Great, you can judge the contest if you do."

Our connection seemed like it would go on. Sherri was 70 years old but had the energy of someone much younger.

"Before coming to Newhouse, she spent years teaching high school journalism in her home state (Texas), and it remained a passion of hers," wrote Loughlin. "Taylor had a positive impact on the thousands of students over the course of her career."

"Sherri loved Newhouse. She dedicated her life to educating the next generation," said Bruce Strong, chair of the visual communications department, in Loughlin's obituary. "With quick wit and candor, she told students exactly what she thought of their work—the good and the bad. She set the bar high and didn't stop pushing students until they reached that bar."

Sherri Taylor had been a great teacher. Her state-wide high school contest validated my journalism program. On one hand, the ESSPA contest for newspapers, yearbooks and literary magazines was just another subjective contest. There were others, even better ones like Columbia University's. But Sherri made it into something Wantagh parents valued and administrators publicized. Without that contest, Wantagh High School administrators would not have continued to run my class with its shrinking numbers by the end of my journalism instruction. And that was all thanks to Sherri Taylor.

Juliet

I didn't have many students named Juliet, a literary character I was very familiar with.

Juliet Watstein had gone to a special journalism school, World Journalism Prep School, in Queens, before moving to Wantagh for ninth grade. I had taught one of her uncles many years before. He gave me a hard time, but he showed up at Wantagh years later and apologized to me for how he behaved. Like so many of my former Wantagh students he had matured and wanted me to know that. However, any torture he had inflicted on me was more than made up by his incredible niece, yet another remarkable teenager I was fortunate to have taught. Juliet was one of my three editors-in-chief in 2019-20. She wrote a retirement article and worked tirelessly to complete the college list, which we posted on our website.

A Groupme text between us, from April 2020 to May 31, 2020 of that horrible pandemic year, had about 200 messages about her article, its editing and the college list. Those texts were about spelling names correctly and hunting down colleges for the last few Wantagh 2020 seniors. Were we in school we would have easily done the same thing during the day. But the 2020 COVID pandemic forced us to figure out novel methods to achieve what we had taken for granted.

Add to that her senior year Assistant Principal Jim Brown ran my Journalism II class, the year-long class that became the primary vehicle for getting the school newspaper out, with only seven students. I had to lean on Juliet even more. My other two editors-in-chief in that difficult year, Jenna Miller and Grace Kane, also came through.

The 2019-20 year wound down. My teaching journalism, advising a student publication and making sure that publication was printed four times a year came to an end. I also contemplated retiring from the profession.

How could a 32-year teaching career zip by like that? Retirement? For years it had been this distant concept. But as colleagues retired, I was forced to contemplate retirement and all that went with it: like cleaning out my classroom. Jennifer did not want me to retire. And she definitely didn't want any of my classroom stuff in our home. Jennifer called me a paper hoarder. Though as a teacher, since most of my career had relied on photocopies of material, I had papers and folders in filing cabinets and in a closet that I shared with Raf. But I hogged the closet and filled it with decades of my papers, books, posters, old photos and of course old newspapers. One filing cabinet featured every issue I had helped students create and old *Warriors* from the 1950s and '60s.

What really scared me about retirement wasn't how I would stay busy, but how would I get rid of a closet and classroom filled with 32 years of stuff.

CHAPTER 26

The Cat Retires

We called David Dubin the Cat, because he had two cats and acted like a cat—not speaking, just sitting there staring at you.

He'd begun his teaching career at Wantagh in 1981, when Jennifer was a senior in high school. Jennifer had had a boyfriend who went to Wantagh, as I mentioned in the first chapter. David remembered his younger sister, who was very mad when Jennifer left her brother for me.

David had an incredible memory, near-total recall for names, people. He remembered the name of every person he'd worked with at Wantagh. He was a personal Google. "Ah David, what was the name of that Spanish teacher from the late 1990s, with the curly hair?" I'd say.

And faster than Google he'd say the name, give details and relate an anecdote. His memory also served him well with literature, especially at his AP (Advanced Placement) Exam reviews—as he remembered the names of every character. My memory only clung to geography and Philadelphia sports trivia.

David retired July 1, 2016. He was 58 and had completed his 35th year of teaching at Wantagh.

An outstanding *Warrior* writer, Karen Kawecki, featured the following great quotes about David's career from teachers in an April 2016 retirement article about him.

From the infamous Kevin Shapiro: "Mr. Dubin has a unique mystique about him. He makes close personal connections with students by revealing absolutely nothing about himself."

Another English teacher, Violet Turner, who would retire one year later said, "No matter what Mr. Dubin presents to students or how he discusses it, they walk out of his class feeling more enlightened than when they came in."

Surprisingly, David never learned to type. Right up until his last year of teaching he asked secretaries to type up tests and assignments for him as he had throughout the computer-less 1980s and early '90s.

That he maintained his brilliant teaching career while never learning to type astounded me. How many times do you have to quickly type up an essay prompt, quiz or assignment and beat Kevin Shapiro to the photocopy machine before school and make a couple of class sets?

A regular in our teacher's poker game, his play was inconsistent. Sometimes he played well. I loved his presence, even to my left, as he made me the second oldest in the game behind him. He hated shuffling. He once obtained a shuffling machine but that didn't last as it chipped the cards. Unlike teaching, dexterity was not his forte.

David purchased a theater in the Long Island town of Lindenhurst for his retirement, while he also subbed at Wantagh. He once said to me about retirement, "I don't talk to another person until the evening when I go to my theater." And that's why he subbed.

I understood that as he was single and didn't have much family around. I vowed that when I retired I would not sub at Wantagh.

* * *

A year-end Wantagh Teacher's Union-sponsored dinner celebrated the careers of retiring teachers.

David spoke about the retirees' careers. His speeches were professional masterpieces, with his delivery timed perfectly. But who would talk about him? Without telling anyone I wrote a retirement speech for David a year before he retired. I enjoyed public speaking and hoped to toast and roast David—and I assumed he'd write one about me one day so I wanted to go first.

Apparently, I had contemplated speaking about David at his retirement as far back as 2009. In one of several tributes to Dubin (no other teachers had kids write a feature about them every four or so years), my features editor Kailey Aiosa quoted me: "For Mr. Dubin there is a great deal of truth to the Shakespearian line, 'All the world's a stage. And all the men and women merely players. They have their exits and their entrances.' We are not looking forward to his exit. Who could possibly speak about him at his retirement?"

It turned out Rich Colavita and Michele Harclerode had already secured the job. Ironically Rich hated public speaking. At the year-end sports dinner, varsity coaches spoke about their teams and handed out the MVP award. I did every one of those speeches. Rich never attended that dinner. Rich described his dislike of public speaking and talking to strangers as "shyness." He was similar to my wife in that respect. Jennifer had an absolute dread of public speaking.

Michelle, like me, loved to speak. David and Michelle had a deep friendship and she warned me not to say anything about his sexual preference. I would speak after Rich but before Michelle's big finish. Speaking about David was pressure-packed. Most of the teachers had never heard me speak, except perhaps for the few who had coached and attended the sports dinner.

"David Dubin has said to me many times that there is nothing about my life that makes him jealous," I began my speech in front of a large crowd of teachers, retired teachers and their spouses. "Especially when he hears about my wife and me journeying to South Africa, Jordan or the Galapagos Islands. In David's mind there is absolutely nothing romantic about flying ten hours to some hot, dusty city where nobody speaks English. David wouldn't drive an extra ten minutes to go anywhere.

"His favorite ferry (I pronounced it as 'fairy' copying him) leads to Fire Island and to his favorite drag queen—Kevin Shapiro's mother. I'm not sure why David calls Kevin's mommy a drag queen. We all love David, one of our all-time most-brilliant educators. But there are some things you just don't want David to explain.

"Yet I'm incredibly jealous about one aspect of David's life. Yes, it's that big, ah (long pause), manly truck he drives. It's my life's dream to own a truck like that.

"The early 1990s were difficult for David and I. Wantagh's staff didn't have the camaraderie it enjoys today. David was stalked by a fellow English teacher named Paul Keryc. Some of you might remember him. He had a fake English accent. David hid from him."

I had written that David hid in his closet (which he actually had) but I figured I shouldn't say that—though for an instant I contemplated ad-libbing it.

I told the story of how Superintendent Dr. George Besculides wasn't going to hire me because of how I left out a line on the application.

"They were going to give the full-time job to a young woman with no experience, fresh out of college. David was enraged. He stormed Dr. Besculides office and convinced that stubborn man to give me the full-time job.

"That young woman, Julie Euston—known to all today as Julie Magnuson—got the part-time job. She was adorable, still is, funny, personable and poised to destroy a 36-year-old cherished Wantagh all-male barbecue tradition. (Julie sat in the audience, laughing.)

"I was 40 pounds lighter, with straight blonde hair, a face not yet ravaged by decades of trying to teach Shakespeare to rambunctious *Lord of the Flies*-like boys. Why on earth would David fight for me and not the fetching young Julie Euston?"

At this point David pantomimed—always the director—with a cutoff sign, which clearly implied I not mention his homosexuality. But I had no intention of going there—just leading up to it.

"To this day David frequently asks the same question—especially every time he sees me enter his favorite domain, the faculty room. 'Why did I get Kravitz this job?' He considers getting me the job the second-greatest blunder of his otherwise brilliant career. The worst blunder, of course, was pushing for Kevin Shapiro's hire.

"Kevin is ahead of me because I never tried to kill David.

"David commuted to work with Kevin for years and it's amazing he survived. Kevin has a habit of not looking at the road while he's driving and talking incessantly about nothing. David would scream, 'Watch out for that truck.'

"'Yo, I got 'dat doobies,'" Kevin said.

"Mercifully David was not in Kevin's truck when he flipped it one day driving to work. I'm not jealous of Kevin's piece of shit truck, especially after that accident. He had the truck righted and drove it to Wantagh and excitedly showed everyone photos of the battered vehicle on its side. Kevin didn't have a scratch. But there's no doubt David would have been killed had he been in it.

"One person who never tried to kill David was former English Chairperson Becky Chowske. Becky observed David teach and said, 'I'm honored to have been able to witness such genius.' As we all know David is not above a little flattery.

"But David deserved Becky's flattery. Nobody brought literature alive like David. He's an entertainer, always on the stage. As a student once wrote about him: 'During his classes you never lose interest.' Nobody taught AP English like David. He taught theater at Wantagh for years, directing 78 plays. For 34 years he gave the announcements in the morning in his magnificent voice, not his phony macho one. And he did not choose Kevin Shapiro to replace him for morning announcements as many people believe. That brilliant decision belongs to Mr. Brown. 'Yo. Yo. What up Wantagh? A fiboo left until homeroom.'

"I will miss sitting in my quiet empty classroom listening to David do a brilliant Mayella Ewell and then an even better Atticus Finch than Gregory Peck. David can command an audience. I admire, respect and love him like an Irish twin, as we are only a year apart in age."

Ok, that was an exaggeration as we were a year and a half apart in age. Though the kids and even young teachers thought that David was a decade older than me.

So, that was a manly chunk of what I said about David. Michelle drew hysterical laughter after me with her crazy stories—that we'd all heard but still roared at. Her embellished delivery helped.

I realized that when I retired I had to ensure that David couldn't make a speech about me. It appeared, however, that there was no way to avoid being lampooned by David's genius. And I'd provided plenty of material. What could save me? That damn union retirement dinner had never been canceled.

CHAPTER 27

2019-20

To Retire or Not to Retire, Amidst Survival and Tragedy

The 2019-20 school year would be my last year of teaching journalism. I considered making it my last as a teacher, too. Should I retire? I still enjoyed teaching. But I would be 60 in July 2020. I had good health. I wanted to enjoy the next ten years and continue to play ice hockey, golf and travel internationally.

Jennifer had convinced me to downsize into a townhouse the year before. While I missed tending to our half-acre with its spacious farm ranch, it proved a brilliant financial maneuver. We could afford my retirement. Though Jennifer, who worried about everything she couldn't control, didn't think so.

"What happens when we are 90?" she said.

"I don't think I'll get to 90," I said. "But I would like to enjoy my 60s."

She badgered me to continue teaching. I had time to decide. I could wait until June.

* * *

My retirement thoughts were interrupted by a shocking illness, which struck a young member of the high school staff that fall. Kathleen Flynn, in her mid 20s and a fourth-year English teacher, was slotted to take over the journalism program for me the next year.

Amazingly, she hadn't been absent for a single day. She was a healthy, fit, friendly, hardworking teacher—who also coached girls' soccer and girls' basketball. She had endless energy and a great sense of humor. I enjoyed chatting with Kathleen. She loved teaching and the kids loved her. She'd figured out the profession quicker than I had.

I had seen her on a fall Friday and she said that she didn't feel well. Suddenly she was in the hospital, then in a coma and intubated. At that time, about five months before the COVID-19 pandemic struck New York, I didn't know precisely what intubation involved. I'd never known an intubated person. I mean, I had a sense it involved having a tube shoved into you but I didn't realize that that tube enabled a person to breathe.

We couldn't get a precise diagnosis about what had happened to her. I told Jennifer I feared she would die. But Jennifer seemed confident that her youth and the doctors at NYU Langone Hospital, formerly Winthrop University Hospital, would enable her to survive. Jennifer was an internet physician—not a recommended source of medical knowledge.

I desperately hoped that Jennifer was right about Kathleen, as I feared she wouldn't survive. Wantagh had lost too many students in my years. We'd never lost a young teacher. Kathleen had to make it.

* * *

Survival was a regular part of my fall freshman instruction. I relied on the short stories "To Build a Fire" and "The Most Dangerous Game." In "To Build a Fire," by Jack London, a man attempts stay alive in temperatures -75 degrees Fahrenheit, while alone in the frozen Yukon territory of Canada. His arrogance creates suspenseful peril for him and his dog. And in "The Most Dangerous Game," a famous hunter, Sanger Rainsford, falls off a ship in the Caribbean on his way to hunt in South America. Rainsford washes up on an island where the hunter becomes the hunted. Those timeless short stories still worked—sans films or videos.

Additionally, I taught other pieces of short fiction and nonfiction, including "The Seventh Man," a short story by Haruki Murakami about one boy's lifelong survivor's guilt after a giant wave struck him and his friend in Japan.

Despite two large freshman English classes, including one of them ninth period, my first semester went smoothly thanks to Kathy Butler—the special education teacher who I collaborated with for both freshman classes. My 55 freshman created scores of essays to grade, but at least there were no behavioral issues—even ninth period. No child dared disrupt class with Kathy hovering. She could put fear into the hearts of freshmen.

I followed up the short story survival unit with tragedy: *Romeo and Juliet*. Would this be the last time I ever taught *Romeo and Juliet* to students? After *Romeo and Juliet* there was more tragedy—the ancient Greek play *Antigone* by Sophocles. A few similarities between the plays convinced me that Shakespeare was influenced by *Antigone*, the last part of the Oedipus trilogy.

The relationship and the outcome between the two pairs of doomed lovers—Antigone and Haimon and Romeo and Juliet—have odd similarities. Antigone and Haimon die in a cave while Romeo and Juliet die in an underground tomb. Another similarity is the fate of Creon's wife Eurydice, who after learning that her son Haimon had died takes her own life in the play's final scene.

After learning that her son Romeo had been exiled, Montague's wife Lady Montague dies: "Grief of my son's exile hath stopped her breath." This also comes in the play's final scene.

The play *Antigone* deals with the failings of leadership—as does *Romeo and Juliet*, with Verona's leader the Prince (Escalus), whose lack of strength leads to the deaths of his kinsmen Mercutio and Count Paris.

I emphasized to the children how Creon, Antigone's uncle and the king of the fictional city-state Thebes, had been a good leader. Indeed, he'd saved Thebes from an attack. But then he made a mistake. He was given several opportunities to correct that mistake but failed to do so, which led to disaster for him and his family. I told my students that I often thought about Creon, and how important it was to make good decisions because one bad one could ruin your life.

* * *

The 2019-20 year included more non-fictional tragedy as reflected by our first *Warrior* front page.

John Michael Martin, a Wantagh grad, passed away at the age of 33 in March of 2019 due to an illness. John had loved the Broadway musical *Rent*. Theater teacher Heather Naughton honored John's memory by staging *Rent* on his birthday. (After a divorce and marriage to Wantagh social studies teacher Sean Naughton, Heather was no longer Heather Romano.)

From my small journalism class Delaney Skelton wrote an excellent front-page article about John and a play preview.

"When he passed away, and all the drama students kept asking for me to have us do *Rent* this year, it felt that the universe was telling me that we were supposed to do this show," Heather said in the article.

John had been in my English class and once came into my room after school while I was listening to the *Rent* soundtrack. He became enraged that I liked the music. As it was his favorite Broadway show, and it was cool, he couldn't process that someone as uncool and old (42 at that time) as me, could possibly like that music, too.

Delaney won a rare award for Best News Story in the 2020 Adelphi contest that year for the article about John Michael Martin and Wantagh students' production of *Rent*. I gave Heather the newspaper as soon as they were printed, before we distributed them. I thought she'd appreciate the article.

Not long after that, maybe an hour, Principal Carolyn Breivogel found me and said, "Could I see you in my office?"

Oh my God, a principal's office visit invitation always meant a time-consuming problem. I hadn't been in there for any trouble in the six years since the infamous Becky meeting. What had I done? I couldn't think of anything. Unless it related to the issue of the *Warrior*, due to be placed in homeroom teachers' mailboxes that afternoon.

Heather and Sean Naughton sat in the principal's office. Heather looked upset. Sean wore his usual silly grin. Assistant principal Jim Brown was there, too.

Carolyn pointed to a page eight article about Bill Bogatz. The Bogatz article? How could that be a problem?

Though Bogatz had retired five years before, he had recently subbed for a week or so for Sean Naughton. Retirement couldn't keep Bogatz away from Wantagh. He announced at football and basketball games and ran a couple of clubs. He even kept a desk in the back of Kevin Shapiro's room, his former room.

"You have to take this article out and replace it with something else," Carolyn said.

"The Bogatz article?" I said, confused.

"Can you reprint the paper?" Carolyn said.

A reprint? Not my third-career reprint. No way.

"Well, Carolyn," I said and took a deep breath. "If I were to do that could you give me the money for it as I have just enough money left in the *Warrior* account to get through this year."

She and Jim Brown quickly discussed that and agreed that they could give me approximately $350 for a full reprint.

"Just please don't let anyone see the paper with this article," Jim said. "Get rid of all of the papers and take the article down from the web site."

The web site? Really? What was going on?

Why was Jim concerned about the article on the website? Though I tried to promote it among the students and their parents, it attracted little traffic. That article had been posted a month before and nobody had said a word about it.

My thoughts sputtered in utter confusion. I knew something had happened with the Naughtons but I wasn't sure precisely what. I mostly ignored faculty gossip. In fact, Rich Colavita and Mike Tallarine teased me incessantly about my disinterest in the lives of teachers—like who had divorced and why.

Carolyn appeared determined so I didn't try to stave off a reprint. Fortunately, one of my editors, Grace Kane, quickly wrote an article and gave me a couple of photos. I swapped out the Bogatz article, emailed the new page to the printer that afternoon and we had new newspapers two days later, with a discount from the printer so I didn't even need the full $350. I hauled the 800 16-page newspapers home to recycle them. That was a pain in the back.

While I did eventually learn about the Naughton's situation, I still don't see how the following line revealed anything to the community: "Mr Bogatz ... went back to teaching as an interim teacher for Mr. Naughton, who was absent until September 23."

That reprint nudged me towards retirement from teaching. I didn't want to deal with student, parent or colleague drama. And as rumors swirled that Carolyn and Jim planned to retire, I didn't want to work for a new principal and assistant principal. For 23 years Terry O'Connor and Carolyn had been exceptional principals of the school; and Jim Brown had been a terrific assistant principal. What if the next principal were a dick, like Joel Dick?

* * *

We'd lost John Michael Martin in 2019. Every high school faculty and staff member desperately hoped that Kathleen would survive as we entered 2020. She awoke from her coma, which gave us all great hope.

On the West Coast, however, retired basketball great Kobe Bryant, his daughter Gianna and seven other people didn't survive a Los Angeles helicopter crash on January 26.

We ran the awful story about Bryant's death on our front page. I couldn't imagine that it would be the last-print front page for me as a newspaper adviser. Twenty-seven years before, my first *Warrior* front page featured a man who had survived a plane crash high in the Andes Mountains with his rugby teammates; my last featured the tragic death of a man who didn't survive a helicopter crash in the mountains of Southern California with his daughter and others connected to her basketball team.

A freshman, Ava Kornbluth, who loved basketball and knew a lot about Gianna Bryant wrote the article. I knew a lot about Kobe. We were both graduates of the Lower Merion School District, though he had graduated from Lower Merion High School and I graduated from Harriton, the township's other public high school.

Ava quoted me for the article: "I started following Kobe's career when he was in high school. I was impressed with what a great student he was and how he was fluent in Italian. (Due to living in Italy during his childhood as his father, Joe Bryant, played professional basketball there.) When he was in high school he beat a 76er's NBA all-star, Jerry Stackhouse, in one-on-one."

Despite never meeting Kobe, his death profoundly saddened me. I saw him in person once, months before, in 2019 at the U.S. Open tennis tournament in Flushing, New York. He signed autographs in a promotion there. I stood perhaps 20 feet from him, amazed at how big he was and how wide his shoulders were. He looked more massive than six feet six inches and 212 pounds. I stared at him until a security guard shooed me away.

Bryant's senior year of high school he led Lower Merion to its first basketball state title in 53 years. He scored more points in high school than perhaps the greatest Philly-area prep hoopster, Wilt Chamberlain. Unless you consider Kobe the greatest prep hoops star from the Delaware Valley.

Bryant was one of the greatest NBA players of all time. He once scored 81 points in a game, second only to Wilt Chamberlain's 100. But Kobe was human, and thus flawed. In 2003 he was accused of raping a 19-year-old hotel employee in Colorado. Bryant claimed that they had had consensual sex. Criminal charges were dropped after the young woman said she would not testify. The *Los Angeles Times* estimated that Bryant settled out of court with the woman for $2.5 million. Yet Bryant's marriage to his wife survived that incident and also a 2011 split when Vanessa Bryant filed for divorce.

After the Colorado case was dropped Bryant made the following statement: "Although I truly believe this encounter between us was consensual, I recognize now that she did not and does not view this incident the same way I did. After months of reviewing discovery, listening to her attorney, and even her testimony in person, I now understand how she feels that she did not consent to this encounter."

Kobe's life ended at age 41—while taking his daughter to play basketball.

* * *

I had to tell the district I would retire by February first if I wanted to get my sick-day payout that year. But I needed more time.

Jennifer and I attended a video conference with a representative of the New York State Teachers' Retirement System and received a pension projection. Jennifer insisted I teach one more year.

It was a difficult decision. Jennifer and I spent a warm February week in Florida visiting cousins and friends. It was great playing golf in the Florida heat. If I retired, I could travel whenever I wanted to. At the same time news of a novel virus trickled out of Wuhan, China in January. It seemed far away.

In New York life went on, as it still seemed that perhaps this virus would be like the SARS and MERS viruses, which while deadly didn't have a global impact. The political leaders of the federal government kept downplaying the virus, though health professionals issued dire warnings. The World Health Organization declared a Global Health Emergency on February first, with only 10,000 cases worldwide and about 200 deaths.

In the schools we maintained a wary interest in the virus. Still, 33 foreign language students went on a field trip to Spain and Italy, with six teacher chaperons, over our February break—Presidents' week—which New York schools and a few other states' public schools had off.

Some of them returned with flu-like symptoms. We didn't even imagine that it could be COVID-19. The focus was on China, not Europe. But it's possible that someone on that trip could have contracted the virus. It was in Europe then.

The virus still had no impact on my thoughts about retirement. Then on March first, I had a brief discussion with Jennifer. I told her I leaned towards retirement; she insisted that I teach one more year. I recalled what the therapist had said to me 14 years before, during our troubled time. I had worked hard for 32 years and was ready to retire. I had a plan to stay busy. This would be my decision, not hers. Though I listened to her concerns, I pushed my laptop return button—and my retirement was now four months away. I would get a pension check every month starting in late July.

To satisfy Jennifer I would continue to coach the varsity golf team at Wantagh. I'd also completed one new coaching gig, a wrestling one at nearby Clarke Middle School, and had been hired to coach baseball at another middle school. While the pandemic canceled my baseball coaching job, I hoped to make a few bucks in 2021 doing it. Little did I know then that there would be no high school sports until January 2021 and my coaching plans wouldn't quite work out.

I posted the following on Facebook on March first: "As my 32nd year as a New York public school educator winds down, I've decided to retire from the classroom. This photo is from my 19th and last Press Day journalism contest at Adelphi University. Three of my students won awards for their writing. Feels like yesterday that I arrived in Wantagh. It has been a privilege to teach there. I tried to do my best every day. Though Philly will always be my home, Wantagh is my second home."

My biggest problem: dodging David Dubin's speech at the retirement dinner.

By early March I had a much bigger problem: COVID-19 exploded in New York. On March 12th, I taught my classes. The next day was Sportsnite: an annual 1950s throwback to a sports and dance competition for girls from the time when they were denied participation in interscholastic athletics.

Our principal had declared earlier in the week that we would still have Sportsnite but nobody would be allowed to attend. It normally drew a massive crowd of parents and family of the girls. Instead they could watch it live on the internet. The girls were distraught. I felt so bad for them. My empathy would soon switch to my thousands of fellow New Yorkers who would become ill and die from the virus.

Meanwhile, there was talk that schools across the state could be closed as the virus was spreading incredibly fast. The World Health Organization declared COVID-19 a world-wide pandemic on March 11th. Federal government officials continued to insist there was no need to be concerned about the virus.

The Nassau County Board of Health found that one parent of a student in Wantagh had the virus and closed all the schools in the district on Thursday, March 12th. Now, Sportsnite was canceled.

In fact, the next day I went to a meeting for the middle school baseball team that I thought I'd coach. Perhaps the virus would abate quickly and we'd be back in school and the kids would be playing sports. Yet, I had already taught what turned out to be my last class in a brick-and-mortar classroom at Wantagh and there would be no spring prep sports in New York in 2020.

Four days later, on Monday March 16th, Governor Andrew Cuomo signed an executive order directing all schools in New York to close by Wednesday, March 18th for two weeks, ending April first. Schools would not open again, however, and we taught remotely for the rest of the school year.

Our district developed a plan to continue instruction. Administrators didn't want us to use a live camera to teach our classes, fearful that a child would see something inappropriate in our homes. We were told to use the software Google Classroom to assign work for students. We had two more weeks left in the third quarter.

I posted daily assignments for students on Google Classroom to complete the third quarter, though I had already had five grades for the freshman and three for my seniors.

For the fourth quarter district officials declared a no-harm policy: If that fourth-quarter grade was lower than their average for the previous three quarters it wouldn't count. If it was higher we would average it in.

As we teachers struggled to figure out how to teach virtually, many students struggled to keep up with work from every class, including physical education. I assigned my freshman work from the novel *Great Expectations*. Without my teaching of the nuances of that novel I knew many freshmen would struggle. As for my seniors, I had the 30 for 30 film *Fantastic Lies*, about the Duke lacrosse scandal, loaded in my Google Classroom. I assigned a little of the video each day and posted questions. The kids opened the DVD from my Google Classroom.

Teaching this way wasn't too difficult. I added an occasional short video. Nonetheless, my students struggled with the workload and younger children struggled more. One quarter of my students took advantage of the no-harm fourth-quarter policy and did little work.

Here's a good example of how two of my seniors approached schoolwork in the fourth quarter, my last as a teacher.

First there was Nick Ginsberg. Nick was the nephew of my great 1990s wrestler Mike Ginsberg. Nick looked exactly like his uncle. Sometimes I'd look at him in his eighth period class, pre-COVID shutdown, and say, "Yes, Mike—"

"Krav I'm not Mike," he said.

Like Mike, Nick was a wrestler. I would see his grandfather, Mr. Ginsberg, at home wrestling meets as I worked the scoreboard.

For the fourth quarter, I learned that the *New York Times* offered free online access to teachers and our students for about three months through the end of the school year—thanks to an email from my former student Angela Cave.

I managed to sign up my 39 seniors for the *Times*. I assigned them a variety of articles and short films. Nick did the second assignment, writing a brief recap on an April second *Times* video titled "It's a Pretty Big Bummer: Olympic Dreams on Hold," in which 2020 Olympians talked about their disappointment at having the games postponed. Nick was one for two on assignments. Then he did assignment No. 6, another short April video, this one by renowned therapist Nayeema Raza titled, "We're All Grieving. This is How We Get Through It."

Both videos were popular with my students. Most students watched them and wrote short responses. Nick was off to a shaky but decent fourth quarter start. He'd done two of the first five assignments. He could finish at any time.

He did No. 9, on an NFL article. At least I seemed to have engaged Nick. Then he did the assignment for a very long *Times* article on a 49-year-old New England lawyer sickened by COVID-19 named Jim Bello who, after 32 days on a ventilator, remarkably survived.

I assigned a total of 25 of these short write ups for the fourth quarter. Nick never did another one. Still Nick had passed for the third quarter so his fourth-quarter collapse would not impact his final semester grade for the class. It seemed like a weak policy.

But considering that students might have sick family members, or crowded homes, the leniency was fair.

Another senior, Nicole Lipski, took a different approach.

Most seniors would not post their work until the afternoon, the next day or several days later. Nicole sent in her work every day immediately after I assigned it at nine a.m. My seniors with that kind of work ethic did more reading remotely during COVID-19 than they had ever done in a second semester.

Nicole was a delightful young lady who had been in my homeroom. Many of the girls in that homeroom harassed me when I sometimes confused their names. They shrieked, "Krav, my name is ..." The girls had no appreciation that as a coffee junkie, my massive infusion of caffeine hadn't kicked in. The homeroom only had a couple of boys and I knew their names. Hey, as you get older as a teacher your short-term memory fades. Didn't the girls understand that?

But Nicole never gave me a hard time. She was cheery and pleasant—a good personality for a cheerleader. She did all 25 assignments. While a few of my other 39 seniors also made very strong efforts, Nicole's was the best.

I spent much of my first year of retirement in 2020-21 trying to get in touch with Nicole, messaging her on Facebook and trying her email but she didn't respond. Then in the spring of 2021 I spotted her on Instagram.

I messaged her on Insta: "Hey, what's up? How's Plattsburgh? You get a 4.0 first semester?"

I instantly got an Insta response.

"Hey Krav! First semester was pretty good, def a lot of restrictions with COVID so I stayed home this semester. I got a 3.76. I was so close to a 4.0."

I knew my star-pandemic-senior student would kill it in her first semester in college. With her work ethic there was no way she wouldn't be successful. You feel a great pride as a teacher when you see your former students succeeding, especially under the very difficult circumstances presented by the pandemic. There were three other students in Nicole's class who also did every assignment, but none who posted them minutes after I assigned them.

In my other second semester senior sports lit/nonfiction class another wrestler did 23 out of 25 assignments. But that young man, only the second four-time state place-winner in Wantagh history, Josiah Encarnacion, was a little more motivated. He's now at the University of Virginia, and on the wrestling team. Josiah's uncle is former UFC middleweight champ Chris Weidman, who was a two-time D1 wrestling All-American at Hofstra.

Josiah and I messaged on Insta in 2021 about his wrestling in the Atlantic Coast Conference and his studies. I encouraged him to work hard in his classes.

"I was a B student first semester," he said. "I'm gonna try for straight A's this semester."

"Yeah. Pick it up. You are at Mr. Jefferson's school. It's a great opportunity for you. Life is about learning. Find something you like in college. I discovered writing when I was in college."

I pushed kids to take advantage of learning opportunities. Josiah could have worked harder in high school but he always showed respect, and he did his best. He had great parents who were on top of him and proud of his enrollment in the University of Virginia, one of the finest state universities in the United States. And Josiah was one of the quickest wrestlers I ever saw. I look forward to watching him wrestle on TV in the 2021-22 season.

As the virus worsened in the New York area, in the spring, Ody Svolos, Wantagh science teacher and my friend, landed in the hospital in late March. He needed supplemental oxygen. He also got a drug cocktail. Ody had joked about his high blood pressure and I warned him he needed to get that under control. He was only in his 40s but he was in the hospital for several days and we all worried about him. He made a full recovery; he lost 30 pounds.

Hospitalizations and death rates in New York City and Long Island soared. Even where we lived in Melville, in Suffolk County, we heard ambulance sirens in the night. The roads, stores and malls were eerily empty; highways had no traffic. Friends and students were sickened by the virus.

It became difficult to get masks and sanitizer. Jennifer and I didn't do very much. We stayed home, wore masks anywhere else and avoided indoor groups.

Then Wantagh lost a beloved staff member. Tony Carter, 57, was an assistant football coach. He didn't teach, rather he worked at a hospital. He'd coached Wantagh football for 18 years, as an assistant, and according to head coach Keith Sachs he was a huge part of the program's success.

Carter had a pre-existing lung condition. He was admitted to the hospital at the end of March with COVID-19 and two weeks later he was gone.

I didn't know Tony Carter well. Though we coached in the fall together, I was quickly off to a golf course. Keith Sachs said he was a brilliant and hard-working coach who the kids loved. Sachs told *Newsday* that Carter "was like a brother to me."

In the fall of 2019, Carter had to coach against his son, Idris, the star quarterback of Uniondale High School. Coach Carter had grown up in Uniondale and played football there himself. It was his community but he had to develop a scheme against his son in the final game of the season and then the first playoff game. Father defeated son in both. Though they were on the same team in both of their last games, as Idris Carter and his dad led their Nassau Conference II-III all-stars to victory over Nassau Conference I-IV. And Idris Carter earned the game's MVP award. He's now at Stony Brook University on the baseball team.

I had many football players in my senior classes. They expressed their devastation at the loss of their beloved coach to me in emails. I wished I could be in school so I could be more supportive.

* * *

Kathleen fought her way out of danger. The diagnosis was encephalitis, caused by a virus. She had to relearn how to walk, drive and breathe.

While at one point it appeared she might not return to school, she regained full health and returned for the 2020-21 school year. She took over the school newspaper from me.

As COVID-19 slammed New York, the U.S. and the world, my last year wound down quickly. I briefly saw the seniors at a graduation car parade for them. There would be a car parade for the retirees and Jennifer would attend with me. I received a yearbook but nobody signed it. We had a chance to virtually sign the seniors' yearbooks but I couldn't figure out how to do it.

My colleagues said that it was a shame that my teaching career had to end this way. I didn't feel bad for myself, only for the Class of 2020 who had missed out on their prom, spring sports seasons, academic and sports award ceremonies, final days of high school with their friends, graduation parties. Jennifer and I patiently waited for the vaccine to arrive and somehow dodged COVID-19.

And while not quite as miraculous as a rapidly created vaccine to save humanity—the union dinner was canceled for the first time ever. David Dubin told me he'd written much of my retirement speech. I didn't have to hear it in front of my colleagues and Jennifer.

I still had to clean out my classroom. I ended up tossing most of what was in my closet and my filing cabinets—stuff that I hoarded for decades. I made several trips to the dumpster. It was cathartic. Though I did keep old gradebooks, seating charts and some year-end observations.

In late June I submitted my last-ever grades and my 32-year New York public-school teaching career ended in an empty, clean, quiet, germ-free school—just me and a few custodians, security guard Bill Colvin walking the halls and Bill Bogatz somewhere in the building— as I emptied out the last remnants of 29 years, most of them spent teaching in Room 129.

I'd barely survived my first year at Wantagh. I was never fired there. Every day I demanded my students learn, think, and respect each other. I hope I'll be remembered fondly. I made mistakes, plenty of them, but no really big, stupid ones—though I'm sure my friend Mike Tallarine would dispute that.

I was inspired to become a teacher on a Parisian street in the spring of 1988 for some barely fathomable reason. Perhaps this memoir has made young folks think that teaching would make a nice career. It worked out for me—despite my early struggles. I wouldn't trade it for any other profession.

Today there are about 3.7 million public school teachers in the United States, many in small towns like Wantagh, who work hard every day. Those millions of teachers truly make America great.

Teachers inspire, educate, and give our children a chance. And if you are one, or hope to be one, just remember to never give up on any child, no matter how much he, she or they torture you and make you miserable—because you would never give up on your own child.

The End
May 1, 2021
Melville, New York

EPILOGUE

From the *The Warrior*, Wantagh High School, Wantagh, New York

Krav Closes Out 32-year Teaching Career in the Time of Corona
By Grace Kane, Editor-in-Chief
April 17, 2020

Where do I even begin? It is with great sadness that we announce Mr. Kravitz's retirement from the classroom on July 1. The man who has made *The Warrior* possible will close out a 32-year public school teaching career.

"Mr. Kravitz has been the inspiration behind *The Warrior* for nearly 30 years," says Wantagh High School Principal Mrs. Breivogel. "We are so grateful for the time and passion he has put into our high school publication. He has championed our students having a voice and as a result, *The Warrior* has received numerous accolades and awards for its professional, exceptional reporting. I thank Mr. Kravitz for his dedication and contributions. He has certainly created a legacy in Wantagh High School."

Mr. Kravitz, 59 years old, has had many roles: Coach, Colleague, Teacher, Friend and of course, the adviser of our school newspaper, *The Warrior*. His dedication to journalism here at Wantagh will be missed. When an article was required for a print issue he popped in classes, stalking editors and insisting their articles be finished 'yesterday.' He emphasized conciseness, short declarative sentences and original verbs and nouns.

"Hemingway didn't trust adjectives and adverbs," he repeatedly told his students. And of course what better way to show them that than to teach Hemingway's short masterpiece 'Hills Like White Elephants.'

Nobody knows Krav as well as his roommate of the past 20 years, fellow English teacher and adventurer, Mr. Rafferty.

"Not a day goes by in English Room 129 without a medley of student passer-by voices saying 'KRAV' as they scuttle by between periods," says Mr. Rafferty. "Mr. Kravitz has rendered such a fun, social, heartfelt and warm atmosphere. He has been the subtle pillar of the goodness in Wantagh High School. 'KRAV' echoes in the hearts of so many lives and certainly, it will remain in mine, encouraging me along the way."

Another English teaching colleague, Mrs. Magnuson, shared a room with Mr. Kravitz their first year at Wantagh. Mr. Kravitz's experience helped a much younger Mrs. Magnuson get through the challenges of first-year teaching.

"If it hadn't been for Pete Kravitz I probably wouldn't still be a teacher," said Mrs. Magnuson. "Anytime I felt discouraged, nervous, or inadequate, he would give me a pep talk so that I would believe in myself again."

Wantagh High School junior Bianca Falco says, "Krav is one of the best teachers and I'm gonna miss him and his stories."

"Mr. Kravitz is the kindest and most supportive colleague anyone could ever ask for," says English teacher Mrs. Nieves. "He is the epitome of a team player, and our English department team is truly going to miss his heart and humor."

He started teaching in Brooklyn at Boys and Girls High School in 1988. He came over to Wantagh in 1991. He taught English (grades 9,10 and 12), journalism and creative writing. The 2020s marked his fifth decade as a New York public school educator.

Former student Chris Eisenhardt said on Facebook, "Four years of journalism with [Krav] made me a better writer and certainly inspired me to teach."

Several of Mr. Kravitz's former students went on to teaching careers including Wantagh Middle School teachers Mr. Liguori, Mrs. Bewick (nee Tepedino), Mrs. Cornella (nee Nallan) and Mrs. Piciullo (nee Fragola). New Hyde Park High School English teacher Mike Stencel was inspired by Krav to teach journalism.

"Stencel did an amazing job as the NHP newspaper advisor," said Mr. Kravitz. "For a few years his kids kicked our butts at the Adelphi Press Day journalism contest. But he didn't last too long as a high school newspaper adviser. It's a grind, but a rewarding one."

And while he is also extremely proud of former students who pursued careers in journalism — like News 12's Erin Colton, *Newsday*'s Owen O'Brien, Jackie Dresch who worked at NBC News and HBO, and Orlando Fox 35 TV reporter Stephanie Buffamonte — he says that pride extends to so many other former students.

"On Facebook I see the courage of former students who are health care workers like nurses Heather Kennedy (nee Cabrera) and Susan Blackmer (nee Bronzino)," said Kravitz. "They are saving lives in this terrible pandemic."

Mr. Kravitz said that ending his career during the coronavirus pandemic is strange and sad, but his first thoughts are with the well-being of the students, his colleagues and the community. "Though I don't miss waking up at 5 a.m. I would rather be in school for the final days of my career," he said. "But I feel for those who are suffering and mourning the loss of loved ones. Nassau County has the second-most corona cases of any county in the nation next to New York City here in mid-April."

Many students have shown their love and support towards Krav's retirement like junior Sarah Benkovic, who had him as an English and journalism teacher. "Through all of the years I have treasured (my moments with) Krav and I'm gonna miss that teddy bear so much," she said. "Not sure what I'm going to do without him for my last year of high school."

"I have very mixed feelings about Krav retiring this June," says Spanish teacher Mr. Espinosa. "I'm really happy that he's going to get to enjoy his life. He brings such youthful enthusiasm and intensity to each day. It's awesome working alongside him. I'll miss the daily banter with him and our friends here at school. As much as I 'hate his voice' when he yells out names in senior study hall, it is a part of my day that will be missed. I wish him only the best in his retirement years."

Mr. Kravitz has coached wrestling and golf here at Wantagh High School. He and Mr. Muzio (current director of guidance) took over the wrestling program in 1991. Had it not been for the two of them, wrestling might have collapsed here. They coached together for eight years and built up the program.

Mr. Muzio continued for another eight years and in his last match as a coach Paul Liguori won a state title — Wantagh's first in over 35 years. "Mr. Muzio put his life into this wrestling program for 16 years," said Mr. Kravitz. "Our time together in the '90s was perhaps the best years of my educational career."

And now the wrestling program is a powerhouse, having dominated Nassau County and New York State for the past decade. Mr. Kravitz always tried to stay connected in a small way to the program by working the scoreboard at meets. And he even returned to the mat this year as a middle school wrestling coach at Clarke, where he had a wrestling renaissance and hopes to coach there next year.

As for golf, Mr. Kravitz and Mr. Colavita have coached the varsity team for the past 11 years, which according to Mr. Kravitz is much more relaxing than coaching wrestling. He hopes to continue coaching golf here post retirement.

A frequent golf partner of Mr. Kravitz is Wantagh H.S. social studies teacher Mr. Tallarine. "Krav's passion for journalism and kids' integrity went unmatched," said Mr. Tallarine, whose wife Lauren (nee Leonard) was a reporter on Mr. Kravitz's very first newspaper staff in 1993. She is now the Math Chairperson at Manhasset High School. "I hope all of his shots in retirement hit the greens except when I play with him."

"Mr. Kravitz and I shared a study hall at the beginning of our careers and shared the golf coaching job up to and hopefully beyond his retirement," says science teacher Mr. Colavita. "I appreciate the way he was always able to handle the things I couldn't, or didn't, want to. I don't know if I'll ever know a more easy-going, good-natured colleague. I wish him all the best and am looking forward to hearing all his retirement stories for years to come."

To Mr. Kravitz, thank you for inspiring my love of journalism and for being a great role model for the past three years. I never would've stayed with the program if it wasn't for you and now I can't imagine my life without it.

A few of the well wishes from students upon my retirement.

Lindsey Cohen
What a nice tribute! Mazel tov on your well deserved retirement-you're officially old!!!

Josh Latzman
Congratulations. You were one of the best teachers. I graduated in 95 and still remember the things you taught us.

Sebastian Muscarella
Congrats Krav! Lots of great years on the mats...but I also enjoyed your class and the paper as well! And go Rangers.

Todd Bloom
Congratulations & well deserved!!!! I know that my brother and Michael Ginsberg were probably key catalysts in you losing your hair but you were without a doubt the most impactful teacher David had......best of luck in retirement and I'll see you on the mat!

Gabrielle Lindau Mitchell
Congratulations Mr. Kravitz! I still remember how much I loved the writing assignments you'd give us - those assignments along with the story content you taught provided a glimpse into a world that existed outside the confines of those rusty high school hallways.

Courtney Allison
What a great and inspiring tribute. Congratulations Krav, best wishes!!! You are the best. I liked the part of the article of you hunting down editors in other classes. This is a sweet story. Thank you for everything.

Megan Gill Carusona
Congrats, Krav! I was lucky to have you in high school. You made teenagers feel heard. Enjoy your next chapter. I hope it's filled with lots of travel and family time!

Kathy DelGais-Butler
What an awesome article.......it was an honor teaching with you this year......I will miss you

Michele Tuzzolo Gebhard
KRAV!!!!!! "You revise and you revise and you revise!"
Congratulations to you!!! So well deserved. Loved having you as my English teacher in high school back in the early 90's.
May this next chapter of your life be full of blessings and all the wonderful things you deserve!
Stay safe and well
xoxoxoxo

Sara Sneddon
Congrats! Krav! Wantagh will miss you.

Michael DelVecchio
You were always so incredibly supportive, funny and an all around great human. We wish you the very best.

Megan Colton Daniels
Krav! What to say... you are certainly one of the best! I had my yearbook out a few days ago and the kids were looking at the pictures, etc. Came across what you wrote. It was so thoughtful and inspiring. I feel honored to have been taught by you and to call you a friend. All the best on this next phase of life. You deserve it!!

Livya Antonacci
Congratulations!! While I certainly cherish that Empire State Press Association award we got for some hard hitting reporting on the hotly contested 1997 school budget issue, I still think the Winter Sniffles expose would have been a winner! But seriously, congratulations again to one of my favorite HS teachers - enjoy your retirement!

Paul Schwartzberg

Congrats, Krav! Were it not for your guidance, support & enthusiasm, I would not be where I am today. Gratitude doesn't quite cover it. After all, it was you who exposed me to the likes of Miller, Burroughs & Bukowski. Their works shaped the course of my life, &, by consequence, so did you. From following the Beats to the Naropa Institute to securing an MFA in Creative Writing from the New School, the journey needed a starting place. That was your classroom. I haven't written my *Tropic of Cancer* or *Naked Lunch* or *Ham On Rye*. Yet. But I hope now, with an empty nest & too much time on your hands that you'll beat me to it. All the best to you on a marvelous career, one whose legacy lives on through those who passed thru your classrooms.

Angela M. Cave

I'm sorry your retirement came at such a strange time! Congratulations and bundles of gratitude to someone who had such a tremendous impact on my life.

Rebecca Kravitz

Makes me so happy to know that you've left an imprint on so many! You've earned this retirement 100x over 5 years ago so enjoy every minute of it! Many adventures to come!!! Love you dad

Brett Kravitz

Maybe with all your extra golf practice you'll have a chance at beating me again.... nahhh

Jennifer Green Kravitz

You had such a rewarding career as a teacher and positively influenced so many. Very few people can say that. I will miss all your great teaching stories but I'm excited to see what your next chapter is!

Rachel Creighton
Best teacher ever!!!! Thank you for making such an impact on my life and helping me become the writer I am today! Wantagh was so lucky to have you!

Kelly Fries Igoe
Congrats mr kravitz!! Always one of my fav teachers!!

Bob Ginsberg
Enjoy your retirement... Wantagh will always be grateful for all the years you touched so many students. I know how highly Michael thought of you. Thanks again!

Liz Tino-LaRosa
So sad to see you go! I was hoping my son would get you as an oncoming 8th grader this year... best of luck! You certainly deserve it

Andrea Markin Stottler

KRAV!!! I really enjoyed reading this article- it brought me back to some (hilarious) memories. Wantagh will miss you! Thanks for being a great teacher and enjoy your retirement- well deserved!

Joseph Giovanniello
I love you, coach Krav. Thanks for everything and congratulations on an amazing career. I can honestly say I am who I am today because of the guidance and support of you and coach Muzio.

Paul Baron
Congrats, Krav, this great tribute definitely gets it right. You made a lasting impact on your students' lives, and you made it fun. Wantagh Wrestling and The Warrior stay with us long after we leave, and that's an awesome testament to your career. Enjoy your next chapter!

Mike Stencel
Congrats once again Kravitz! You were my teacher, advisor, coach and school newspaper rival. It was certainly a privilege. Enjoy the golf course.

Frank Cammarata
Congratulations you were a great coach and teacher.
Well-deserved retirement!!

Lawrence Thomas
So happy for you and your family! You were an awesome teacher and a great coach. I wish you all the best in your retirement!

Irwin M. Loew
Gonna miss you Krav! -Jon Loew

Kristy Nallan-Cornella
What?!?! You're retiring?? I'm soooooo sad!!!! I will miss you so very much! Thanks for being the best teacher.

Ashley Exner
A great end to a great career...the one and only Krav! Wishing my favorite teacher many long and happy years as a retired man!

Jackie Dresch
Congratulations, Krav! You were a tremendous influence on my writing and my career - I didn't know about Syracuse/Newhouse until I took your journalism class in the 7th grade and you and my experience with *The Warrior* are the reason why I ended up there (and I loved it!) Thanks again for being such a great teacher and editor. Wantagh was lucky to have you all these years!

Audrey Abbate
I'm so thankful for those four years that you've guided me. I wouldn't have developed a passion for writing without those important four years. Enjoy your free time and congratulations you deserve it!

Maria Tsimis Ebbets
Congrats to one of the best, definitely left a lasting impression on this student. Good luck on this next chapter.

Daniella Marie
Oh Krav! So many memories of WHS that I can think of. You truly are one of the best teachers. I was so lucky to have you. I wish I would have been a little bit less of a pain in the ass! Enjoy the next chapter of your life. You will always be a huge part of Wantagh #warriors

Tracy E. Hill
The fact that you thought 32 years flew by is a testament to the love you have and gave to the thousands of students you've taught over the last three decades. Bravo to a tremendous career and doing what you love!

Jamie Bush
Enjoy your retirement. Just as my daughter is gonna be joining the middle school next year. Was hoping that when she got to hs she would have had you. Loved having you as a 9th grade teacher. You made learning fun.

Jared R
Congratulations on a fantastic career. Inspired many, including me. Best of luck!

Megan Rutherford
Such great memories. What a great career, Krav. Hope you can plan some retirement trips sometime soon. Celebratory drinks in NYC (or Philly?!) will be in order post COVID.

Stina Dani
Your class was one of my most memorable. Good luck on your retirement.

Tina Treiber Racette
Congratulations Krav. Wantagh is losing an amazing teacher. Good luck traveling, writing, golfing and spending time with your family! Well deserved!

Stefanie Martorano Zimmerman
One of my very favorite teachers! Congrats Krav! I believe my love of teaching was influenced by how much you loved teaching us.

ABOUT THE AUTHOR

Peter Kravitz was a Philadelphia newspaper reporter in the 1980s before becoming a teacher. He has more recently published articles in *Newsday* and *The Philadelphia Inquirer* and is a regular contributor to *Silversage Magazine*.

ABOUT THE PUBLISHER

The Sager Group was founded in 1984. In 2012, it was chartered as a multimedia content brand, with the intention of empowering those who create art—an umbrella beneath which makers can pursue, and profit from, their craft directly, without gatekeepers. TSG publishes books; ministers to artists and provides modest grants; designs logos, products and packaging, and produces documentary, feature, and commercial films. By harnessing the means of production, The Sager Group helps artists help themselves. For more information, visit TheSagerGroup.net

MORE BOOKS FROM THE SAGER GROUP

The Swamp: Deceit and Corruption in the CIA
An Elizabeth Petrov Thriller (Book 1)
by Jeff Grant

Chains of Nobility: Brotherhood of the Mamluks (Book 1)
by Brad Graft

Meeting Mozart: A Novel Drawn From the Secret Diaries of Lorenzo Da Ponte
by Howard Jay Smith

Labyrinth of the Wind: A Novel of Love and Nuclear Secrets in Tehran
by Madhav Misra

A Boy and His Dog in Hell: And Other Stories
by Mike Sager

Miss Havilland: A Novel
by Gay Daly

The Orphan's Daughter: A Novel
by Jan Cherubin

Lifeboat No. 8: Surviving the Titanic
by Elizabeth Kaye

Shaman: The Mysterious Life and Impeccable Death of Carlos Castaneda
by Mike Sager

See our entire library at TheSagerGroup.net

Artifex Te Adiuva

Made in United States
North Haven, CT
30 October 2021